HIKING THE ABSAROKA- BEARTOOTH WILDERNESS

HELP US KEEP THIS GUIDE UP TO DATE

Every effort has been made by the authors and editors to make this guide as accurate and useful as possible. However, many things can change after a guide is published—trails are rerouted, regulations change, techniques evolve, facilities come under new management, etc.

We appreciate hearing from you concerning your experiences with this guide and how you feel it could be improved and kept up to date. While we may not be able to respond to all comments and suggestions, we'll take them to heart and we'll also make certain to share them with the authors. Please send your comments and suggestions to the following address:

FalconGuides
Reader Response/Editorial Department
Falconeditorial@rowman.com

Thanks for your input, and happy trails!

HIKING THE ABSAROKA-BEARTOOTH WILDERNESS

A GUIDE TO 63 GREAT WILDERNESS HIKES

FOURTH EDITION

Bill Schneider

With Fishing Information by Richard K. Stiff,
Former High Mountain Lakes Survey Coordinator,
Montana Department of Fish, Wildlife & Parks

FALCONGUIDES

ESSEX, CONNECTICUT

FALCONGUIDES®

An imprint of Globe Pequot, the trade division of The Rowman & Littlefield Publishing Group, Inc.
4501 Forbes Blvd., Ste. 200
Lanham, MD 20706
www.rowman.com

Falcon and FalconGuides are registered trademarks and Make Adventure Your Story is a trademark of The Rowman & Littlefield Publishing Group, Inc.

Distributed by NATIONAL BOOK NETWORK

Library of Congress Cataloging-in-Publication Data

Names: Schneider, Bill, author.
Title: Hiking the Absaroka-Beartooth Wilderness : a guide to 63 great wilderness hikes / Bill
    Schneider.
Description: Fourth edition. | Essex, Connecticut : Falcon Guides, [2024] |
    Includes index. | Summary: "This guide, a thoroughly revised and updated
    edition of Hiking the Absaroka-Beartooth Wilderness, explores 63 trails
    in Montana's Absaroka-Beartooth Wilderness. The wilderness area, located
    north and northeast of Yellowstone, is renowned for its spectacular
    scenery and abundant wildlife"—Provided by publisher.
Identifiers: LCCN 2022035987 (print) | LCCN 2022035988 (ebook) | ISBN
    9781493063277 (paperback) | ISBN 9781493063284 (epub)
Subjects: LCSH: Hiking—Absaroka-Beartooth Wilderness (Mont. and
    Wyo.)—Guidebooks. | Backpacking—Absaroka-Beartooth Wilderness (Mont.
    and Wyo.)—Guidebooks. | Trails—Absaroka-Beartooth Wilderness (Mont.
    and Wyo.)—Guidebooks. | Absaroka-Beartooth Wilderness (Mont. and
    Wyo.)—Guidebooks.
Classification: LCC GV199.42.M92 A272 2023 (print) | LCC GV199.42.M92
    (ebook) | DDC 796.5109786/6—dc23/eng/20220917
LC record available at https://lccn.loc.gov/2022035987
LC ebook record available at https://lccn.loc.gov/2022035988

Printed in India

CONTENTS

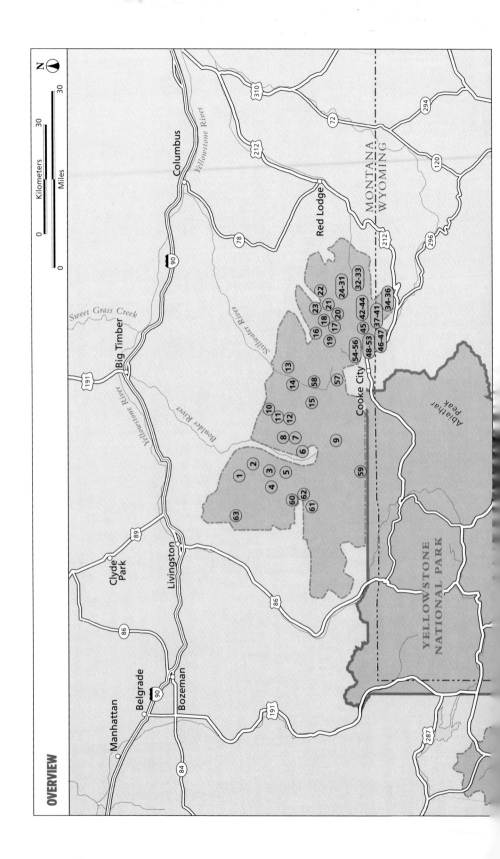

OVERVIEW

N

Kilometers
0   30

Miles
0   30

Manhattan

Belgrade

Bozeman

Clyde
Park

Livingston

Big Timber

Columbus

Sweet Grass Creek

Yellowstone River

Boulder River

Stillwater River

Yellowstone River

Red Lodge

MONTANA
WYOMING

YELLOWSTONE
NATIONAL PARK

Cooke City

Abiathar
Peak

86

89

90

84

191

86

191

287

90

78

212

310

72

294

212

120

296

1
2
3
4
5
6
7
8
9
10
11
12
13
14
15
16
17
18
19
20
21
22
23
24-31
32-33
34-36
37-41
42-44
45
46-47
48-53
54-56
57
58
59
60
61
62
63

ACKNOWLEDGMENTS

No book, especially a hiking guidebook, ever makes it into print without a lot of help from a lot of people. This book is an excellent example of the collaborative effort required to have a complete and accurate product.

First, I'd like to thank my family, who not only spent many days and nights in the wilderness with me, but also spent many days and nights without me while I was hiking and running the trails. Also, thanks to my hiking partners, Mike Cannon and Jim Melstad, who suffered through some major power hiking to finish off all the trails before the snows reclaimed the wilderness for the winter. I also received invaluable information from other hikers—Ann Boyd, Cathy Wright, Dick Krott, and Mike Sample.

The good folks in the Forest Service helped me by reviewing the draft manuscript and answering a lot of questions they didn't have time to answer to make sure all the details in this book are as accurate as possible. They are Jeremy Baker, Kathryn Barker, Frank Cifala, Jeff Gildehaus, Lyle Hancock, Dan Tyers, Allie Wood, Bill Frost, Jeremy Zimmer, and Lawson Maclean. I also learned a lot from chance meetings out on the trails and long chats with wilderness rangers Dorothy Houser and Susan Nicholas.

I also owe a big thank-you to the staff at Falcon, who endured my distractions while researching and writing the original edition of the book back in the mid-1990s and helped in a hundred other ways to make it happen—especially Randall Green, Will Harmon, Eric West, and Chris Stamper. Now, an equal thank you goes to the staff of FalconGuides, who worked with me to make the second, third, and fourth editions a reality. They are Jeff Serena, Ann Seifert, Meredith Dias, Gillian Belnap, Nancy Freeborn, Julie Marsh, David Legere, and Mason Gadd.

Anyone seeing this sign has made a good decision and will relish the days ahead.

INTRODUCTION: A TALE OF TWO WILDERNESSES

The Absaroka-Beartooth Wilderness isn't a national park. It's even better. It's a national treasure.

This guidebook details trips of varying lengths, including day hikes and overnighters. Interestingly, though, most people quickly discover that a day or two in the Absaroka-Beartooth isn't nearly enough. Actually, it's probably impossible to get enough of this place, so I've also included several multiday backpacking adventures to help you get your fill of paradise.

The 943,377-acre Absaroka-Beartooth Wilderness is one of the most visited wild areas in the United States. This is surprising considering the hiking season is so short with snow usually covering the area until July and often reclaiming the highlands again in early September.

This book covers both the high-elevation, lake-strewn uplift, commonly called the Beartooth Plateau or, more simply, the Beartooths, and the gentler, forested mountains of the Absaroka. The vast majority of the hiking occurs in the Beartooths, and the high-elevation plateau can, fortunately, absorb a lot of use in a way that gives you the illusion you have the wilderness to yourself. Instead of competing for designated campsites or huts, backcountry travelers can camp almost anywhere. And anywhere is a big place in the Beartooths.

Almost all use on the Beartooth Plateau occurs from July through September. Even in July, snow may still cling to some sections of trail, and in September, winter can come early and with a dangerous vengeance, so most use is concentrated into a six-week period from mid-July through August.

In the Absaroka and a few lower-elevation sections of the Beartooths, the season can be slightly longer, but the winter snows still don't give up some trails until at least late June. In September and October, large numbers of hunters and outfitters head into the Absaroka Mountains and more or less take over the area.

Most people admire the Beartooth Mountains for their sheer, unbridled beauty. But many geologists marvel at this range for a different reason. A band of igneous rock rich in rare minerals lies along the northern edge of these mountains, often called the Beartooth Front. The uplifted granite that comprises most of the range dates back more than 3 billion years and contains some of the oldest rocks on Earth. The Beartooths also boast the highest mountain in Montana: Granite Peak, at 12,799 feet. From the top of Granite or many other peaks in the range, the view is dizzying.

With 944 lakes and nine major drainages, the Beartooths are also an angler's paradise. Rainbow, cutthroat, brook, golden, and lake trout thrive in the waterways of the plateau.

Soaking up the spirit of the wilderness.

About 350 lakes have stocked or naturally reproducing trout populations. Though the area is extremely popular, a persistent angler can usually find an unoccupied lake or stream to call his or her own for a day or two. Conversely, the Absaroka has limited fishing opportunities, and the streams, not lakes, offer the most fishing.

Much of the Beartooth Plateau rests at about 10,000 feet and is covered with delicate alpine tundra. Because of the high use, zero-impact camping practices are essential to the preservation of this fragile ecosystem. Most people visiting the Beartooths nowadays take great care to leave no trace of their visit. This is, of course, one reason this great masterpiece of the national forest system still seems pristine and uncrowded. It's the responsibility of all future visitors to carry on this tradition.

The Absaroka could be compared to the second child, a quieter, less aggressive sibling. Fans of the Absaroka must put up with the "firstborn" getting all the fanfare and friends and fame and fortune while they sulk in obscurity. The Absaroka is like that—wild and magnificent but almost forgotten next to its big sister, the Beartooths.

Unlike the Beartooths, the Absaroka is a more stereotypical western mountain range with fewer lakes and alpine areas, but more streams. The Absaroka is a quiet wilderness, less rock but more greenery. And if you want to get up to 10,000 feet, you have to climb up there. You aren't parking your vehicle at 10,000-foot trailheads and hiking all day at close to that elevation as you can in the Beartooths.

Also, unlike the Beartooths, the Absaroka has great trails begging for hikers—with the exception of a few hot spots like Passage Falls, Pine Creek Lake, and Elbow Lake

Hidden Lake, but they're all hidden, right? CASEY SCHNEIDER

that get heavy use. When you get tired of people but still want a pristine wilderness, try the Absaroka.

Not all Absaroka trails are included in this guidebook. Some are only outfitter trails, leading more or less nowhere, unless you're looking for a hunter's spike camp. Others are little used and with no real destination such as a mountaintop or lake that might test an experienced hiker's route-finding skills. For this reason, this guidebook covers only selected routes in the Absaroka Range, not the entire trail system.

HOW TO USE THIS GUIDE

This guidebook won't answer every question you have concerning your planned excursions into the Absaroka-Beartooth. But then, most people don't want every question answered before they head for the trailhead, lest they remove the thrill of making their own discoveries while exploring a magnificent wilderness. This book does, however, provide the basic information needed to plan a successful trip to the AbsarokaBeartooth Wilderness.

Types of Trips

In this book, hikes are designated into four types.

Loop: Starts and finishes at the same trailhead, including "lollipop" loops with some retracing of your steps when starting and finishing the hike. Sometimes the definition of a loop is stretched to include trips that involve a short walk on a road at the end of the hike to get back to your vehicle.

Shuttle: A point-to-point trip that requires two vehicles or an arrangement to be picked up at a designated time. The best way to manage the logistical problems of shuttles is to arrange for another party to start at the other end of the trail, meet in the middle, and trade keys. When finished, drive each other's vehicles home.

Out and Back: Traveling to a specific destination such as a lake or mountaintop and then retracing your steps back to the trailhead.

Base Camp: An out-and-back trip involving a multi-night stay while you enjoy short day trips back and forth from your base camp.

Distances

It's almost impossible to get precisely accurate distances for most trails. The distances used in this guidebook are based on a combination of actual experience hiking the trails, distances stated on Forest Service signs, and estimates from topographic maps. In some cases distances may be slightly off, so consider this when planning a trip. Keep in mind that distance is often less important than difficulty—a rough, steep, 2-mile cross-country trek may take longer than 5 or 6 miles on an easy, flat trail. Also, keep mileage estimates in perspective; they are all at least slightly inaccurate. Knowing exact mileage does not improve your wilderness experience.

Ratings

The estimates of difficulty should serve as a general guide only, not the final word. What is difficult to one person may be easy to the next. In this guidebook, difficulty ratings take into account both how long and how strenuous the route is, but they do not consider your physical condition. Here are general definitions of the ratings.

Easy: Suitable for any hiker, including small children or the elderly; without serious elevation gain; no off-trail or hazardous sections; and no places where the trail is faint.

Moderate: Suitable for hikers who have some experience and at least an average fitness level; probably not suitable for small children or the elderly unless they have an above-average level of fitness; perhaps with some short sections where the trail is difficult to follow; and often with some hills to climb.

Difficult: Suitable for experienced hikers with an above-average fitness level; often with some sections of trail that are hard to follow or some off-trail sections that could require knowledge of route-finding with topo map and compass; often with serious elevation gain; and possibly with some off-trail hiking and hazardous conditions such as difficult stream crossings, snowfields, or cliffs.

In a few sidebars the ratings have more colorful definitions of Human, Semi-human, and Animal. These ratings roughly equal the definitions of easy, moderate, and difficult, although the Animal rating could be described as very difficult or strenuous.

Special Regulations

Compared to hiking in many national parks, hiking in the Absaroka–Beartooth Wilderness is almost unregulated. Nonetheless, the Forest Service has special regulations for hikers such as group size (fifteen maximum), and the regulations vary with the ranger district and even from trail to trail. Check with the Forest Service before you leave on your trip, and be sure to read and follow any special regulations posted at the trailhead. The Forest Service doesn't come up with these regulations to inconvenience backcountry visitors. Instead, the agency issues regulations to promote safely sharing and preserving the wilderness.

Inconsistent Names

Some names of places and features used in this guidebook may not match the names found on some maps and in other books. In some cases, lakes named in this book are unnamed on some maps. The US Geological Survey (USGS) maps, for example, list only officially approved names, but many lakes, streams, and mountains have common names that appear on other maps and trail signs and in guidebooks, including this one.

Trails Only

As mentioned several times in this guidebook, off-trail travel is the essence of the Beartooths. However, this guidebook does not, with a few exceptions, cover off-trail travel. Even those exceptions are cases where there has been so much off-trail travel on a certain unofficial route that it has resulted in a definable trail. Off-trail travel should be tried only after you've gained enough experience to feel confident with your physical and route-finding abilities. Perhaps the best way to achieve this experience is to go on a few trips with an experienced off-trail hiker.

Following Faint Trails

Trails receiving infrequent use often fade away in grassy meadows, on ridges, or through rocky sections. Don't panic. These sections are usually short, and you can look ahead to see where the trail goes. Often the trail is visible going up a hill or through a hallway of trees ahead. If so, focus on that landmark and don't worry about being off the trail for a short distance.

Mighty East Rosebud Creek leaving the heart of the Beartooths and heading for New Orleans.

Also watch for other indicators that you are indeed on the right route, even if the trail isn't clearly visible. Watch for cairns, metal markers, blazes, downfall cut with saws, and trees with the branches cut off on one side. Follow only official Forest Service blazes, which are shaped like an upside-down exclamation point, and don't follow blazes made by hunters, outfitters, or other hikers. And remember, making your own blazes to mark your route is very old school and no longer acceptable.

Sharing

We all want our own wilderness all to ourselves, but that only happens in our dreams. Lots of people use the Absaroka-Beartooth Wilderness, and to make everyone's experience better, we all must work at politely sharing it.

Hikers not only must share with other hikers, but also with backcountry horseback riders. Both groups have every right to be on the trail, so please don't let it become a confrontation. Keep in mind that horses and mules are much less maneuverable than hikers, so it becomes the hiker's responsibility to yield the right-of-way. All hikers should stand on the downhill side of the trail, well off-trail for safety's sake, and quietly let the stock pass.

Another example of politely sharing the wilderness is choosing your campsite. If you get to a popular lake late in the day and all the good campsites are taken, don't crowd in on another camper. This is most aggravating, as these sites rightfully go on a first-come, first-served basis. If you're late, you have the responsibility to move on or take a less desirable site a respectful distance away from other campers.

Always another lake over the next hill on the Beartooth Plateau. CASEY SCHNEIDER

Elevation Profiles

All hikes have elevation profiles to give you a general idea of the elevation gain and loss on the route. Be sure to check the scale on the axis of the profiles to get a better picture of the route's difficulty.

Rating the Hills

In the process of publishing dozens of FalconGuides, Falcon has been working to develop a consistent rating system to help hikers determine how difficult those "big hills" really are. Such a system would help hikers decide how far they wanted to hike that day or even whether they wanted to take that trail at all. In the past, guidebook authors have described hills to the best of their ability, but subjectively. What is a big hill to one hiker might be a slight upgrade to the next.

Also, it isn't only going up that matters. Some hikers hate going down steep hills and the knee problems that go with descending with a big pack. These "weak-kneed" hikers might want to avoid Category 1 and Category H hills.

This new system combines the elevation gain and the length of that section of trail in a complicated mathematical formula to come up with a numerical hill rating similar to the system used by cyclists. The system only works for climbs of 0.5 mile or longer, not short, steep hills.

FALCON HILL RATING CHART

ELEVATION GAIN (in feet)	DISTANCE (in miles)											
	0.5	1.0	1.5	2.0	2.5	3.0	3.5	4.0	4.5	5.0	5.5	6.0
200	4.2	5.0	5.4	5.5	5.6	5.6	5.7	5.7	5.7	5.7	5.7	5.7
300	3.3	4.5	4.9	5.2	5.3	5.4	5.5	5.5	5.5	5.5	5.6	5.6
400	1.8	4.0	4.5	4.8	5.1	5.2	5.3	5.3	5.4	5.4	5.4	5.4
500	1.0	3.5	4.2	4.5	4.7	5.0	5.1	5.2	5.2	5.2	5.3	5.3
600	H	3.0	3.8	4.2	4.4	4.6	4.9	4.9	5.0	5.1	5.1	5.1
700	H	2.5	3.4	3.9	4.2	4.3	4.5	4.8	4.9	4.9	4.9	5.0
800	H	1.4	3.1	3.6	3.9	4.1	4.2	4.3	4.7	4.7	4.8	4.9
900	H	H	2.7	3.3	3.6	3.9	4.0	4.1	4.2	4.6	4.7	4.7
1,000	H	H	2.3	2.9	3.4	3.6	3.8	3.9	4.0	4.1	4.5	4.6
1,100	H	H	1.9	2.7	3.1	3.4	3.6	3.7	3.8	3.9	3.9	4.5
1,200	H	H	H	2.4	2.8	3.1	3.4	3.5	3.6	3.7	3.8	3.9
1,300	H	H	H	2.1	2.6	2.9	3.2	3.3	3.5	3.5	3.6	3.7
1,400	H	H	H	1.8	2.3	2.7	2.9	3.1	3.3	3.4	3.5	3.5
1,500	H	H	H	1.6	2.1	2.4	2.7	2.9	3.1	3.2	3.3	3.3
1,600	H	H	H	H	1.9	2.2	2.3	2.7	2.9	2.9	3.1	3.2
1,700	H	H	H	H	1.7	1.9	2.3	2.5	2.7	2.8	2.9	3.0
1,800	H	H	H	H	1.5	1.8	2.0	2.3	2.5	2.6	2.7	2.8
1,900	H	H	H	H	1.3	1.7	1.9	2.1	2.3	2.4	2.6	2.6
2,000	H	H	H	H	H	1.5	1.7	1.9	2.1	2.2	2.4	2.5
2,100	H	H	H	H	H	1.3	1.6	1.8	1.9	2.0	2.2	2.3
2,200	H	H	H	H	H	1.2	1.4	1.6	1.8	1.9	1.9	2.1
2,300	H	H	H	H	H	1.0	1.3	1.5	1.7	1.8	1.9	1.9
2,400	H	H	H	H	H	H	1.2	1.4	1.5	1.6	1.8	1.8
2,500	H	H	H	H	H	H	1.0	1.2	1.4	1.5	1.6	1.7
2,600	H	H	H	H	H	H	H	1.1	1.3	1.4	1.5	1.6
2,700	H	H	H	H	H	H	H	H	1.1	1.3	1.4	1.5
2,800	H	H	H	H	H	H	H	H	H	1.1	1.3	1.4
2,900	H	H	H	H	H	H	H	H	H	1.0	1.2	1.3
3,000	H	H	H	H	H	H	H	H	H	H	1.0	1.1

Here is a rough description of the categories, listed from easiest to hardest.

Category 5: A slight upgrade.

Category 4: Usually within the capabilities of any hiker.

Category 3: A well-conditioned hiker might describe a Category 3 climb as "gradual," but a poorly conditioned hiker might complain about the steepness. It's definitely not steep enough to deter you from hiking the trail, but these climbs will slow you down.

Category 2: Most hikers would consider these "big hills," steep enough, in some cases, to make hikers choose an alternative trail, but not the real lung-busting, calf-stretching hills.

Category 1: These are among the steepest hills hikers will ever encounter. If you have heart or breathing problems or simply dislike climbing big hills, you might look for an alternative trail.

Category H: These are hills that make you wonder if the person who laid out the trail was on drugs. Any trail with a Category H (for "Horrible") hill is steeper than any trail should be.

The hills in this book are rated according to the accompanying chart. Some climbs are rated in the hike descriptions of this book, but if not included (or to use this formula in other hiking areas), get the mileage and elevation gain off the topo map and look them up on the rating chart.

Map Sense

The Absaroka-Beartooth Wilderness has several options for maps. And good maps are essential to any wilderness trip. For safety reasons maps help you find routes and "stay found." For non-safety reasons, most people would not want to miss out on the unending joy of mindlessly whittling away untold hours staring at a map and wondering what the world looks like here and there.

For trips into the Absaroka-Beartooth, there are at least three excellent maps covering the entire wilderness:

- The Forest Service Absaroka-Beartooth Wilderness map, which is currently somewhat outdated, but a new version is in the works. Until the new wilderness map comes out, a good choice would be the Gallatin National Forest Central map, which will soon be replaced by a new map for the recently combined Custer Gallatin National Forest.

- The Absaroka-Beartooth Wilderness map published by Beartooth Publishing of Bozeman, Montana.

- The Trails Illustrated/National Geographic Maps (East and West) covering the entire wilderness.

For more detailed maps covering, usually in larger scale and with more detail, parts of the wilderness:

- US Geological Survey (USGS) topographic maps.

- Rocky Mountain Survey (RMS), a private company in Billings, Montana, sells a series of six topo maps designed especially for serious hikers and anglers.

- Ranger district maps published by the Forest Service.

Finding Maps

You can find maps at the following locations:

USGS: Check sporting goods stores in the Absaroka-Beartooth area or write directly to the USGS at the following address and refer to the specific quad you need. You can also print out your own maps from several map websites and topo map software programs. Note the grid on page 11.

Map Distribution
US Geological Survey
Box 25286, Federal Center
Denver, CO 80225
(303) 202-4700

Forest Service Maps: The Absaroka-Beartooth Wilderness map hasn't been updated since 1997 and is now difficult to find. A new map for the combined Custer Gallatin National Forest is currently under production, so if that map becomes available, it will probably be the best choice. In the meantime, the best choice is the Gallatin National Forest Central map, which was published more recently and before the merger with the Custer National Forest. You can also get ranger district maps at Forest Service offices and some sporting goods stores in towns around the wilderness. You can also call or write any of these Forest Service offices to buy maps:

Custer-Gallatin National Forest
Beartooth Ranger District
6811 Highway 212
Red Lodge, MT 59068
(406) 446-2103

Custer Gallatin National Forest
Gardiner Ranger District
805 Scott Street
Gardiner, MT 59030
(406) 848-7375

Custer Gallatin National Forest
Yellowstone Ranger District
5242 Highway 89 South
Livingston, MT 59047
(406) 222-1892

Shoshone National Forest
Clarks Fork, Greybull, Wapiti Ranger
District
203A Yellowstone Avenue
Cody, WY 82414
(307) 527-6241

Note: The new, yet-to-be-published map to the combined national forest will include new trail numbers for some trails.

Rocky Mountain Survey: Look for RMS maps at sporting goods stores near the wilderness.

Beartooth Publishing: Available at regional sporting goods stores or online from www.beartoothpublishing.com.

Trails Illustrated/National Geographic: Available at most regional sporting goods stores or online from www.natgeomaps.com.

Map index grid (overlay region labels: **MONTANA / WYOMING** state boundary; **ABSAROKA-BEARTOOTH WILDERNESS**; **YELLOWSTONE NATIONAL PARK**).

	COLUMBUS EAST	SHANE RIDGE	COONEY RESERVOIR	ROBERTS	RED LODGE EAST	TOLMAN FLAT	CLARK
	COLUMBUS WEST	WHITEBIRD SCHOOL	ROSCOE NE	CASTAGNE	RED LODGE WEST	MOUNT MAURICE	NORTH BENNETT CREEK
	SPRINGTIME	ASBAROKEE	ROSCOE NW	ROSCOE	BARE MOUNTAIN	BLACK PYRAMID MOUNTAIN	DEEP LAKE
	REED POINT	SANDBORN CREEK	FISHTAIL	MACKAY RANCH	SYLVAN PEAK	SILVER RUN PEAK	BEARTOOTH BUTTE
	WORK CREEK	COW FACE HILL	BEEHIVE	EMERALD LAKE	ALPINE	CASTLE MOUNTAIN	MUDDY CREEK
GREYCLIFF	PACKSADDLE BUTTE	WILDCAT DRAW	NYE	MOUNT WOOD	GRANITE PEAK	FOSSIL LAKE	JIM SMITH PEAK
BIG TIMBER	BOSS CANYON	SLIDEROCK MOUNTAIN	MEYER MOUNTAIN	CATHEDRAL POINT	LITTLE PARK MOUNTAIN	COOKE CITY	PILOT PEAK
CARNEY	MCLEOD	SQUAW PEAK	PICKET PIN MOUNTAIN	TUMBLE MOUNTAIN	PINNACLE MOUNTAIN	CUTOFF MOUNTAIN	ABIATHAR PEAK
KELLY HILLS	SPRINGDALE	MCLEOD BASIN	CHROME MOUNTAIN	MOUNT DOUGLAS	HAYSTACK PEAK	ROUNDHEAD BUTTE	MOUNT HORNADAY
ELTON	MOUNT RAE	WEST BOULDER PLATEAU	THE NEEDLES	IRON MOUNTAIN		HUMMINGBIRD PEAK	LAMAR CANYON
MISSION	LIVINGSTON PEAK	MOUNT COWEN	THE PYRAMID	MOUNT WALLACE		SPECIMEN CREEK	TOWER JUNCTION
LIVINGSTON	BRISBIN	DEXTER POINT	KNOWLES PEAK	MINERAL MOUNTAIN		ASH MOUNTAIN	BLACKTAIL DEER CREEK
HOPPERS	CHIMNEY ROCK	PRAY	EMIGRANT	MONTOR PEAK		GARDINER	MAMMOTH
BOZEMAN PASS	BALD KNOB	BIG DRAW	DAILEY LAKE	DOME MOUNTAIN		ELECTRIC PEAK	QUADRANT MOUNTAIN
KELLY CREEK	MOUNT ELLIS	FRIDLEY PEAK	LEWIS CREEK	MINER		SPORTSMAN LAKE	JOSEPH PEAK
BOZEMAN	WHEELER MOUNTAIN	MOUNT BLACKMORE	THE SENTINEL	RAMSHORN PEAK		BIG HORN PEAK	DIVIDE LAKE
BOZEMAN HOT SPRINGS	GALLATIN GATEWAY	GARNET MOUNTAIN	HIDDEN LAKE	LONE INDIAN PEAK		SUNSHINE POINT	UPPER TEPEE BASIN

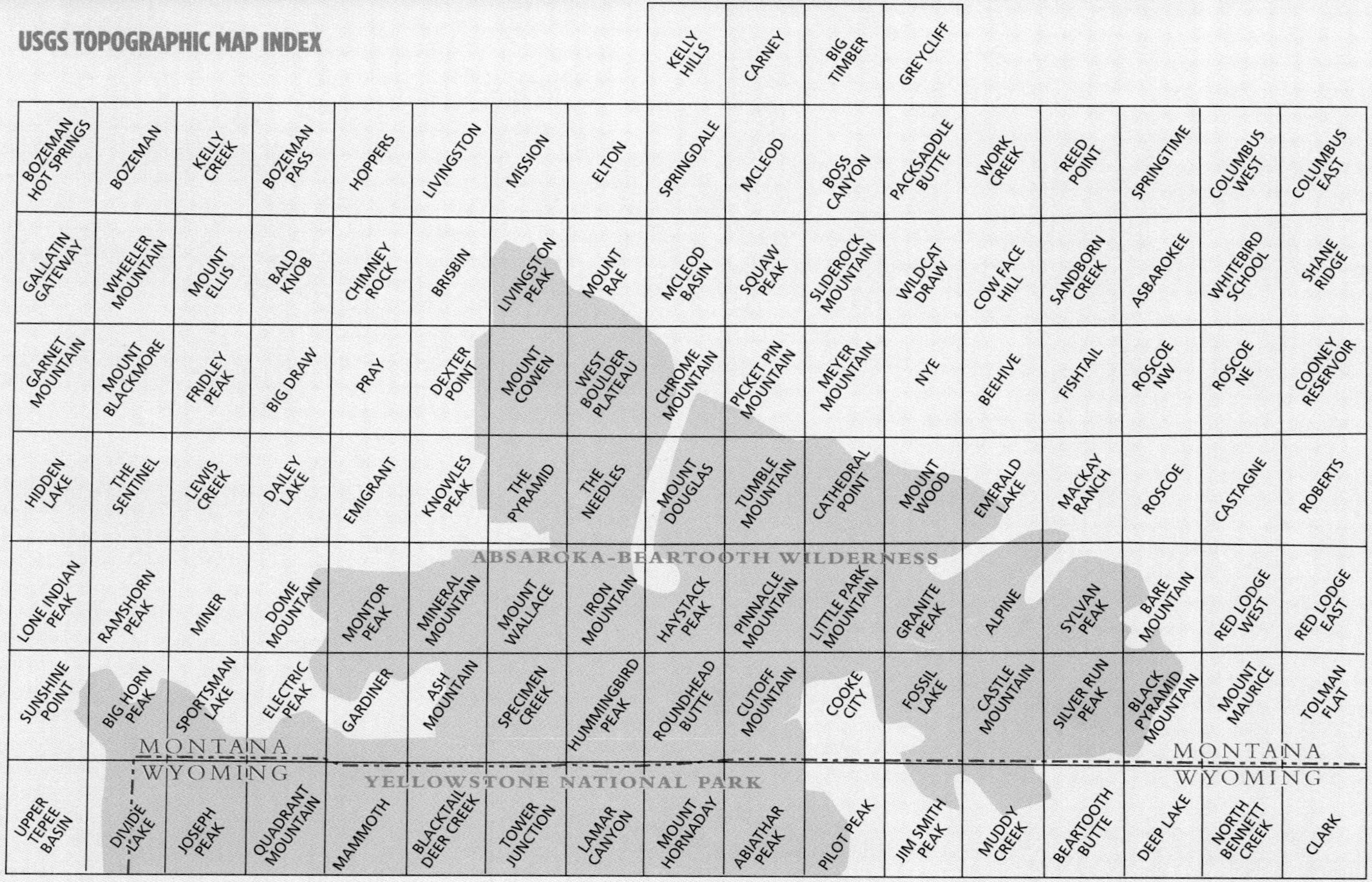

Which Maps Do You Need?

The well-prepared wilderness traveler will take at least two—one covering the entire wilderness and one covering the specific area of the hike. In the hike descriptions to follow, I suggest taking at least one wilderness-wide map and then give the specific maps for the area covered in the hike.

The Vehicle You Need to Reach the Trailheads

Usually this isn't a huge problem, but in the Absaroka-Beartooth, it can be. At least three trailheads require a high-clearance, four-wheel-drive vehicle with low-range gearing and the four-wheeling expertise to go with it. Those trailheads are Hellroaring, Lake Abundance, and Goose Lake. Other trailheads have bumpy, dusty roads but are accessible with any vehicle. They are West Rosebud, East Rosebud, and all the trailheads in the West Fork of Rock Creek. To reach the West Fork Stillwater Trailhead and most trailheads along the Boulder River south of Big Timber, you'll feel more comfortable with a 4WD, but with great care, you can make it to the trailhead with any vehicle. The rest of the trailheads are on paved roads.

Expect to see lots of four-legged hikers in the Absaroka-Beartooth. CASEY SCHNEIDER

For More Information

The Forest Service is the best source of information on the Absaroka-Beartooth Wilderness. Unfortunately, four different ranger districts manage parts of this wilderness, and the exact areas of management can be confusing. Also, some trails go from one ranger district to another. The best approach is to contact the ranger district closest to the trailhead you intend to use.

Contact ranger districts at the following addresses:

Beartooth Ranger District
Custer Gallatin National Forest
6811 Highway 212
Red Lodge, MT 59068
(406) 446-2103

Yellowstone Ranger District
Custer Gallatin National Forest
5242 Highway 89 South
Livingston, MT 59047
(406) 222-1892

Gardiner Ranger District
Custer Gallatin National Forest
PO Box 5
805 Scott Street
Gardiner, MT 59030
(406) 848-7375

Clarks Fork Greybull Wapiti Ranger District
Shoshone National Forest
203A Yellowstone Avenue
Cody, WY 82414
(307) 527-6921

VACATION PLANNER

Keeping in mind that any hike can be extended or shortened, here is a breakdown to help you select your next destination in the Absaroka-Beartooth.

Adventures, 3-5 Nights or Longer:

Base camps: Lake Plateau North, Lake Plateau East, Martin Lake, and Aero Lakes

Loops: Three Passes, Columbine Pass, Lake Plateau West, Green Lake, Copeland Lake, and Horseshoe Lake

Shuttles: Slough Creek Divide, Stillwater to Stillwater, The Beaten Path, Jordan Lake, and The Complete Stillwater

Moderate Backpacking Trips, 1-2 Nights:

Base camps: Island Lake, Quinnebaugh Meadows, and Native Lake

Loops: Beartooth Recreation Loop, Claw Lake, and The Hellroaring

Out and back: West Boulder River, Great Falls Creek Lakes, Silver Lake, Bridge Lake, Breakneck Park Meadows, Timberline Lake, Quinnebaugh Meadows, Lake Mary, Crow Lake, Upper Granite Lake, Lower Granite Lake, Ivy Lake, Curl Lake, Rock Island Lake, Fox Lake, Goose Lake, Elbow Lake, Thompson Lake, and Pine Creek Lake

Shuttles: Sundance Pass, Beartooth High Lakes, and Crazy Lakes

Easy Backpacking Trips, Overnighters:

Out and back: Sioux Charley Lake, Elk Lake, Hellroaring Plateau, Hauser Lake, Becker Lake, Beauty Lake, Native Lake, and Lady of the Lake

Serious Day Trips for Well-Conditioned Hikers:
Loops: Claw Lake
Out and back: Great Falls Creek Lakes, Silver Lake, Bridge Lake, Sylvan Lake, Lake Mary, Crow Lake, Curl Lake, and Elbow Lake
Shuttles: Rosebud to Rosebud and Silver Run Plateau

Moderate Day Hikes:
Out and back: Breakneck Park Meadows, Quinnebaugh Meadows, Upper Granite Lake, Lower Granite Lake, Ivy Lake, Rock Island Lake, Fox Lake, Thompson Lake, and Pine Creek Lake

Easy Day Hikes:
Out and back: West Boulder River, East Fork Boulder River, Sioux Charley Lake, Mystic Lake, Elk Lake, Slough Lake, Basin Creek Lakes, Timberline Lake, Broadwater Lake, Hellroaring Plateau, Glacier Lake, Gardner Lake, Hauser Lake, Becker Lake, Beartooth High Lakes, Beauty Lake, Native Lake, Lake Vernon, Lady of the Lake, and Passage Falls

Hiking the Beartooths, always scenic, especially in the East Rosebud.

ZERO IMPACT

Going into a national park or wilderness area is like visiting a famous museum. You obviously do not want to leave your mark on an art treasure in the museum. If everybody going through the museum left one little mark, the piece of art would be quickly destroyed—and of what value is a big building full of trashed art? The same goes for a pristine wilderness, which is as magnificent as any masterpiece by any artist. If we all left just one little mark on the landscape, the wilderness would soon be despoiled.

A wilderness can accommodate human use as long as everybody behaves. A few thoughtless or uninformed visitors can ruin it for everybody who follows. All wilderness users have a responsibility to know and follow the rules of zero-impact hiking and camping.

Nowadays most wilderness users want to walk softly, but some aren't aware that they have poor manners. Often their actions are dictated by the outdated habits of a past generation of campers who cut green boughs for evening shelters, built campfires with fire rings, and dug trenches around tents. In the 1950s, these "camping rules" may have been acceptable, but they leave long-lasting scars, and today such behavior is absolutely unacceptable. The wilderness is shrinking, and the number of users is mushrooming. More and more camping areas show unsightly signs of heavy use.

Consequently, a new code of ethics is growing out of the necessity of coping with the unending waves of people who want a perfect wilderness experience. Today we all must leave no clues that we have gone before. Canoeists on a wild river can look behind and see no sign of their passing. Hikers, backcountry horseback riders, mountain bikers, and four-wheelers should have the same goal. Enjoy the wilderness, but make it a zero-impact visit.

Most of us know better than to litter—in or out of the wilderness. Be sure you leave nothing, regardless of how small it is, along the trail or at the campsite. This means you should pack out everything, including orange peels, cigarette butts, and gum wrappers. Also, pick up any trash that others, possibly accidentally, leave behind. In addition, please follow this zero-impact advice.

- Follow the main trail. Avoid cutting switchbacks and walking on vegetation beside the trail.

- Don't pick up "souvenirs" such as rocks, antlers, or wildflowers. The next person wants to see them too.

- Avoid making loud noises that may disturb others. Remember, sound travels easily to the other side of the lake. If you have a dog, don't let it bark.

- Carry a lightweight trowel to bury human waste 6 to 8 inches deep and pack out used toilet paper. Keep human waste at least 300 feet from any water source.

- Finally, and perhaps most importantly, strictly follow the pack-in/pack-out rule. If you carry something into the backcountry, consume it or carry it out.

Leave zero impact of your passing—and put your ear to the ground in the wilderness and listen carefully. Thousands of people coming behind you are thanking you for your courtesy and good sense.

HAVE A SAFE TRIP

Scouts have been guided for decades by what is perhaps the best single piece of safety advice—be prepared. For starters, this means carrying survival and first-aid kits, proper clothing, compass or GPS unit, and topographic maps—and knowing how to use them.

Perhaps the second-best piece of safety advice is to tell somebody where you're going and when you plan to return. Pilots file flight plans before every trip, and anybody venturing into a blank spot on the map should do the same. File your "flight plan" with a friend or relative before taking off.

Close behind your flight plan and being prepared with proper equipment is physical conditioning. Being fit not only makes wilderness travel more fun, it also makes it safer. To whet your appetite for more knowledge of wilderness safety and preparedness, here are a few more tips.

- Check the weather forecast. Be careful not to get caught at high altitude by a bad storm or along a stream in a flash flood. Watch cloud formations closely so you don't get stranded on a ridgeline during a lightning storm. Avoid traveling during prolonged periods of cold weather.

- Avoid traveling alone in the wilderness.

- Keep your party together.

- Study basic survival and first aid before leaving home.

- Don't eat wild plants unless you have positively identified them and know they are safe to eat.

- Before you leave for the trailhead, find out as much as you can about the route, especially any potential hazards.

- Don't exhaust yourself or other members of your party by traveling too far or too fast. Let the slowest person set the pace.

- Don't wait until you're confused to look at your maps. Follow them as you go along, from the moment you start moving up the trail, so you have a continual fix on your location.

- If you get lost, don't panic. Sit down and relax for a few minutes while you carefully check your topo map and take a reading with your compass. Confidently plan your next move. It's often smart to retrace your steps until you find familiar ground, even if you think it might lengthen your trip. Lots of people get temporarily lost in the wilderness and survive, usually by calmly and rationally dealing with the situation.

- Stay clear of all wild animals.

- Take a first-aid kit that includes, at a minimum, the following items: sewing needle, snakebite kit, aspirin, antibacterial ointment, two antiseptic swabs, two butterfly bandages, adhesive tape, four adhesive strips, four gauze pads, two triangular bandages, codeine tablets, two inflatable splints, Moleskin or Second Skin for blisters, one roll of 3-inch gauze, CPR shield, rubber gloves, and lightweight first-aid instructions.

- Take a survival kit that includes, at a minimum, the following items: compass, whistle, matches in a waterproof container, cigarette lighter, candle, signal mirror, flashlight and extra batteries, fire starter, aluminum foil, water purification tablets, space blanket, and flare.

Last but not least, don't forget that the best defense against unexpected hazards is knowledge. Read up on the latest in wilderness safety information.

You Might Never Know What Hit You

The high-altitude topography of the Absaroka-Beartooth is prone to sudden thunderstorms, especially in July and August. If you get caught by a lightning storm, take special precautions. Remember:

- Lightning can travel far ahead of the storm, so be sure to take cover before the storm hits.

- Don't try to make it back to your vehicle. It isn't worth the risk. Instead, seek shelter even if it's only a short way back to the trailhead. Lightning storms usually don't last long, and from a safe vantage point, you might enjoy the sights and sounds.

- Be especially careful not to get caught on a mountaintop or exposed ridge, under large solitary trees, in the open, or near standing water.

- Seek shelter in a low-lying area, ideally in a dense stand of small, uniformly sized trees.

Be alert for afternoon thunderstorms common in the high country.

- Stay away from anything that might attract lightning, such as metal tent poles, graphite fishing rods, or pack frames.

- Get in a crouch position and place both feet firmly on the ground.

- If you have a pack (without a metal frame) or a sleeping pad with you, put your feet on it for extra insulation against an electrical shock.

- Don't walk or huddle together when hiking with others. Instead, stay 50 feet or more apart, so if somebody gets hit by lightning, others in your party can give first aid.

- If you're in a tent, stay there, in your sleeping bag with your feet on your sleeping pad.

The Silent Killer

Be aware of the danger of hypothermia—a condition in which the body's internal temperature drops below normal. It can lead to mental and physical collapse and death. This is a special item of concern when hiking in the Absaroka-Beartooth, particularly on the Beartooth Plateau, where it can snow heavily any day of the year.

Hypothermia is caused by exposure to cold and is aggravated by wetness, wind, exhaustion, and dehydration. The moment you begin to lose heat faster than your body produces it, you're suffering from exposure. Your body starts involuntary exercise, such as shivering, to stay warm and makes involuntary adjustments to preserve normal temperature in vital organs, restricting blood flow in the extremities. Both responses drain your energy reserves. The only way to stop the drain is to reduce the degree of exposure.

With full-blown hypothermia, as energy reserves are exhausted, cold reaches the brain, depriving you of good judgment and reasoning power. You won't be aware that this is happening. You lose control of your hands. Your internal temperature slides downward. Without treatment, this slide leads to stupor, collapse, and death.

To defend against hypothermia, stay dry. When clothes get wet, they lose most of their insulating value. High-tech synthetics are your best choice for retaining heat and repelling moisture. Choose rain clothes that cover the head, neck, body, and legs and provide good protection against wind-driven rain. Most hypothermia cases develop in air temperatures between 30° and 50°F, but hypothermia can develop in warmer temperatures.

If your party is exposed to wind, cold, and wet, automatically and instantly think hypothermia. Watch yourself and others for these symptoms: uncontrollable fits of shivering; vague, slow, slurred speech; memory lapses; incoherence; immobile, fumbling hands; frequent stumbling or a lurching gait; drowsiness (to sleep is to die); apparent exhaustion; and inability to get up after a rest. When a member of your party has hypothermia, he or she may deny any problem. Believe the symptoms, not the victim. Even mild symptoms demand treatment, as follows:

- Get the victim out of the wind and rain.

- Remove wet clothing.

- If the victim is only mildly impaired, give him or her warm drinks. Then get the victim into warm clothes and a warm sleeping bag. Place well-wrapped water bottles filled with heated water close to the victim.

- If the victim is badly impaired, attempt to keep him or her awake. Put the victim in a sleeping bag with another person—both naked. If you have a double bag, put two warm people in with the victim.

BE BEAR AWARE

The first step of any hike in bear country is an attitude adjustment. Nothing guarantees total safety. Hiking in bear country adds a small additional risk to your trip. However, that risk can be greatly minimized by adhering to this age-old piece of advice: Be prepared. And being prepared doesn't only mean having the right equipment. It also means having the right information. Knowledge is your best defense.

You can—and should—thoroughly enjoy your trip to bear country. Don't let the fear of bears ruin your vacation. This fear can accompany you every step of the way. It can be constantly lurking in the back of your mind, preventing you from enjoying the wildest and most beautiful places left on Earth.

Being prepared and knowledgeable gives you confidence. It allows you to fight back the fear that can burden you throughout your stay in bear country. You won't—nor should you—forget about bears and the basic rules of safety, but proper preparation allows you to keep the fear of bears at bay and let enjoyment rule the day.

And on top of that, do we really want to be totally safe? If we did, we probably would never venture into a wilderness—bears or no bears. We certainly wouldn't, at much greater risk, drive hundreds of miles to get to the trailhead. Perhaps a tinge of danger adds a desired element to our wilderness trip.

Hiking in Bear Country

Bears don't like surprises. The majority of bear encounters occur when a hiker surprises a bear. Therefore, it's vital to do everything possible to avoid these surprise meetings. If you follow the following five rules, the chance of encountering a bear on the trail sinks to the slimmest possible margin.

- Be alert.
- Hike with a group and stay together.
- Stay on the trail.
- Hike in the middle of the day.
- Make noise.

No substitute for alertness: As you hike, watch ahead and to the sides. Don't fall into the all-too-common and particularly nasty habit of fixating on the trail 10 feet ahead. It's especially easy to do this when lugging a heavy pack up a long hill or when carefully watching your step on a rocky or eroded trail.

Using your knowledge of bear habitat and habits, be especially alert in areas most likely to be frequented by bears such as avalanche chutes, berry patches, streams, and stands of whitebark pine.

Watch carefully for bear signs, and be especially watchful (and noisy) if you see any. If you see a track or a scat, but it doesn't look fresh, pretend it's fresh. The area is obviously frequented by bears.

Safety in numbers: There have been very few instances where a large group has had an encounter with a bear. On the other hand, a large percentage of hikers mauled by bears were hiking alone. Large groups naturally make more noise and put out more smell and probably appear more threatening to bears. In addition, if you're hiking alone and get injured, there is nobody to go to for help. For these reasons, rangers often recommend

WARNING

BEAR
FREQUENTING AREA

Removal of this sign may result in INJURY to others
and is punishable by law

THERE IS NO GUARANTEE OF YOUR SAFETY
WHILE HIKING OR CAMPING IN BEAR COUNTRY

A bear warning sign in the Absaroka-Beartooth Wilderness.

parties of four or more hikers when going into bear country.

If the large party splits up, the advantage is lost, so stay together. If you're on a family hike, keep the kids from running ahead. If you're in a large group, keep the stronger members from going ahead or weaker members from lagging behind. The best way to prevent this natural separation is to have the slowest member of the group lead the way. This keeps everybody together.

Stay on the trail: Although bears use trails, they don't often use them during midday when hikers commonly use them. Through generations of associating trails with people, bears probably expect to find hikers on trails, especially during midday.

On the other hand, bears probably don't expect to find hikers off trails. Bears rarely settle down in a daybed right along a heavily used trail. However, if you wander around in thickets off the trail, you're more likely to stumble into an occupied daybed or cross paths with a traveling bear.

Sleeping late: Bears—and most other wildlife—usually aren't active during the middle of a day, especially on a hot summer day. Wild animals are most active around dawn and dusk. Therefore, hiking early in the morning or late afternoon increases your chances of seeing wildlife, including bears. Likewise, hiking during midday on a hot summer day greatly reduces the chance of an encounter.

Sounds: Perhaps the best way to avoid a surprise meeting with a bear is to make sure the bear knows you're coming, so make lots of noise. Some experts think metallic noise is superior to human voices, which can be muffled by natural conditions, but the important point is to make lots of noise, regardless of what kind of noise.

Watch the wind: The wind can be a friend or foe. The strength and direction of the wind can make a significant difference in your chances of an encounter with a bear. When the wind is blowing at your back, your smell travels ahead of you, alerting any bear that might be on or near the trail ahead. Conversely, when the wind blows in your face, your chances of a surprise meeting with a bear increase, so make more noise and be more alert.

A strong wind can also be noisy and limit a bear's ability to hear you coming. If a bear can't smell or hear you coming, the chances of an encounter greatly increase, so watch the wind.

Running: Many avid runners like to get off paved roads and running tracks and onto backcountry trails. But running on trails in bear country can be seriously hazardous to your health. Bears can't hear you coming, you approach them faster than expected, and, of course, it's nearly impossible to keep alert while running when you have to watch the trail closely to keep from falling.

Leave the night to the bears: Like running on trails, hiking at night can be very risky. Bears are more active after dark, and you can't see them until it's too late. If you get caught at night, be sure to make lots of noise, and remember that bears commonly travel on hiking trails at night.

You can be dead meat, too: If you see or smell a carcass of a dead animal when hiking, immediately vacate the area. Don't let

Grizzly bears are currently expanding their range into all sections of the Absaroka-Beartooth Wilderness, so be prepared and aware on all trails. NATIONAL PARK SERVICE

your curiosity keep you near the carcass a second longer than necessary. Bears commonly hang around a carcass, guarding it and feeding on it for days until it's completely consumed. Your presence could easily be interpreted as a threat to the bear's food supply, and a vicious attack could be imminent.

If you see a carcass ahead of you on the trail, don't go any closer. Instead, either abandon your hike and return to the trailhead or take a very long detour around it, upwind from the carcass, making lots of noise along the way. Be sure to report the carcass to the local ranger. This might prompt a temporary trail closure or special warnings and prevent injury to other hikers. Rangers will, in some cases, go in and drag the carcass away from the trail.

Cute, cuddly, and lethal: If you see a bear cub, don't go one inch closer to it. It might seem abandoned, but it is not. Mother bear is very close, and female bears fiercely defend their young.

It doesn't do you any good in your pack: Always carry bear pepper spray when hiking in bear country, know how to use it, and don't bury it in your pack. Keep it as accessible as possible. It won't do you any good if you can't have it ready to fire in one or two seconds. Most pepper spray comes in a holster or somehow conveniently attaches to your belt or pack. Before hitting the trail, read the directions carefully and test fire the spray.

But I didn't see any bears: You know how to be safe: Walk up the trail constantly clanging two metal pans together. It works every time. You won't see a bear, but you'll hate your "wilderness experience." You left the city to get away from loud noise.

Yes, you can be very safe, but how safe do you want to be and still be able to enjoy your trip? It's a balancing act. First, be knowledgeable and then decide how far you want to go. Everybody has to make his or her own personal choice.

Here's another conflict. If you do everything listed here, you most likely will not see any bears—or any other wildlife. Again, you make the choice. If you want to be as safe as possible, follow these rules religiously. If you want to see wildlife, including bears, do all of this in reverse, but then, you're increasing your chance of an encounter instead of decreasing it.

Camping in Bear Country

Staying overnight in bear country is not dangerous, but it adds a small additional risk to your trip. The main difference is the presence of more food, cooking, and garbage. Plus, you're in bear country at night when bears are more active. Once again, however, following a few basic rules greatly minimizes this risk.

Storing food and garbage: If the campsite doesn't have a bearproof storage box or bear pole, be sure to find a good tree to hang your food and garbage and do it before it gets dark. It isn't only difficult to hang food and garbage after darkness falls, but it's easier to forget some juicy morsel on the ground. Also, store food in airtight, waterproof bags to prevent food odors from circulating throughout the forest. For double protection, put food and garbage in ziplock bags and then seal them tightly in a larger plastic bag.

The illustrations on the next page depict three popular methods for hanging food bags. In all cases, try to get food and garbage at least 10 feet off the ground.

Special equipment: It's not really that special, but one piece of equipment you definitely need is a good supply of ziplock bags to store most food and garbage. They also keep food smell to a minimum and help keep food from spilling on your pack, clothing, or other gear.

Take a special bag for storing food. The bag must be sturdy and waterproof. You can get dry bags at most outdoor specialty stores, but you can get by with a trash compactor bag. Regular garbage bags can break and leave your food spread on the ground.

You also need 100 feet of nylon cord. You don't need a heavy climbing rope to store food. Go light instead. Parachute cord will usually suffice unless you plan to hang large quantities of food and gear, which might be the case on a long backpacking excursion with a large group.

You can also buy a small pulley system to make hoisting a heavy load easier. Again, you can usually get by without this extra weight in your pack unless you have a massive load to hang.

What to hang: To be as safe as possible, store everything that has any food smell. This includes cooking gear, eating utensils, bags used to keep food in your pack, all garbage, and even clothes with food smells on them. If you spilled something on your clothes, change into other clothes for sleeping and hang clothes with food smells with the food and garbage. If you take them into the tent, you aren't separating your sleeping area from food smells. Try to keep food odors off your pack, but if you failed, put the food bag inside and hang the pack.

What to keep in your tent: You can't be too careful in keeping food smells out of the tent. Just in case a bear has become accustomed to coming into that campsite looking for food, it's vital to keep all food smells out of the tent. This often includes your pack, which is hard to keep odor-free. Most important, take your bear pepper spray into the tent with you every night along with valuables (like cameras and binoculars), clothing, headlamp, and sleeping gear.

The campfire: Regulations prohibit campfires in most campsites in the Absaroka-Beartooth, but if you're in an area where fires are allowed, treat yourself. Besides adding the nightly entertainment, the fire might make your camp safer from bears.

The campfire provides the best possible way to get rid of food smells. Build a small but hot fire and thoroughly burn everything that smells of food—garbage, leftovers, fish entrails, everything. If you brought food in cans or other incombustible containers, burn

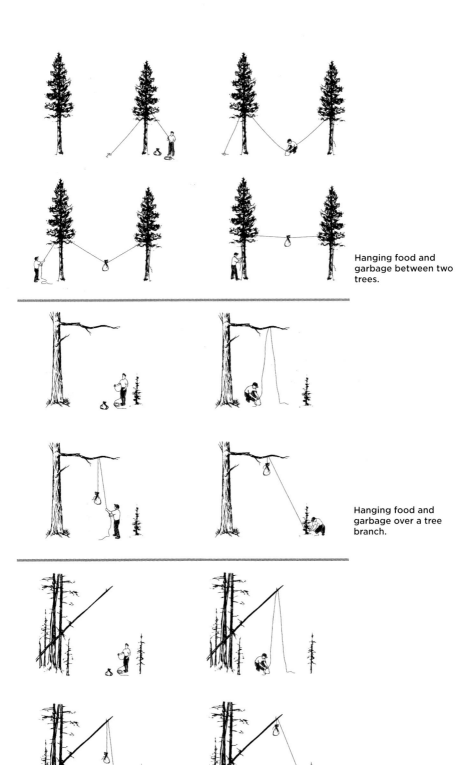

Hanging food and garbage between two trees.

Hanging food and garbage over a tree branch.

Hanging food and garbage over a leaning tree.

When at lower elevations where campfires are possible without causing undue resource damage, thoroughly burn leftover food and garbage. Be sure to dig any unburned material out of the firepit the next morning and pack it out.

them too. You can even dump extra water from cooking or dishwater on the edge of the fire to minimize the smell.

Be very sure you have the fire hot enough to completely burn everything. If you leave partially burned food scraps in the fire, you're setting up a dangerous situation both for you and the next camper who uses this campsite.

Before leaving camp the next morning, dig out the firepit and pack out anything that has not completely burned, even if you believe it no longer carries food smells. For example, many foods like dried soup or hot chocolate come in foil packages that might seem like they burn, but they really don't. Pack out the scorched foil and cans (now with very minor, if any, food smells). Also pack out foil and cans left by other campers.

Types of food: Don't get paranoid about the types of food you bring. All food has some smell, and you can make your trip much less enjoyable by fretting over food.

Perhaps the safest option is freeze-dried food. It carries very little smell, and it comes in convenient envelopes that allow you to "cook it" by merely adding boiling water. This means you don't have smelly cooking pans to wash or store. However, freeze-dried food is expensive, and many backpackers don't use it—and still safely enjoy bear country.

Dry, prepacked meals (often pasta- or rice-based) offer an affordable compromise to freeze-dried foods. Also, take your favorite high-energy snack and don't worry about it. Avoid fresh fruit and canned meats and fish.

The key point is this: What food you have is much less critical than how you handle it, cook it, and store it. A can of tuna fish, for example, might put out a smell, but if you eat all of it in one meal, don't spill it on the ground or on your clothes, and burn the can later, it can be quite safe.

Hanging food at night is not the only storage issue. Also make sure you place food correctly in your pack. Use airtight packages as much as possible. Store food in the containers it came in or, when opened, in ziplock bags. This keeps food smells out of your pack and off your other camping gear and clothes.

How to cook: The overriding philosophy of cooking in bear country is to create as little odor as possible. Keep it simple. Use as few pans and dishes as possible.

Unless it's a weather emergency, never cook in the tent. If you like winter backpacking, you probably cook in the tent, but you should have a different tent for summer backpacking.

If you can have a campfire and decide to cook fish, try cooking them in aluminum foil envelopes instead of frying them. Then, after removing the cooked fish, quickly and completely burn the fish scraps off the foil. Using foil also means you don't have to wash the pan you used to cook the fish.

Be careful not to spill on yourself while cooking. If you do, change clothes and hang the clothes with food odor with the food and garbage. Wash your hands thoroughly before retiring to the tent.

Don't cook too much food, so you don't have to deal with leftovers. If you do end up with extra food, however, you have only two choices: Carry it out or burn it. Don't bury it or throw it in a lake or leave it anywhere in bear country. A bear will find and dig up any food or garbage buried in the backcountry.

Taking out the garbage: In bear country, you have only two choices: Burn garbage or carry it out. Prepare for garbage problems before you leave home. Bring along airtight ziplock bags to store garbage. Be sure to hang your garbage at night along with your food. Also, carry in as little garbage as possible by discarding excess packaging while packing.

FOOD STORAGE ORDER

The national forests in Montana have issued a legally binding "Food Storage Order," which is posted at most trailheads.

A Food Storage Order requires the following:
- Food must be actively attended while transporting, preparing and eating it.
- All attractants must be stored in a locked bear-resistant container or a closed vehicle constructed of solid, nonpliable material, *or*
- Suspended at least 10 feet clear of the ground at all points and 4 feet horizontally from supporting tree or pole.

The Food Storage Order prohibits the following:
- Camping within one-half mile of any animal carcass or within 100 yards of any acceptably stored animal carcass.
- Leaving an animal carcass unless it is (a) at least one-half mile from any sleeping area, trail, or recreation site or (b) at least 100 yards from any sleeping area, trail, or recreation area and acceptably stored or (c) being eaten, being prepared for eating, or being transported.

For questions and clarification call your local Forest Service office. To learn more about bear-resistant containers or the Interagency Grizzly Bear Committee, visit www.igbconline.org.

Washing dishes: This is a sticky problem, but there is one easy solution. If you don't dirty dishes, you don't have to wash them. So try to minimize food smell by using as few dishes and pans as possible. If you use the principles of zero-impact camping, you're probably doing as much as you can to reduce food smell from dishes.

If you brought paper towels, use one to carefully remove food scraps from pans and dishes before washing them. Then, when you wash dishes, you have much less food smell. Burn the dirty towels or store them in ziplock bags with other garbage. Put pans and dishes in ziplock bags before putting them back in your pack.

If you end up with lots of food scraps in the dishwater, drain out the scraps and store them in ziplock bags with other garbage or burn them. You can bring a lightweight screen to filter out food scraps from dishwater, but be sure to store the screen with the food and garbage. If you have a campfire, pour the dishwater around the edge of the fire. If you don't have a fire, take the dishwater at least 200 feet downwind and downhill from camp and pour it on the ground or in a small hole. Don't put dishwater or food scraps in a lake or stream.

Although possibly counter to accepted rules of cleanliness for many people, you can skip washing dishes altogether on the last night of your trip. Instead, simply use the paper towels to clean the dirty dishes as much as possible. You can wash them when you get home. Pack dirty dishes in ziplock bags before putting them back in your pack.

Finally, don't put it off. Do dishes immediately after eating, so a minimum of food smell lingers in the area.

Choosing a tent site: Try to keep your tent site at least 100 feet from your cooking area. Unfortunately, some campsites do not adequately separate the cooking area from the tent site. Store food at least 100 yards from the tent. You can store it near the cooking area.

Not under the stars: Some people prefer to sleep out under the stars instead of using a tent. This might be okay in areas not frequented by bears, but it's not a good idea in

THE BEAR ESSENTIALS OF HIKING IN BEAR COUNTRY
- Knowledge is the best defense.
- There is no substitute for alertness.
- Hike with a large group and stay together.
- Don't hike alone in bear country.
- Stay on the trail.
- Hike in the middle of the day.
- Make lots of noise while hiking.
- Never approach a bear.
- Females with cubs are very dangerous.
- Stay away from carcasses.
- Carry bear pepper spray and know how to use it.
- Choose a safe campsite.
- Camp below timberline.
- Separate sleeping and cooking areas.
- Sleep in a tent.
- Cook just the right amount of food and eat it all.
- Store food and garbage out of reach of bears.
- Never feed bears.
- Keep food odors out of the tent.
- Leave the campsite cleaner than you found it.
- Leave no food rewards for bears.

bear country. The thin fabric of a tent certainly isn't any real physical protection from a bear, but it does present a psychological barrier to a bear that wants to come closer.

Do somebody a big favor: Report all bear sightings to the ranger after your trip. This might not help you, but it could save another camper's life. If rangers get enough reports to spot a pattern, they manage the area to prevent potentially hazardous situations.

BE MOUNTAIN LION AWARE, TOO

The most important safety element for recreation in mountain lion country is simply recognizing their habitat. Mountain lions primarily feed on deer, so these common ungulates are a key element in cougar habitat. Fish and wildlife agencies usually have good information about deer distribution from population surveys and hunting results.

Basically, where you have a high deer population, you can expect to find mountain lions. If you aren't familiar with identifying deer tracks or scat, seek the advice of someone knowledgeable, or refer to a book on animal tracks such as the FalconGuides Scats and Tracks series.

To stay as safe as possible when hiking in mountain lion country, follow this advice.

- Travel with a friend or group. There's safety in numbers, so stay together.
- Don't let small children wander away by themselves.
- Don't let dogs run unleashed.
- Avoid hiking at dawn and dusk—the times mountain lions are most active.
- Watch for warning signs of mountain lion activity such as cougar tracks or high deer numbers.
- Know how to behave if you encounter a mountain lion.

What to Do If You Encounter a Mountain Lion

In the vast majority of mountain lion encounters, the animals exhibit avoidance, indifference, or curiosity that does not result in human injury. But it is natural to be alarmed if you have an encounter of any kind. Try to keep your cool and consider the following:

Recognize threatening mountain lion behavior: There are a few clues that may help you gauge the risk of attack. If a mountain lion is more than 50 yards away and directs its attention to you, it may be only curious. This situation represents only a slight risk for adults, but a more serious risk to unaccompanied children. At this point you should move away while keeping the animal in your peripheral vision. Also look for rocks, sticks, or anything else to use as a weapon, just in case. If you have bear pepper spray, get it ready to discharge. If a mountain lion is crouched and staring intently at you less than 50 yards away, it may be assessing the chances of a successful attack. If this behavior continues, the risk of attack may be high.

Do not approach a mountain lion: Instead, give the animal the opportunity to move on. Slowly back away, but maintain eye contact if close. Mountain lions are not known to attack humans to defend young or a kill, but they have been reported to "charge" in rare instances and may want to stay in the area. It's best to choose another route or time to hike through the area.

Do not run from a mountain lion: Running may stimulate a predatory response.

Make noise: If you encounter a mountain lion, be vocal and talk or yell loudly and regularly. Try not to panic. Shout to make others in the area aware of the situation.

Maintain eye contact: Eye contact presents a challenge to the mountain lion, showing you're aware of its presence. However, if the behavior of the mountain lion isn't threatening (if it is, for example, grooming or periodically looking away), maintain visual contact through your peripheral vision and move away.

Appear larger than you are: Raise your arms above your head and make steady waving motions. Raise your jacket or another object above your head. Do not bend over, as this will make you appear smaller and more "prey-like."

Grab the kids: If you're with small children, bring them close to you, maintaining eye contact with the mountain lion, then pull the children up without bending over. If you're with other children or adults, band together.

Defend yourself: If attacked, fight back. Try to remain standing. Don't "play dead" or feign death. Use whatever weapon you have—bear pepper spray, sticks, rocks, knives, anything you have. Almost anything is a potential weapon, and hikers have fought off mountain lions with blows from rocks, tree limbs, cameras, even fists.

Defend others: Defend your hiking partners, but don't risk your life defending your dog. In past attacks on children, adults have successfully stopped attacks. However, such encounters are very dangerous, which is why physically defending a dog is not recommended.

Respect any warning signs posted by agencies.

Spread the word: Before leaving on your hike, discuss lions and teach others in your group how to behave in case of a mountain lion encounter. For example, let the group know that anyone who starts running could bring on an attack.

Report encounters: If you have an encounter with a mountain lion, record your location and the details of the encounter, and notify the nearest landowner or land-management agency. The agency (federal, state, or county) may want to visit the site and, if appropriate, post education/warning signs. Fish and wildlife agencies should also be notified because they record and track such encounters. If physical injury occurs, it's important to leave the area and not disturb the site of the attack. Mountain lions that have attacked people must be killed, and an undisturbed site is critical for effectively locating the dangerous mountain lion.

HOW TO GET REALLY AWARE

Most of the bear and lion information in this book comes from *Bear Aware* and *Lion Sense*, handy, inexpensive FalconGuides. These small, packable books contain the essential tips you need to reduce the risk of being injured by a bear or mountain lion to the slimmest possible margin, and they are written for both beginner and expert.

In addition to covering the all-important subject of how to prevent an encounter, these books include advice on what to do if you are involved in an encounter. Find copies at booksellers specializing in outdoor recreation or order online at www.falcon.com.

THE BEARTOOTH FISHERY
By *Richard K. Stiff*
Former High Mountain Lakes Survey Coordinator
Montana Department of Fish, Wildlife & Parks

The Absaroka-Beartooth Wilderness contains about 944 lakes, and of these, 328 support fisheries and 616 are barren. Only a few lakes in the entire wilderness (within the Slough Creek drainage) are thought to contain native fish, with surviving original Yellowstone cutthroat stock. All other fisheries within the wilderness were created when fish were introduced to lakes or streams. In some cases, introduced fish migrated and established populations in new locations. Lakes are currently managed by drainage due to the nature of the drainages and fish migration within each drainage, although this has not always been the case.

More than 60 percent of the lakes within the wilderness are barren of fish, their natural condition. These provide an opportunity for backcountry travelers to get away from anglers and find more solitude. While most anglers would probably enjoy seeing fish in many of these lakes, leaving them in their natural state is a tribute to the Absaroka-Beartooth as a true "wilderness." Current laws prohibit the stocking of fish, without an environmental review, in lakes that have no history of a fishery.

The distribution of lakes (with and without fish) by drainage is as follows:

Boulder River	103
Clarks Fork	426
East Rosebud	76
Rock Creek	91
Slough Creek	10
Stillwater River	154
West Rosebud	84
Total	**944**

The majority of the lakes are above 8,500 feet, with a number of these above 10,000 feet. Because of the high elevation, lakes often remain ice-covered until late June and have surface temperatures that seldom reach 60°F. The size of the fish in a lake is generally related to the size of the population. There are usually a few large fish, many medium-size fish, or lots of smaller fish.

Lakes that harbor self-sustaining populations of fish often tend to become overpopulated, resulting in slower growth rates. Since brook trout have the least restrictive spawning requirements, they are most often the victims of poor growth rates. Lakes with brook trout tend to have stunted populations, although there are exceptions such as Cairn and Lower Aero Lakes.

Many of the lakes managed within the wilderness do not have a suitable place for trout to spawn and must be stocked to maintain a fishery. Most stocked lakes are planted with fish on a rotating cycle of three, four, six, and eight years, depending on use and management goals. Knowing the year these lakes are stocked can increase an angler's chance of catching good fish. Three- to four-year-old fish provide the best fishing for nice-size trout.

Three- and four-year stocking cycles are generally used on lakes that receive significant fishing pressure and where a persistent good catch is desired. A six-year cycle allows at

Lonesome Lake in the shadow of mighty Lonesome Mountain, visible from many trails, and of course, the home of Smaug, the fearsome dragon.

least some of the fish to grow larger, while still maintaining a constant fishery. Stocking at eight-year intervals is based on the premise that fish will live for seven years, and there will be a fallow year to allow the food population to recover. The eight-year cycle is used in lakes where a trophy-type fishery is desired, as well as in remote, relatively unproductive lakes. More lakes are being considered for the eight-year cycle.

There are many different species of fish in the Beartooths, although the majority of the lakes support only one species of fish. Cutthroat trout are the principal fish stocked because the area is in their original geographic range, and the hatchery in Big Timber provides an economical source of cutthroat trout. But many lakes were planted with brook trout in the first half of this century, and these have established populations.

Analysis of the fisheries reveals the following distribution of fish species:

Arctic grayling	11 lakes
Cutthroat trout	117 lakes
Eastern brook trout	85 lakes
Golden trout	25 lakes
Rainbow trout	22 lakes
Mixed fishery	56 lakes
Undecided	12 lakes
Total	**328 lakes**

Lake trout and brown trout are found in several mixed fisheries, mostly outside the wilderness boundaries.

Stream fisheries are different than lake fisheries. Since the Montana Department of Fish, Wildlife & Parks (FWP) no longer plants fish in streams, the fish found there are self-supporting populations. Alpine streams, like alpine lakes, have a limited food supply. But in a stream the trout not only have to find food, they must also fight the current of the stream.

Trout rely on the current of the stream to bring food to them, while hiding from the current themselves. Places that do both of these things are at a premium, and the largest fish get the best spots. The number of good feeding spots and the amount of food available limit the number of fish that can be present in a given reach of stream. Streams tend to support fewer fish than lakes, but fish in streams are easier to locate. Anglers should note that stream and lake fishing regulations differ.

Trout can usually find suitable places to spawn in a stream, so reproduction is not a problem. The type of fish present usually reflects a combination of what was originally found in the stream, the fish that were planted, and the fish that have migrated down from lakes above.

One final note: The southeastern arm of the Beartooths straddles the border between Montana and Wyoming. Anglers in this area must be careful to fish only in the state for which they hold a valid fishing license. In some places, particularly where lakes actually straddle the border (as does Granite Lake, for example), it might be wise to carry licenses for both states. Also know and heed the appropriate regulations.

(For more information on the Absaroka-Beartooth fishery, get a copy of *Fishing the Beartooths* by Pat Marcuson.)

THE AUTHOR'S FAVORITES

For That First Night in the Wilderness

25. Timberline Lake

32. Hellroaring Plateau

35. Beartooth Recreation Loop

36. Hauser Lake

37. Becker Lake

39. Beauty Lake

40. Claw Lake

41. Native Lake

54. Lady of the Lake

For Anglers

1. West Boulder River

7. Columbine Pass

9. Slough Creek Divide

12. Stillwater to Stillwater

20. The Beaten Path

32. Hellroaring Plateau

33. Glacier Lake

44. Green Lake

55. Aero Lakes

Sierra Creek, one of the many hidden off-trail jewels in the Beartooths.

For Photographers

7. Columbine Pass

18. Rosebud to Rosebud

20. The Beaten Path

26. Silver Run Plateau

30. Sundance Pass

33. Glacier Lake

38. Beartooth High Lakes

For Climbers

17. Granite Peak

20. The Beaten Path

55. Aero Lakes

60. Elbow Lake

For People Who Don't Want to See a Grizzly Bear

18. Rosebud to Rosebud

22. Sylvan Lake

30. Sundance Pass

32. Hellroaring Plateau

33. Glacier Lake

37. Becker Lake

38. Beartooth High Lakes

40. Claw Lake

41. Native Lake

For People Who Wouldn't Mind Seeing a Grizzly Bear

9. Slough Creek Divide

49. Crazy Lakes

57. Horseshoe Lake

59. The Hellroaring

For Parents with Small Children Who Want a Really Easy Hike

14. Sioux Charley Lake

31. Broadwater Lake

36. Hauser Lake

54. Lady of the Lake

For People Who Like Long, Hard Day Hikes So They Can Eat Anything They Want for Dinner

18. Rosebud to Rosebud

26. Silver Run Plateau

60. Elbow Lake

For People Who Just Can't Get Enough Adventure, Who Are Wilderness-wise, and Who Like a Variety of Off-Trail Side Trips

4. Three Passes

7. Columbine Pass

12. Stillwater to Stillwater

20. The Beaten Path

43. Martin Lake

44. Green Lake

55. Aero Lakes

For Trail Runners

10. Breakneck Park Meadows

18. Rosebud to Rosebud

22. Sylvan Lake

27. Quinnebaugh Meadows

28. Lake Mary

30. Sundance Pass

38. Beartooth High Lakes

40. Claw Lake

63. Pine Creek Lake

For Backcountry Horseback Riders

9. Slough Creek Divide

45. Jordan Lake

47. Copeland Lake

49. Crazy Lakes

58. The Complete Stillwater

59. The Hellroaring

For People Who Like Four-Wheel-Drive Access Roads

32. Hellroaring Plateau

57. Horseshoe Lake

MAP LEGEND

Municipal

≡⟨90⟩≡ Freeway/Interstate Highway

≡⟨89⟩≡ US Highway

≡⟨18⟩≡ State Road

≡⟨202⟩≡ County/Paved Road

≡ ≡ ≡ ≡ Gravel Road

≡ ≡ ≡ ≡ Unimproved Road

⸱⸱⸱—⸱⸱⸱ State Boundary

Trails

------ Featured Trail

------ Trail or Fire Road

Land Management

▭ National Park

⬚ Wilderness

Symbols

⏝ Bridge

■ Building/Point of Interest

⛰ Campground

⚑ Guard Station

▲ Mountain/Peak

⟩⟨ Pass

○ Towns and Cities

㉑ Trailhead

Water Features

◯ Body of Water

Marsh/Swamp

Glacier

River/Creek

Waterfall

Spring

BOULDER RIVER ROAD

Most locals see the Boulder River as the dividing line between the Beartooths to the east and the Absarokas to the west. The Boulder River Road ends nearly 50 miles south of Big Timber, Montana, at the Box Canyon Trailhead. In the 1970s there was a controversial proposal to punch the road all the way from Box Canyon to Cooke City, Montana, splitting the great wilderness into two smaller wild areas. Look at a topo map and the feasibility of such a road becomes obvious. Wilderness advocates mounted an epic battle and won. After a long, hard fight, politicians dropped the road proposal, and a roadless corridor between the two spectacular mountain ranges became part of the designated wilderness.

The Boulder River is a popular place. The road is lined with vehicle campgrounds, dude ranches, church camps, and private cabins and summer homes. During the early hunting season in September, hunters and outfitters and their horse trailers fill up the spacious Box Canyon Trailhead parking lot.

The Lake Plateau region of the Beartooths is a unique and spectacular section of the Beartooths and is as popular as any spot in the entire wilderness. Both Lake Plateau trailheads along the Boulder River Road (Box Canyon and Upsidedown Creek) attract many backpackers. Few backcountry horseback riders use the Upsidedown Creek Trail, but many use Box Canyon. The Lake Plateau can also be accessed from the West Fork Stillwater River and Stillwater River trailheads.

The trailheads for trails heading west into the Absaroka Mountains (West Boulder River, Great Falls Creek, Fourmile Creek, Speculator Creek, and Bridge Creek) receive much less use during the summer and moderate use (again mostly by hunters and outfitters) during September and October.

To find Boulder River Road, take CR 298 (locally referred to as Boulder River Road) south from Big Timber. The road doesn't take off from either of the two exits off I-90. Instead, drive into Big Timber and watch for signs for CR 298 (also called McLeod Street), which heads south and passes over the freeway from the middle of town between the two exits.

It's a long 48 miles from Big Timber to the Box Canyon Trailhead, so make sure to top off the gas tank. At 16 miles you'll pass the small community of McLeod, and at 24 miles the pavement ends, which, of course, means 24 more miles of bumpy, dusty gravel road to Box Canyon. It's passable with any vehicle, but the last 10 miles or so can be slow and bumpy. I drove to Box Canyon again in 2021, and the last 6 miles of the road had deteriorated badly, almost requiring a high-clearance, four-wheel-drive vehicle. You can still make it, barely, to Box Canyon in any vehicle, but it will be very slow, and you might wish you had not taken your vehicle up there.

From Big Timber, mileage to the trailheads is as follows:

West Boulder River turnoff—18 miles   Upsidedown Creek—46.5 miles

Great Falls Creek—30 miles   Bridge Creek—47 miles

Speculator Creek—38.5 miles   Box Canyon—48 miles

Fourmile Creek—42.5 miles

A jeep road continues on from Box Canyon to the Independence Pass area, where signs of early 1900s mining operations still remain. But all the hiking trails in this region can be accessed without bumping and grinding up this four-wheel-drive road.

1 WEST BOULDER RIVER

An easy route suitable for a moderate day hike or overnighter along a scenic, trout-filled river.

Start: West Boulder Trailhead
Distance: Up to 16 miles out and back
Difficulty: Easy

Maps: USGS Mount Rae and Mount Cowen; RMS Mount Cowen Area; and at least 1 wilderness-wide map

FINDING THE TRAILHEAD

Drive 18 miles south from Big Timber on Boulder River Road, to about a half mile past McLeod, and cross the West Boulder River. About a half mile later, turn right (west) onto West Boulder Road, which starts as pavement but quickly turns to gravel. After 7.4 miles turn left (west) at a well-signed junction, continuing on West Boulder Road. (Don't go straight here—it's private land. West Boulder Road also crosses private land, but it's a public road.) Drive 6.2 more miles until you see West Boulder Campground on your right. Park at the trailhead just past the campground entrance. Toilet in campground, but not at trailhead. The road continues on past the trailhead, but it's a private road, so don't drive on it. **GPS:** 45.54698 N, 110.30740 W

THE HIKE

One of the highlights of this hike is the drive to the trailhead. West Boulder Road winds through a scenic slice of the "real Montana"—wide-open spaces, snowcapped mountains, big valleys with rustic cattle ranches, aspens coloring the transitions between grassland and forest, and, of course, a beautiful stream all the way. If you drive to the trailhead near dawn or dusk, it resembles a video game trying to dodge all the deer on the road.

From the trailhead, hike up the private dirt road, through an open gate, for about 100 yards. Watch for a sign on the left up on the hill away from the road and a defined trail angling off toward it. Turn left here. Don't continue on the road, which goes to a private residence. This is all private land, but the landowner has been cooperative in allowing public access. Please show your appreciation by respecting the landowner's private property rights.

The first part of the trail is very well constructed—raised, drained, graveled, lined with logs—a regular hiker's highway. About a half mile up the trail, you go through a gate. Be sure to lock it behind you. Just before the bridge over the West Boulder River (and another gate) about a mile down the trail, you enter the Absaroka-Beartooth Wilderness, where the trail becomes more like a wilderness trail.

The first mile is flat, but then you climb two switchbacks and get a good view of the river. From here the trail goes through a partially burned forest interspersed with gorgeous mountain meadows; West Boulder Meadows is especially large and beautiful. Several of the meadows have excellent campsites, and the river offers good fishing all the way. After West Boulder Meadows you can see a beautiful waterfall.

This hike provides a reminder that wilderness is a multiple-use land designation with livestock grazing allowed. A local rancher holds a grazing allotment in West Boulder

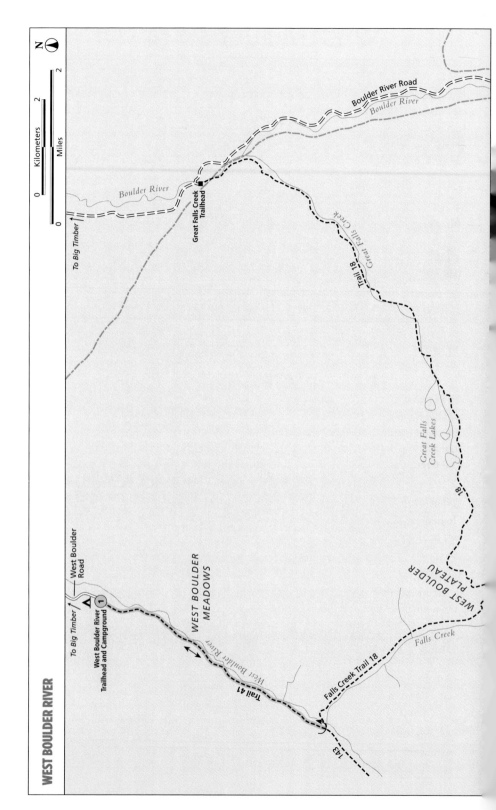

WEST BOULDER RIVER

N

Kilometers

Miles

To Big Timber

Boulder River

Boulder River

Boulder River Road

Boulder River

Great Falls Creek Trailhead

Great Falls Creek

Trail 18

Great Falls Creek Lakes

18

WEST BOULDER PLATEAU

To Big Timber

West Boulder Road

West Boulder River Trailhead and Campground

1

WEST BOULDER MEADOWS

West Boulder River

Trail 41

Falls Creek Trail 18

Falls Creek

143

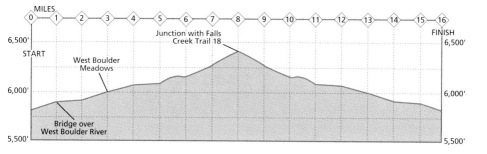

Meadows. You'll see an unsightly steel-post fence at the west end of the meadows, very out of character for the surroundings. About 5 miles up the trail, you go through another barb-wire fence with a gate over the trail. And, of course, expect to see a few cows and cow pies.

The entire trail is in great shape, with a gradual stream-grade incline all the way. Unlike many trails, this one stays by the stream throughout its length. Recent forest fires, however, have burned large sections of the valley.

OPTIONS

This trip provides the option of going as far as you choose, instead of targeting a specific destination. You can make this trip any length that suits you. It's 8 miles to the junction with the Falls Creek Trail, but there is no need to hike that far. The West Boulder is a great day hike, but it also makes an easy overnighter for beginning backpackers or families.

SIDE TRIPS

An ambitious and experienced hiker staying two nights and wanting a long side trip could try Kaufman Lake, which is partly off-trail hiking, or a long trek up the trail to Mill Creek Pass.

CAMPING

No designated campsites, but many opportunities to set up a zero-impact camp in meadows or along the stream.

FISHING

In the lower stretches of the river, you can catch cutthroats, rainbows, and browns, but as you proceed upstream and get close to the Falls Creek junction, it's mostly cutthroats.

MILES AND DIRECTIONS

0.0 Start at West Boulder Trailhead.

0.1 Trail turns off private road; turn left.

1.0 Bridge over West Boulder River and wilderness boundary.

3.0 West Boulder Meadows.

8.0 Junction with Falls Creek Trail 18.

16.0 Arrive back at West Boulder Trailhead.

2 GREAT FALLS CREEK LAKES

A long walk in the woods to three beautiful mountain lakes, best suited for one or two nights out.

Start: Great Falls Creek Trailhead
Distance: 16 miles out and back
Difficulty: Difficult

Maps: USGS Chrome Mountain and West Boulder Plateau; RMS Mount Cowen Area; and at least 1 wilderness-wide map

FINDING THE TRAILHEAD

Drive south from Big Timber on Boulder River Road for 30 miles and park in the small trailhead on the right (west) side of the road at the end of a short spur road. Falls Creek Campground, a full-service vehicle campground, is about a half mile before the trailhead. Ample parking. No toilet at trailhead. **GPS:** 45.48695 N, 110.21761 W

THE HIKE

It's a tough 8 miles to reach Upper Great Falls Creek Lake, but it's worth the effort. Not many hikers go up this trail, so you'll probably have the entire lake basin to yourself.

The Great Falls Creek Trail is different than trails up Bridge Creek and Fourmile Creek, which climb at the beginning and then level out. With a few minor flat sections, this trail climbs the entire way—not a steep grade, but steadily uphill. The steepest section is a short stretch at the beginning of the trail, unless you hike the precipitous extra mile from the upper lake to the pass, which is called West Boulder Plateau.

The beginning of the trail could be slightly confusing. You walk along the Boulder River for about 100 yards before taking a sharp right then a sharp left. These two junctions were well signed when I hiked this route, but if the signs have disappeared, you could get on the wrong trail at either of these junctions.

About a mile up the trail, you get a nice view of a falls on the Boulder River, and about a half mile farther, you can take a short (about 100 yards), steep spur trail to see a waterfall on Great Falls Creek. This is a nice place for your first break, after finishing the first, steep section of the trail.

After that, the trail stays away from the stream for about 5 miles. This means no water, not even any small feeder streams, so carry an extra bottle for the first part of the hike. After this you'll have all the water you need because you cross Great Falls Creek five times. Sorry, no bridges, but the fords aren't dangerous. Between crossings the trail closely follows the creek. You can see some old mining ruins at the second crossing.

About a mile after the last crossing, the trail takes a sharp left (south). At this point you can bushwhack about a half mile over to the lower lake. Use your compass or GPS to make sure you hit the lake, which can be difficult to find because of the thick forest. You can't see the lake until you're almost in it. I found a faint social trail going to the lower lake, but it was difficult to follow.

Whitebark pines, killed by pine beetles in many places, still flourish in the high-altitude Beartooths.

The first two lakes are in the forest, but the upper lake is barely above timberline at 9,452 feet. If you haven't had enough climbing, tackle a few switchbacks on the fairly easy, Category 3 climb up to the West Boulder Plateau. The view from the lake is great, but it's even better on the 10,000-foot plateau, which provides a good look at all three lakes and at mighty Mount Cowen, the highest point in the Absaroka Range, to the west.

The trail is in good shape and easy to follow all the way to the West Boulder Plateau. It stays in the forest until just before the upper lake.

SIDE TRIPS

The major side trip is the 2-mile round trip from the upper lake to the West Boulder Plateau, definitely worth taking. In big snow years, a large and potentially dangerous snowbank forms over the trail just before reaching the plateau and sometimes holds out until late July, so if you're up here early in the season, be careful crossing it. Also, regardless of which lake you camp at, you'll want to take time to visit the other two.

CAMPING

The upper lake has the best campsites and best view but no fish. The upper lake is above timberline and fragile, so make sure you have a zero-impact camp. You can camp at the other two lakes, of course, but they are more difficult to reach.

GREAT FALLS CREEK LAKES

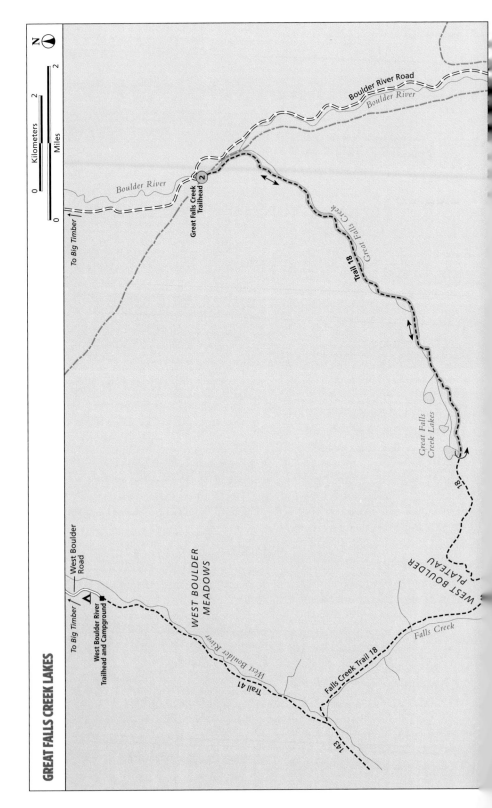

N

Kilometers
0   2

Miles
0   2

To Big Timber

Boulder River

Great Falls Creek
Trailhead 2

Boulder River Road

Boulder River

Great Falls Creek

Trail 18

Great Falls
Creek Lakes

18

WEST BOULDER
PLATEAU

To Big Timber   West Boulder
Road

West Boulder River
Trailhead and Campground

WEST BOULDER
MEADOWS

West Boulder River

Trail 41

Falls Creek Trail 18

Falls Creek

143

143

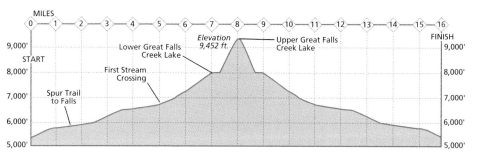

FISHING

The lower lake has a few rainbows that may require some patience but can be caught. The other two lakes are fishless.

MILES AND DIRECTIONS

0.0 Start at Great Falls Creek Trailhead.

1.5 Spur trail to falls.

5.0 First stream crossing.

7.0 Leave trail for Lower Great Falls Creek Lake.

8.0 Upper Great Falls Creek Lake.

16.0 Arrive back at Great Falls Creek Trailhead.

3 SILVER LAKE

A long day hike or overnighter to the heart of the Absaroka ending in a super-scenic cirque containing Silver Lake.

Start: Fourmile Creek Trailhead
Distance: 17 miles out and back
Difficulty: Difficult

Maps: USGS Mount Douglas and The Needles; RMS Mount Cowen Area; and at least 1 wilderness-wide map

FINDING THE TRAILHEAD

Drive 42.5 miles south from Big Timber on Boulder River Road to the Fourmile Creek Trailhead. A parking area is on the left and the trail starts on the right. Minimal parking; no toilet. **GPS:** 45.34211 N, 110.23158 W

THE HIKE

Silver Lake probably gets more use than most places in the Absaroka Range, but traffic is still light, mainly because it's an 8.5-mile hike through a thick, mostly lodgepole forest to reach the lake, making it a tough day hike. If you're backpacking, the 8.5 miles may be more than you want on your first day, especially since it's all uphill, which is why backpackers commonly stay more than one night once they have made the effort to get to the lake.

The first 2 miles are quite steep, but then the trail becomes a gradual uphill grade. The mature lodgepole forest lining the trail most of the way is broken here and there by big grassy meadows. Watch for big game in the meadows. Water sources are scarce, so plan on taking an extra bottle.

Silver Lake is, of course, the highlight of the trip. After you get there, you'll definitely believe it was worth the effort.

SIDE TRIPS

If you set up a base camp at Silver Lake and have an extra day, you can spend part of it going to Silver Pass and back. Another possibility for more experienced hikers is the off-trail scramble to two unnamed lakes above Silver Lake, or perhaps even as far as West Boulder Lake.

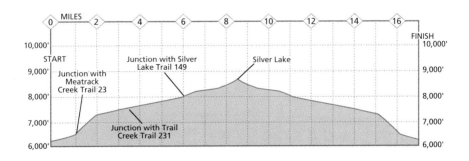

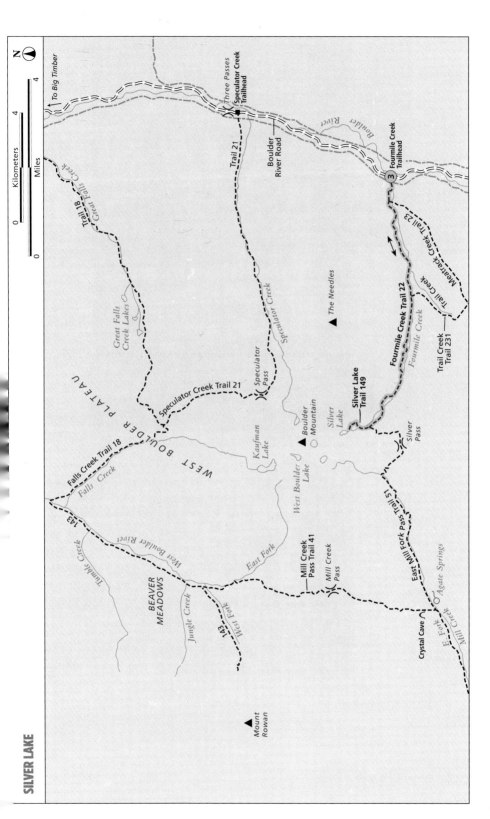

SILVER LAKE

N

To Big Timber

Kilometers
0   4

Miles
0   4

Three Passes

Speculator Creek
Trailhead

Trail 21

Boulder
River Road

Boulder River

Fourmile Creek
Trailhead

3

Great Falls Creek

Trail 18

Great Falls
Creek Lakes

Meadrack Creek Trail 23

Trail Creek 23

The Needles

Speculator Creek

Fourmile Creek Trail 22

Fourmile Creek

Speculator Creek Trail 21

Speculator
Pass

Silver Lake
Trail 149

Trail Creek
Trail 231

WEST BOULDER PLATEAU

Kaufman
Lake

Boulder
Mountain

Silver
Lake

Silver
Pass

Falls Creek Trail 18

Falls Creek

West Boulder
Lake

143

West Boulder River

East Fork

East Mill Fork Pass Trail 51

Tumble Creek

BEAVER
MEADOWS

Jungle Creek

Mill Creek Pass Trail 41

Mill Creek
Pass

Agate Springs

143

West Fork

Crystal Cave

E. Fork

Mill Creek

Mount
Rowan

Nothing like a big trout to hook a youngster on fishing for the rest of his life.

CAMPING

You can find five-star campsites at both the upper and lower ends of Silver Lake, but both sites show the wear and tear of past use, so be sure to set up a zero-impact camp in this fragile environment.

FISHING

Silver Lake has a good population of ultrasmart rainbow trout. They tend to rush to the other side of the lake at the first sign of a fly line on the water. West Boulder Lake has some sizeable cutthroats.

MILES AND DIRECTIONS

- **0.0** Start at Fourmile Creek Trailhead.
- **1.0** Junction with Meatrack Creek Trail 23; turn right.
- **3.5** Junction with Trail Creek Trail 231; turn right.
- **6.0** Junction with Silver Lake Trail 149; turn right.
- **8.5** Silver Lake.
- **17.0** Arrive back at Fourmile Creek Trailhead.

4 THREE PASSES

A demanding, multiday backpacking adventure through the remote and uncrowded heart of the Absaroka Mountains, including scenic trips over three high-altitude passes.

Start: Fourmile Creek Trailhead
Distance: 42.5-mile loop
Difficulty: Difficult and quite strenuous, especially Speculator Pass
Maps: USGS Chrome Mountain, Mount Douglas, The Needles, The

Pyramid, Mount Cowen, and West Boulder Plateau; RMS Mount Cowen Area; and at least 1 wilderness-wide map

FINDING THE TRAILHEAD

Drive 38.5 miles south from Big Timber on Boulder River Road to the Speculator Creek Trailhead (**GPS:** 45.39019 N, 110.21191 W), where this hike finishes, and then 4 more miles to the Fourmile Creek Trailhead. Large parking area, toilet and primitive camping area. (**GPS:** 45.34211 N, 110.23158 W). Minimal parking at both trailheads; no toilet.

RECOMMENDED ITINERARY

We did this route in four days, but I wish we had taken five. It would have been a more enjoyable (but still difficult) trip. Even though it's 8.5 miles uphill (most of it gradual), I suggest trying to make it to Silver Lake, a delightful place, for the first night out. The next best option for the first campsite would be the junction of the Silver Lake and Fourmile Creek Trails, which means a shorter day but a less spectacular campsite. Spend the second night along East Fork Mill Creek somewhere near the junction of the East Fork Mill Creek Pass Trail and Agate Springs, and the third night along the West Boulder River or first part of Falls Creek. The last night out probably won't be ideal, with the best choice probably being somewhere in the open meadows just over Speculator Pass. Once you get out of the meadows and into the thick lodgepole forest of Speculator Creek, good campsites are scarce. When we did this trip, we hiked from Silver Lake to Falls Creek in one day, which was too much, but we didn't have the extra day we needed.

- First night: Silver Lake
- Second night: East Fork Mill Creek near Agate Springs
- Third night: Falls Creek junction
- Fourth night: Upper Speculator Creek

THE HIKE

Some of us take long backpacking trips to leave civilization way behind and feel alone in a great wilderness, correct? If you agree, this route perfectly fits that goal. I have hiked thousands of miles through the decades, often with a heavy pack on my back, and I'll always remember this hike as one of the most memorable of them all.

As a general rule, the farther from the trailhead, the better the hiking. That's true with most of this trip, except for the first few miles and the last few miles, which could be considered boring as you walk through mile after mile of a mature lodgepole forest that obstructs the view. In between, though, it doesn't get much better than this hike, anywhere.

Two notes of caution: This is not a national park or a popular wilderness area. One disadvantage (or advantage?) of this is getting exact distances from maps or signs. Consequently, I had to estimate mileage more than I did for any other trip in this book. And second, it's for well-conditioned backpackers only. After getting to the top of Speculator Pass, you won't need to hit the StairMaster machine for a while. But if you want to get ready for this trip, you should spend many hours on it.

Fourmile Creek Trail 22 starts right at the Forest Service guard station and climbs steeply for about a mile before settling into a gradual ascent through lodgepole all the way to the junction with the Silver Lake Trail 149, 6 miles from the trailhead. Two trails veer off to the left (south)—Meatrack Creek Trail 23 (1 mile) and Trail Creek Trail 231 (3.5 miles). You stay right (west) at both junctions. Just after the junction with Meatrack Creek Trail, a major social trail goes off to the right. You stay left on Fourmile Creek Trail.

Along the way to the Silver Lake Trail junction, you pass through two large meadows. Finding water is not a problem as several small feeder streams come in from the north on their way to Fourmile Creek. The trail is in great shape all the way to the Silver Lake Trail junction, kept that way by horse traffic, primarily during the fall hunting season. There definitely is not enough backpacker traffic to keep the trail distinct through the meadows. We did not, however, see a single horse or mule during our August trip.

At the Silver Lake Trail junction, you have a decision. You've hiked 6 miles, most of it gradually uphill, and might be ready to pitch the tent. You can find a campsite along the stream near the junction, but you probably will enjoy staying at Silver Lake much more than along Fourmile Creek. Plan to start early in the day to leave enough time and energy for the climb up to Silver Lake. You follow Fourmile Creek to its source, Silver Lake, and the last mile to the lake is quite steep. You'll definitely be ready to stop and shed your heavy pack when you get there.

Silver Lake is a truly beautiful place. Boulder Mountain and an awesome, serrated ridge extending from it provide a gorgeous backdrop. The horseshoe of mountain ridges rising up from three sides of the lake keeps the sun out of camp in the early morning and evening. The lake has three or four good campsites, but this is a most fragile place, so please use the strictest zero-impact camping techniques. The lake has a healthy population of rainbows, but they're smart and skittish. One fly line on the water sends them to the other end of the lake.

After a wonderful night (or two nights, if you're lucky enough to have the time) in the five-star hotel called Silver Lake, retrace your steps back to the Silver Lake Trail junction and turn right. You might get your feet wet, depending on how high the water is, when you cross Fourmile Creek.

From here it's about 2.5 miles and 1,700 feet to 9,673-foot Silver Pass, a demanding Category 1 climb. However, the trail has a nice grade with well-designed switchbacks that make it easier. The steepest parts are right after Fourmile Creek and the last quarter mile or so to the pass.

Unfortunately, we hiked this section in a pouring rain and fog, so I didn't see what was surely some stunning scenery. The trail is well defined up to about a half mile from the pass, where it can get confusing. In fact, there is one place where it is easy to get off the main trail and onto a major social trail veering to the right (north). If you start going downhill on a trail marked with cairns, hit the brakes and backtrack to the main trail.

Silver Pass is an austere, knife-edged ridge. You can see an old "silvery" sign marking the pass from a half mile below. When we hiked, it was so wet that we couldn't keep our footing and had to virtually crawl up the last hundred yards, which is super steep. Once on top, though, we experienced the exhilaration of unbridled remoteness. I loved the old, weathered sign on Silver Pass—oh, the stories it could tell!

But keep in mind that this is only the first of three major passes on this trip—and definitely not the most difficult.

Silver Pass is part of the major east–west divide that forms the backbone of the Absaroka Range. On the pass, Fourmile Creek Trail 22 becomes East Fork Mill Creek Trail 51. After enjoying Silver Pass, head down toward East Fork Mill Creek on switchbacks for about a mile before the trail enters a fairly open forest. On the way to Agate Springs, you cross East Fork Mill Creek two more times than those crossings shown on the topo maps for the area. Sorry, no bridges. This is the wilderness, not a national park. Normally, finding water wouldn't be a problem, but when we hiked this route, heavy rain had turned East Fork Mill Creek into a brown, silt-laden torrent. We had a hard time finding water clean enough to filter (tip, throw a few coffee filters in your pack), but we did find lots of juicy huckleberries to eat.

After spending a night along East Fork Mill Creek somewhere near the junction (no trail sign when I was there), go right (north) on East Fork Mill Creek Pass Trail 41, heading toward Mill Creek Pass. About a quarter mile up the trail from East Fork Mill Creek, stop briefly to see Crystal Cave. As you'll note, this isn't much of a cavern, but there are several major caves in this area. Local cavers spend lots of time around here exploring and mapping caves—and carefully concealing their locations to preserve them from the overuse that routinely follows notoriety.

The trail climbs steeply for the first 1.5 miles, but switchbacks make the climb easier. Then, the switchbacks end, the trail straightens out, and the grade gets gradual for about a mile before heading up another series of switchbacks all the way to the pass. The well-defined trail stays in the timber until just before the pass and gains 2,400 feet in 4 miles from East Fork Mill Creek, another Category 1 climb (but easier than Silver Pass) to another spot on the Absaroka Divide.

From Mill Creek Pass you get an outstanding view to the north down the West Boulder River valley, to the south of The Pyramid and Crow Mountain, and in all directions a sweeping panorama of some of the wildest country left in America.

As the trail descends into the West Boulder from the pass, it fades away twice. You can stay on track, however, by following a series of well-placed cairns. After a short, steep section on top, the mostly well-defined trail gradually descends all the way to Falls Creek. The West Boulder valley is more open with lots of beautiful meadows, and is arguably more scenic than Fourmile Creek or East Fork Mill Creek. The West Boulder River is also a larger stream, especially after Tumble Creek and Falls Creek join in, and supports a healthy trout population all the way.

You can go all the way to Falls Creek to camp, or you can pick one of many campsites along the way. It would be challenging to find a bad campsite in this scenic valley.

So far on this trip, you've had many stream crossings, but crossing the West Boulder at Falls Creek might qualify as a ford, so be careful, especially early in July when the river will be close to maximum levels. After crossing Falls Creek and start heading toward Speculator Pass, you enter one of the wildest drainages in the Absaroka Range.

The trail is less defined and brushy as it follows cascading (and well-named) Falls Creek. The scenery is amazing in this, the fourth of five mountain valleys you hike through on this trip. As you hike up Falls Creek, you're treated to views of Boulder Mountain, The Needles, and, in the distance, The Pyramid.

About 3.5 miles up from the West Boulder River, you see the junction with Speculator Creek Trail 21. Trail 18 goes left (east) to Great Falls Creek Lakes and out to the Boulder River Road. You can take this route, but you'll be a long way from your vehicle, and you'll miss Speculator Pass, so go right (south) toward the pass.

This seldom-used section of trail becomes difficult to follow, and you might have to use some route-finding skills and even get the compass or GPS out here and there. However, the route to the pass is fairly obvious, even if you get off the trail momentarily.

The scenery is incredible and rugged as you climb 3,300 feet in 5.5 miles from the West Boulder River. Actually, the last 2 miles up to Speculator Pass, a rare Category H hill, is the steepest designated trail I have ever hiked. Your lungs will feel it, and your calves will get stretched out to the maximum.

On top of the pass—finally!—we had fun speculating on why it was named Speculator Pass. One theory was that there was speculation whether you could make it up here without having a heart attack. Another theory was that some mountain man couldn't spell "spectacular," so he jotted down "speculator." In any case, you'll never forget Speculator Pass.

On the south side of Speculator Pass, the trail goes through open Upper Speculator Creek and disappears in several places. This section will test your route-finding skills. While trying to stay on the trail, keep your eye open for a good campsite.

After spending your last night in the extreme wildness of Upper Speculator Creek (sorry, no good campsites), you hike through a lodgepole forest similar to Fourmile Creek all the way to the Boulder River Road. This stretch of trail seems to go on forever. We were wasted after climbing three major passes, but I made the time pass by visualizing that big steak I planned to attack as soon as I could find a restaurant.

At the Speculator Creek Trailhead, you need to hang your packs and take an easy 4-mile stroll to the Fourmile Creek Trailhead where you left your vehicle. When we

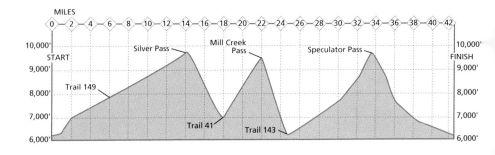

THREE PASSES

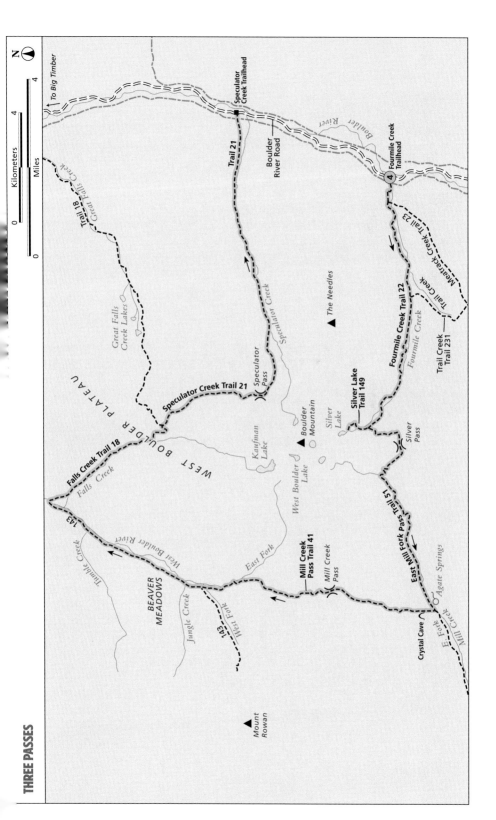

N

Kilometers
0   4

Miles
0   4

To Big Timber

Speculator Creek Trailhead

Trail 21

Boulder River Road

Boulder River

Fourmile Creek Trailhead

Great Falls Creek

Trail 18

Great Falls Creek Lakes

Speculator Creek

The Needles

Meantrack Creek Trail 23

Trail Creek

Fourmile Creek Trail 22

Fourmile Creek

Trail Creek Trail 231

WEST BOULDER PLATEAU

Speculator Creek Trail 21

Speculator Pass

Kaufman Lake

Boulder Mountain

Silver Lake

Silver Lake Trail 149

Falls Creek Trail 18

Falls Creek

West Boulder Lake

Silver Pass

East Mill Fork Pass Trail 15

143

Tumble Creek

West Boulder River

BEAVER MEADOWS

Jungle Creek

East Fork

West Fork

143

Mill Creek Pass Trail 41

Mill Creek Pass

Crystal Cave

Agate Springs

E. Fork

Mill Creek

Mount Rowan

did this trip, I stashed an old bicycle at the Speculator Creek Trailhead and rode back to my vehicle.

OPTIONS

If you aren't quite ready for the extreme wildness and steepness of the Speculator Pass area, you can hike out from Falls Creek to the Boulder River Road by going out Great Falls Creek, which is, oddly, only 1 to 2 miles shorter than going out Speculator Creek. If you didn't stash a bicycle at the Great Falls Creek Trailhead, you'll need two vehicles to do this route because it's 11 miles up the Boulder River Road to get back to the Fourmile Creek Trailhead.

You can also skip Falls Creek and keep going out the West Boulder for 8 gradually descending miles to the West Boulder River Trailhead and a vehicle campground. This option has a long shuttle, so you'll need two vehicles.

And for a really, really long shuttle, you can keep going down East Fork Mill Creek and come out at the Mill Creek Trailhead in Paradise Valley near Pray, Montana. It's an easy 7 miles from Agate Springs to the Mill Creek Trailhead.

SIDE TRIPS

Silver Lake could be a side trip instead of the first campsite. Depending on how early you hit the trail, you can pitch your tent somewhere around the junction with Silver Lake Trail and day hike up to the lake. Great Falls Creek Lakes might look like a nice side trip, but make sure you have plenty of daylight left to get over the intensely demanding Speculator Pass.

From Silver Lake, try an off-trail trek to two unnamed lakes at the head of the cirque. From the Falls Creek Trail, try the climb up to the divide above Great Falls Creek or to Kaufman Lake.

CAMPING

Regulations allow you to set up a zero-impact campsite anywhere along this route. Be especially careful not to leave your mark in the nearly untouched meadows at the head of Upper Speculator Creek.

FISHING

Silver Lake has some nice rainbows, but they're stealthy. East Fork Mill Creek has some nice cutthroats, as well as a few rainbows and browns, but fishing is fairly lean in the upper stretches of the creek along the route of this hike. The upper stretches of the West Boulder are great fishing for small cutthroat, and as you get farther downstream, you might snag a brown or rainbow.

MILES AND DIRECTIONS

0.0 Start at Fourmile Creek Trailhead.

1.0 Junction with Meatrack Creek Trail 23; turn right.

3.5 Junction with Trail Creek Trail 231; turn right.

6.0 Junction with Silver Lake Trail 149; turn right.

8.5 Silver Lake.

11.5 Backtrack to Fourmile Creek Trail 22; turn right to Silver Pass.

14.0 Silver Pass and start of East Fork Mill Creek Trail 51.

18.0 Agate Springs and junction with Mill Creek Pass Trail 41; turn right.

18.3 Crystal Cave.

22.0 Mill Creek Pass.

24.5 Junction with West Boulder Trail 143; turn right.

25.5 Jungle Creek and start of Beaver Meadows.

28.0 Falls Creek and junction with Falls Creek Trail 18; turn right.

31.5 Junction with Speculator Creek Trail 21; turn right.

33.5 Speculator Pass.

42.5 Arrive at Speculator Creek Trailhead and Boulder River Road.

5 BRIDGE LAKE

A very long day hike or strenuous overnighter to a super-remote, rarely visited mountain lake, one of the nicest places in the entire National Wilderness Preservation System that hardly anybody sees.

Start: Bridge Creek Trailhead
Distance: 20 miles out and back
Difficulty: Difficult

Maps: USGS Mount Douglas and The Needles; RMS Mount Cowen Area; and at least 1 wilderness-wide map

FINDING THE TRAILHEAD

 Drive 47 miles south from Big Timber on Boulder River Road to the Bridge Creek Trailhead on your right (west), less than a mile past the Upsidedown Creek Trailhead. Hicks Park Campground, a full-service vehicle campground, is right at the trailhead. Minimal parking. No toilet. **GPS:** 45.28736 N, 110.24260 W

THE HIKE

Like trails to Silver Lake and Great Falls Creek Lakes, this route is long for a day hike or an overnighter. Only well-conditioned hikers can make it into Bridge Lake and back in one day and not many want to haul a heavy pack in for an overnighter. The upshot? Not many hikers go to Bridge Lake, so if you go, you'll probably have it to yourself.

The trail starts out with a serious upgrade for about 2.5 miles. Then it levels out for about 5 miles until you start the last steep pitch up to the lake. Also at 2.5 miles you'll see one of the few private cabins still remaining in the wilderness. This cabin is on public land, and the Forest Service has decided to let nature gradually reclaim it instead of destroying it.

After you cross Bridge Creek on a bridge shortly after leaving the trailhead, you stay on the north side of the stream until about 2 miles before the lake, crossing several feeder streams with no bridges along the way. After about 4 miles from the trailhead, the trail leaves the thick forest and winds through a series of scenic meadows before breaking out above timberline.

The trail is in great shape over the entire route. I especially liked the "no nonsense" switchbacks on the first climb and on the last pitch up to the lake. These switchbacks are

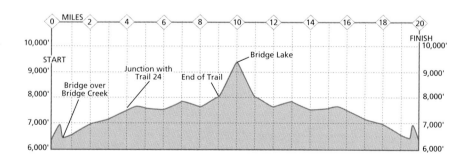

The Absaroka-Beartooth Wilderness has many thousands of five-star campsites. Try to keep them that way by leaving as little disruption as possible.

generous curves in the trail as opposed to the type of near-level switchbacks that double the length of a trip. If the switchbacks on this route were like those on the Upsidedown Creek Trail, it would probably add 2 or 3 miles to the route.

You might think the map is wrong because the trail doesn't go all the way to the lake, but the map is correct. The trail ends about a mile before the lake, and you go off-trail the rest of the way. This is well above timberline, though, and easy hiking, with the exception of one 50-foot stretch along the creek just before the lake. Stay on the left (south) side of Bridge Creek even though it looks easier on the other side. Keep your topo map or GPS out so you can see where the lake is.

OPTIONS

You could camp along Bridge Creek about 6 or 7 miles up the trail and day hike to Bridge Lake. This option spares you the pain of lugging your overnight pack up the last steep pitch and the off-trail section before the lake.

CAMPING

If you decide to camp at Bridge Lake, look for a good campsite on the bench above the right (north) side of the lake. This involves a little more climbing, but it's worth it. If

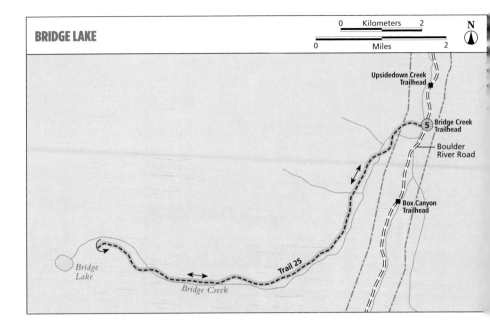

you're wasted and can't make that last quarter mile to this campsite, you can camp on the bench just before you get to the lake, but this camping area isn't as nice. If you decide to camp along the creek before doing the last climb to the lake, you'll find several nice campsites there, but not as nice as camping at the lake. Bridge Lake is almost free of signs of past campers, so please help keep it that way. No campfires, please!

FISHING

Bridge Lake has nice-size cutthroats, but they can be quite temperamental, so you could go home skunked.

MILES AND DIRECTIONS

0.0   Start at Bridge Creek Trailhead.

0.5   Bridge over Bridge Creek.

2.5   Wilderness cabin.

4.0   Junction with Trail 24; turn left.

9.0   End of trail.

10.0 Bridge Lake.

20.0 Arrive back at Bridge Creek Trailhead.

6 EAST FORK BOULDER RIVER

An easy day hike or overnighter along a beautiful stream with good fishing.

Start: Box Canyon Trailhead
Distance: 7 miles out and back
Difficulty: Easy
Maps: USGS Mount Douglas and Haystack Peak; RMS Mount Douglas–

Mount Wood and Cooke City–Cutoff Mountain; and at least 1 wilderness-wide map

FINDING THE TRAILHEAD

Drive 48 miles south from Big Timber on Boulder River Road to the Box Canyon Trailhead, which is at the end of the improved road. Large trailhead with toilets and plenty of parking most of the year, but can be crowded with horse trailers in September and October. **GPS:** 45.27344 N, 110.25000 W

THE HIKE

This trail is actually the "approach" to the popular routes into Lake Plateau and Slough Creek. Consequently, even though many people use this area, most hurry right through the East Fork Boulder River on their way to somewhere else. This makes it a pleasant day hike or an easy overnighter for beginning backpackers.

From the Box Canyon Trailhead, Trail 27 climbs gradually along the East Fork. The trail stays a fair distance from the river for about 3 miles. The first part of this trail was once a wagon road, and it still looks like one. Fortunately, this isn't because of heavy traffic, although the area receives moderate use during July and August and heavy use from stock parties in September during the early hunting season.

The trail leads to a great camping area about 3.5 miles from the trailhead and then crosses the East Fork on a big bridge. The large camping area just before the bridge can handle a large party or several parties. However, stock users should check the Forest Service regulations for the area (including group size limits) when planning to stay here.

Day hikers can easily spend a few hours fishing or lounging around this area, and even those bound for higher regions might want to linger. The stream is as charming as they get, and the fishing is great. The bridge marks a good turnaround point for day hikers. Those with more time and energy can continue east to where the trail forks, leading to extended trips up to Lake Plateau or south to the Slough Creek Divide.

CAMPING

If you're staying overnight, set up a zero-impact camp at the large camping area just before the bridge over the East Fork.

FISHING

Above Box Canyon the East Fork Boulder River contains mostly cutthroat trout, although rainbows dominate the fishery below. Some of these cutthroats may be descendants of

EAST FORK BOULDER RIVER

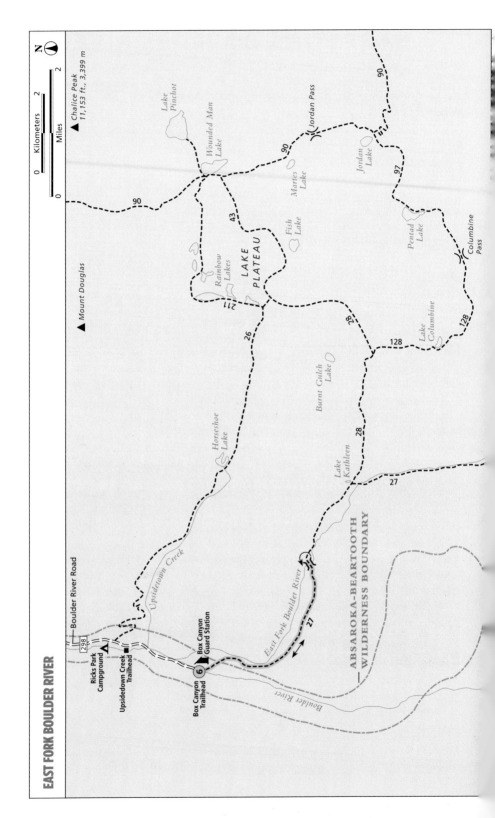

Ricks Park Campground

298

Boulder River Road

Upsidedown Creek Trailhead

Box Canyon Guard Station

Box Canyon Trailhead

6

27

East Fork Boulder River

Boulder River

ABSAROKA-BEARTOOTH WILDERNESS BOUNDARY

27

28

Lake Kathleen

28

128

Lake Columbine

128

Columbine Pass

Pentad Lake

97

Jordan Lake

Jordan Pass

90

Burnt Gulch Lake

Horseshoe Lake

Upsidetown Creek

26

211

211

LAKE PLATEAU

Rainbow Lakes

Fish Lake

43

Martes Lake

90

Wounded Man Lake

90

Lake Pinchot

▲ Mount Douglas

▲ Chalice Peak
11,153 ft., 3,399 m

N

0   Kilometers   2

0   Miles   2

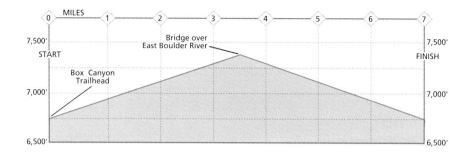

native stocks. A smattering of rainbows (immigrants from Rainbow Lakes above) can be found near where Rainbow Creek enters the East Fork Boulder River.

Cutthroat trout are aggressive and often easy to catch. As a result, where cutthroats dominate the fishery, fishing tends to be great. While this has been the fish's downfall in lower streams, most anglers in the Beartooths only keep enough for dinner, and populations seem stable.

None of the lakes near this route supports a fishery, but Lake Kathleen provides an opportunity to observe a lake in its natural, untarnished state.

MILES AND DIRECTIONS

0.0   Start at Box Canyon Trailhead.

3.5   Bridge over East Fork Boulder River.

7.0   Arrive back at Box Canyon Trailhead.

7 COLUMBINE PASS

A weeklong backpacking vacation over magnificent Columbine Pass and into a gorgeous, lake-dotted plateau with a myriad of side-trip opportunities; nicely suited to backpackers who like to set up a base camp.

Start: Box Canyon Trailhead
Distance: 34.3-mile (without side trips) loop with shuttle and base-camp options
Difficulty: Moderate but long

Maps: USGS Mount Douglas, Tumble Mountain, Pinnacle Mountain, and Haystack Peak; RMS Mount Douglas–Mount Wood and Cooke City–Cutoff Mountain; and at least 1 wilderness-wide map

FINDING THE TRAILHEAD

Drive 48 miles south from Big Timber on Boulder River Road to the Box Canyon Trailhead at the end of the improved road. Large trailhead with toilets. Plenty of parking most of the year, but can be crowded with horse trailers in September and October. **GPS:** 45.27344 N, 110.25000 W

The Upsidedown Creek Trailhead is 1.5 miles before Box Canyon. The Upsidedown Creek Trail comes out to the road about 50 yards south of the parking area. **GPS:** 45.29571 N, 110.24012 W

RECOMMENDED ITINERARY

This trip works best if you get an early start from Box Canyon, but since the drive to the trailhead is long, it might be difficult to hit the trail early. If you start later in the day, try the East Fork Boulder River for the first night out. This may lengthen the trip by one day—not a bad price to pay for sleeping late. The following recommended itinerary lays out a five-day trip, but you could easily spend more time on Lake Plateau.

- First night: Lake Columbine
- Second night: Lake Pinchot, Wounded Man, Owl, or nearby lakes
- Third night: Same campsite
- Fourth night: Diamond or Horseshoe Lake

THE HIKE

Hikers can choose from a variety of options for hiking into the Lake Plateau, but this route is special because there aren't many opportunities like this one to see so much wild country without working out a burdensome shuttle or retracing your steps for half of the trip.

From the Box Canyon Trailhead, Trail 27 climbs gradually through timber and open parks along the East Fork Boulder River for about 3.5 miles before crossing a bridge sturdy enough to support horses. If you started late, you may wish to stay the first night

Expect to see horse parties throughout the wilderness, especially in the Lake Plateau area.

in one of several excellent campsites located just before the bridge. If you started early, forge on.

After crossing the East Fork, the trail follows the river for about a half mile before climbing away through heavy timber. Several trout-filled pools beckon along this stream-side stretch, so be prepared to fight off temptations to stop and rig up the fly rod.

In less than 2 miles you reach the junction with Trail 28. Trail 27 goes straight and eventually ends up in Yellowstone National Park. Turn left here onto Trail 28. In about a quarter mile, watch for tranquil little Lake Kathleen off to the left, another option for a first-night campsite.

The trail joins Trail 128 to Columbine Pass 2.5 miles above Lake Kathleen. Turn right onto this trail, which immediately climbs a short, steep hill and then breaks out of the forest into a subalpine panorama. It's about 1.5 miles to Lake Columbine. With an early start on the first day, this would also make a good first campsite. If it's your second day out, consider pushing on to Pentad Lake or Jordan Lake for the second night's camp.

From Lake Columbine continue another scenic 2 miles up to 9,850-foot Columbine Pass. In a good snow year, snowbanks cover the trail on Columbine Pass well into July. The trail fades away a couple of times between Lake Columbine and the pass, so watch the topo map carefully to stay on track. A few well-placed cairns make navigation here easier.

After the Category 2 climb to Columbine Pass, take a break and enjoy a snack and the stunning vistas, including 10,685-foot Pinnacle Mountain to the south. From here the trail leaves the Boulder River drainage behind and heads into the Stillwater River drainage. Hereafter the trip leapfrogs from one lake to the next for 14 miles. There's a good reason they call it the Lake Plateau.

EXPLORING THE LAKE PLATEAU

Any trip to the Lake Plateau should include some extra time for exploring the many hidden treasures in the area. Here's a few suggestions rated for difficulty as follows: Human (easy for almost everyone, including children), Semi-human (moderately difficult), or Animal (don't try it unless you're very fit and wilderness-wise). Also refer to more detailed rating information in "How to Use This Guide" (page 4).

Destination	Difficulty
Lake Pinchot	Human
Flood Creek lakes	Semi-human
Asteroid Lake Basin	Animal
Chalice Peak	Animal
Lightning Lake	Animal
Lake Diaphanous	Human
Fish Lake	Human
Barrier Lake	Animal
Mirror Lake	Semi-human
Chickadee Lake	Animal
Squeeze Lake	Animal
Mount Douglas	Animal
Lake Plateau Loop	Human
Martes Lake	Semi-human
Columbine Pass	Human
Jordan Lake	Human
Sundown Lake	Semi-human
Pentad and Favonius Lakes	Human
Burnt Gulch Lake	Animal

Those who camped at Lake Columbine can make it all the way into the Lake Plateau for the next night's campsite. Otherwise, plan to pitch a tent at Pentad or Jordan Lake. Pentad is more scenic, but Jordan offers better fishing (and suffers more from overuse). You can also camp at several smaller lakes near Pentad—Mouse, Favonius, Sundown, and several unnamed lakes. You can find many great campsites in the area that won't be as crowded as at Jordan Lake, so don't be in a hurry and take the first campsite you see. Look around for a while and you'll probably find a better one. It might be wise to stop at the south end of Pentad anyway, as the trail is difficult to follow because of all the tangent trails created by backcountry horseback riders to going to various campsites. To untangle the maze, stop and study the topo map.

The trail skirts the east shore of Pentad Lake heading north. Jordan Lake, another 2 miles down the trail from Pentad, has limited camping, with one heavily used camping area at the foot of the lake large enough for a big group or several groups—and probably too heavily impacted to be used by parties with stock animals.

At Jordan Lake the trail meets Trail 90, coming out of Lake Plateau and dropping east down into the Middle Fork of Wounded Man Creek. Turn left (north) here onto Trail 90, which climbs gradually 1.5 miles over Jordan Pass and drops into the Lake Plateau. This isn't much of a pass, but it's a great spot to take 15 minutes to marvel at the mountainous horizons in every direction.

If you camped at Jordan or Pentad Lake, you have lots of options for the next night out or for a base camp. The closest site is at Wounded Man Lake, but this is a busy place. The

Lush open meadows on the way to Columbine Pass.

best campsite is along the North Fork of Wounded Man Creek just southwest of the lake. But consider hiking the short mile northeast from Wounded Man Lake to Lake Pinchot to stay at the crown jewel of the Lake Plateau. The third option is to turn left onto Trail 211 at the junction on the west side of Wounded Man Lake and stay at Owl Lake or one of the Rainbow Lakes that follow shortly thereafter. These offer some of the best base camps in the area because there are innumerable sights to see, all within a short walk.

After a night or two or three or more on the plateau, follow Trail 211 along the west shore of Rainbow Lakes down to the junction with Trail 26 at the south end of Lower Rainbow Lake. Turn right (west) here and spend the last night out at Diamond or Horseshoe Lake (sometimes called Upper and Lower Horseshoe Lakes). Horseshoe Lake is probably better because it has more campsites and leaves the shortest possible distance along Upsidedown Creek for the last day. That's still about 8.5 miles, plus the 1.5 miles some lucky volunteer has to walk or try to catch a ride up to the Box Canyon Trailhead to retrieve your vehicle. There are no suitable campsites anywhere from Horseshoe Lake to the Boulder River Road.

OPTIONS

If you can arrange transportation for a long, difficult shuttle, you can hike out the West Stillwater River or the main Stillwater River. You might need a four-wheel-drive vehicle to get to the West Stillwater River Trailhead. You can also make this an out-and-back trip from either the Box Canyon or Upsidedown Creek Trailheads.

COLUMBINE PASS

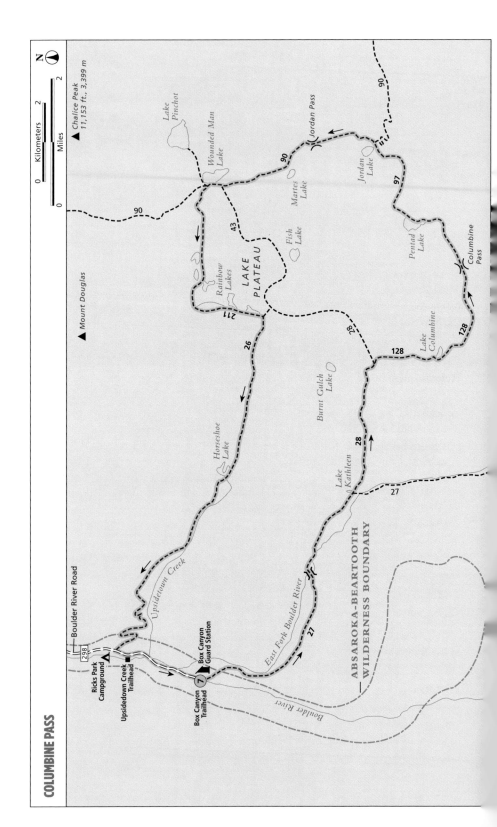

N

▲ Chalice Peak
11,153 ft., 3,399 m

Lake Pinchot

Wounded Man Lake

Jordan Pass

90

Jordan Lake

97

Martes Lake

43

Fish Lake

LAKE PLATEAU

Rainbow Lakes

211

Pentad Lake

Columbine Pass

26

28

128

Lake Columbine

128

Burnt Gulch Lake

▲ Mount Douglas

Horseshoe Lake

28

Lake Kathleen

27

Upsidetown Creek

ABSAROKA-BEARTOOTH WILDERNESS BOUNDARY

27

East Fork Boulder River

Boulder River Road

298

Ricks Park Campground

Upsidedown Creek Trailhead

Box Canyon Guard Station

Box Canyon Trailhead

Boulder River

0   Kilometers   2
0   Miles   2

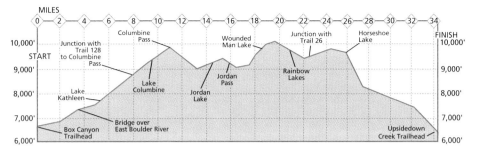

SIDE TRIPS
Refer to "Exploring the Lake Plateau" (page 62).

CAMPING
The Lake Plateau has hundreds of terrific campsites, all undesignated. Find one for your base camp, and please make it a zero-impact camp because this area rightfully deserves the heavy use it receives.

FISHING
Refer to "Fishing the Lake Plateau" (page 68).

MILES AND DIRECTIONS

0.0   Start at Box Canyon Trailhead.

3.5   East Fork Boulder River (follow Trail 27).

5.2   Junction with Trail 28; turn left.

5.4   Lake Kathleen.

7.9   Junction with Trail 128; turn right.

9.3   Lake Columbine.

11.1   Columbine Pass.

12.5   Pentad Lake.

14.5   Jordan Lake and junction with Trail 90; turn left.

15.9   Jordan Pass.

18.7   Wounded Man Lake and junction with Trail 43; turn left.

18.9   Junction with Trail 211; turn left.

21.0   Rainbow Lakes.

22.5   Junction with Trail 26, turn right.

25.9   Horseshoe Lake.

34.3   Arrive at Upsidedown Creek Trailhead.

8 LAKE PLATEAU WEST

An extended backpacking adventure into the fabulous Lake Plateau; an ideal base-camp trip.

Start: Box Canyon Trailhead
Distance: 25.5-mile (not counting side trips) loop with out-and-back option
Difficulty: Moderate but long

Maps: USGS Mount Douglas, Tumble Mountain, and Haystack Peak; RMS Mount Douglas–Mount Wood and Cooke City–Cutoff Mountain; and at least 1 wilderness-wide map

FINDING THE TRAILHEAD

Drive 48 miles south from Big Timber on Boulder River Road to the Box Canyon Trailhead at the end of the improved road. Large trailhead with toilet. Plenty of parking most of the year, but crowded horse trailers in September and October. **GPS:** 45.27344 N, 110.25000 W

The Upsidedown Creek Trailhead is 1.5 miles before Box Canyon. The Upsidedown Creek Trail comes out on the road about 50 yards south of the parking area. **GPS:** 45.29571 N, 110.24012 W

RECOMMENDED ITINERARY

Since it's such a long drive to Box Canyon Trailhead from just about anywhere, most hikers don't hit the trail until afternoon. This actually works well for this route because there aren't many good camping areas between the East Fork Boulder River. Rainbow Lakes, more than 12 miles down the trail, is too far for a single day for many backpackers. If you stay at the East Fork Boulder River, though, you only have 8.8 miles to the Rainbow Lakes for the second night out. You could also set up a base camp at Rainbow Lakes or hike 2 to 3 miles farther the second day to set up the base camp.

- First night: East Fork Boulder River
- Second night: Along Rainbow Creek or at Rainbow Lakes
- Third night: Set up base camp somewhere on the Lake Plateau
- Fourth night: Same campsite
- Fifth night: Same campsite
- Sixth night: Horseshoe or Diamond Lake

THE HIKE

From the Box Canyon Trailhead, Trail 27 climbs gradually through timber and open parks along the East Fork Boulder River for about 3.5 miles before crossing a sturdy bridge. If you started late, you may wish to stay the first night at the excellent camping area just before the bridge.

Camping here is not a bad idea. Otherwise, it's a tough 12- to 14-mile day to get onto the Lake Plateau, depending on where you decide to set up base camp. And there really aren't any great campsites at the convenient 5- to 7-mile range to split up the distance. So

Taking a break at one of the dozens of lakes on the Lake Plateau. MARNIE SCHNEIDER

either plan to camp at the 3.5-mile mark or aim for the valley just below the Lake Plateau, about 10 miles in, where several great campsites are nestled along Rainbow Creek.

After crossing the East Fork, the trail follows the river for about a half mile before climbing away through heavy timber. Several trout-filled pools beckon along this riverside stretch, so be prepared to fight off temptations to stop and rig up the fly-casting gear.

In less than 2 miles, Trail 27 heads south toward Slough Creek Divide. Turn left here onto Trail 28. In a quarter mile or less, the trail passes little Lake Kathleen on the left. Then, 2.5 miles farther, Trail 128 breaks off to the right and heads for Columbine Pass. Stay left on Trail 28.

After another 2.6 miles the trail meets Trail 211. At this point you need to decide where you intend to base camp. Here are a few options: (1) Head left up the steep switchbacks 0.75 mile to the junction with Trail 26 and turn right to any of six Rainbow Lakes to the northwest; (2) go right less than 1 mile up Trail 211 to Fish Lake, reached after a short, steep climb; or (3) continue past Fish Lake another 3.5 miles on Trail 211 to Lake Pinchot. All three options have plenty of great campsites.

On the way to Lake Pinchot, Wounded Man Lake might look like a good place to base camp, but it has limited camping. Lake Pinchot might add an extra mile when you really don't want it, but this beautiful lake is the heart of the Lake Plateau. If you don't base camp there, be sure to visit it on a day trip—then you'll be sorry you didn't camp there.

If you can't make up your mind on where to base camp, set up a temporary camp for one night and then spend the next day trekking around, enjoying the scenery, fishing, and searching for that five-star campsite for your base camp.

FISHING THE LAKE PLATEAU

Anglers who want to fish the first day of the trip should camp near the East Fork Boulder River or Rainbow Creek. Above Box Canyon the East Fork Boulder River contains mostly cutthroat trout, although rainbows dominate the fishery below. Some of these cutthroats may be descendants of native stocks. A smattering of rainbows (immigrants from Rainbow Lakes above) can be found near where Rainbow Creek enters the East Fork Boulder River.

The Lake Plateau offers a variety of fishing opportunities, consisting mostly of rainbow and cutthroat trout. Cutthroats are frequently found along rocky shorelines on the downwind sides of lakes. Anglers often fish past the fish by casting out into the lake.

Cutthroat trout are aggressive and often easy to catch. As a result, where cutthroats dominate the fishery, the fishing tends to be great. This has been the cutthroats' downfall in lower streams, so take only enough for dinner to help keep populations stable.

The lakes of the Lake Plateau are located in both the Stillwater and Boulder River drainages and offer cutthroat, rainbow, and some golden trout fishing. Keep in mind that not all lakes contain fish, but most of the lakes along the trails have self-sustaining populations and contain plenty of fish. Golden trout were once planted on the plateau, but only a few remain. Flood Creek, including Lake Pinchot, has beautiful mixed species of fish (golden, cutthroat, rainbow) due to migrations of planted fish. A small drainage south of Flood Creek (Asteroid Lake) contains pure goldens.

Wounded Man Creek supports a mainly cutthroat trout fishery, although rainbows share Pentad and Favonius Lakes with cutts. Jordan Lake holds nice cutthroats that can be counted on to provide dinner.

For solitude, try off-trail trips to Burnt Gulch, Barrier, and Martes Lakes, all good fishing. Aufwuchs Lake is a tough cross-country hike but has good cutthroat fishing. Many high mountain streams are too steep to harbor large populations of trout, so look for the slow spots.

Once you've set up your base camp, start taking advantage of the numerous adventures waiting in all directions. For anglers, there are two dozen lakes within reach of an easy day hike. For peak baggers, there are 11,298-foot Mount Douglas, 11,153-foot Chalice Peak, and other summits to conquer.

To return to the Box Canyon Trailhead, follow whichever leg of the Lake Plateau loop trail (211 or 43) you didn't take on the way in. This way you'll have covered the entire Lake Plateau circle (about a 6-mile loop). Then drop back to the junction with Trail 28 and retrace the route down Rainbow Creek.

To avoid backtracking on Trail 28 take Upsidedown Creek Trail 26, which heads west from the foot of Lower Rainbow Lake. Plan on two days to get out, camping at Horseshoe or Diamond Lake (sometimes called Upper and Lower Horseshoe Lakes) before heading out Upsidedown Creek. This route may be slightly shorter, but it involves a steep downhill after a 600-foot climb, some of it on annoying "'mall-walk" switchbacks which add a couple miles to the hike. The trail hits Boulder River Road about 1.5 miles north of the Box Canyon Trailhead. Here, pick the most energetic member of your party to jog up to Box Canyon to get your vehicle.

The Lake Plateau gets more use than most areas in the Beartooths, but a large number of destinations and campsites dilute the crowd to a tolerable level. A week in this wonderland will undoubtedly be a memorable vacation. But expect a few remorseful

Fishing Rainbow Lakes on the Lake Plateau.

moments when you realize that you must return to your hectic lifestyle back home. Be forewarned: The first days back at work may seem quite unpleasant.

OPTIONS

It seems slightly easier to do this trip as described above, but the route can be reversed: going in Upsidedown Creek and out along the East Fork. This option, however, involves a steady, dry, 8.3-mile climb to Horseshoe Lake. If you take this option, carry extra water. You can also retrace your steps down Rainbow Creek to Box Canyon and skip the Upsidedown Creek Trail.

SIDE TRIPS

You could spend weeks exploring the Lake Plateau. Check out the list of possible side trips in "Exploring the Lake Plateau" (page 62).

CAMPING

The Lake Plateau has hundreds of terrific campsites, all undesignated. Find one for your base camp, and please make it a zero-impact camp.

FISHING

Refer to "Fishing the Lake Plateau" (page 68).

LAKE PLATEAU WEST

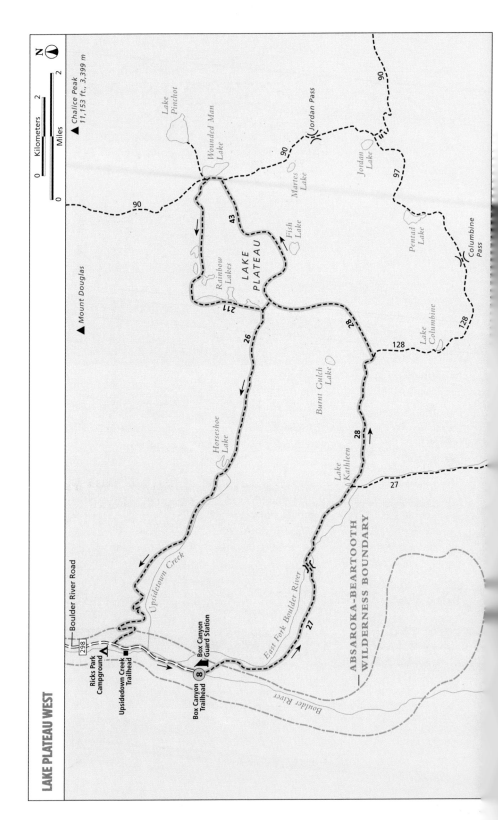

N

▲ Chalice Peak
11,153 ft., 3,399 m

0   Kilometers   2

0   Miles   2

▲ Mount Douglas

Boulder River Road

298

Ricks Park
Campground

Upsidedown Creek
Trailhead

Box Canyon
Guard Station

8
Box Canyon
Trailhead

Upsidetown Creek

Horseshoe
Lake

26

211

211

43

90

90

LAKE
PLATEAU

Rainbow
Lakes

Wounded Man
Lake

Lake
Pinchot

Fish
Lake

Martes
Lake

Jordan Pass

Jordan
Lake

90

97

82

128

Pentad
Lake

Columbine
Pass

Lake
Columbine

128

Burnt Gulch
Lake

28

28

Lake
Kathleen

27

27

East Fork Boulder River

Boulder River

ABSAROKA-BEARTOOTH
WILDERNESS BOUNDARY

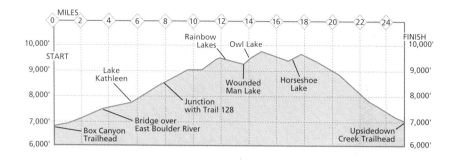

MILES AND DIRECTIONS

0.0 Start at Box Canyon Trailhead.

3.5 East Fork Boulder River.

5.2 Junction with Trail 28; turn left.

5.4 Lake Kathleen.

7.9 Junction with Trail 128; turn left.

10.5 Junction with Trail 211; turn left.

11.4 Junction with Trail 26; turn right.

12.3 Rainbow Lakes.

13.2 Wounded Man Lake and junction with Trail 90; turn right.

13.5 Junction with Trail 43; turn right.

15.0 Junction with Trail 28; turn right.

15.9 Junction with Trail 26; turn left.

17.2 Horseshoe Lake.

25.5 Arrive at Upsidedown Creek Trailhead.

9 SLOUGH CREEK DIVIDE

A long trek through a lot of extreme remoteness with a beautiful stream all the way and an excellent chance of seeing wildlife, including grizzly bears.

Start: Box Canyon Trailhead
Distance: 39.4-mile very long shuttle
Difficulty: Difficult
Maps: USGS Mount Douglas, Haystack Peak, Roundhead Butte, and Mount Hornaday; RMS Mount Douglas–Mount Wood and Cooke City–Cutoff Mountain; and at least 1 wilderness-wide map. A Yellowstone National Park map would also be helpful.

FINDING THE TRAILHEADS

Drive 48 miles south from Big Timber on Boulder River Road to the Box Canyon Trailhead, which is at the end of the improved road. Large trailhead with toilets. Plenty of parking most of the year, but can be crowded in September and October. **GPS:** 45.27344 N, 110.25000 W

To leave a vehicle at the Slough Creek Trailhead in Yellowstone National Park, drive 5.8 miles east of Tower Junction or 22.6 miles west of the Northeast Entrance and turn north onto the unpaved road to the Slough Creek Campground. Go 1.7 miles and park at the trailhead, which is on your right just before the campground. **GPS:** 44.94354 N, 110.30825 W

RECOMMENDED ITINERARY

A three-night itinerary means approximately 10 miles per day. If this is too ambitious for you, make this a four-night trip by spending the first night along the East Fork Boulder River. To follow this itinerary, you probably want to do the shuttle the day before and vehicle camp somewhere along Boulder River Road.

- First night: Slough Creek Divide area

- Second night: Along Slough Creek halfway between the divide and the park boundary

- Third night: Along Slough Creek in Yellowstone National Park (permit required)

THE HIKE

Most of the Beartooths is subalpine—open, rocky country full of mountainous panoramas—but not this route. Instead, this trail starts in the deep forest of the upper Boulder River valley and stays below timberline for almost 40 miles.

This is one of the most phenomenal hiking routes in the Absaroka-Beartooth Wilderness, if not any wilderness. Yet, during the summer it doesn't get much use, mainly because the trail doesn't go to a lake or the top of a mountain, and it requires a very time-consuming shuttle. In the fall, however, many hunters and outfitters use the area in search of elk, deer, and other big game common in Boulder River/Slough Creek country. If you're looking for solitude and remoteness and the chance to see all kinds of wildlife, including the mighty grizzly bear, put this trail high on your list of priorities.

Paintbrush, one of many wildflowers found throughout the wilderness. MARNIE SCHNEIDER

The first step is to arrange a shuttle. This route can be done from either end, but starting at the north end is slightly better because it allows a net loss in elevation and the trip ends in Yellowstone National Park. If your group is big enough to split in two, start at opposite ends and trade keys when you meet each other. This greatly reduces the trouble in arranging the shuttle. If not, leave a vehicle at the Slough Creek Trailhead in the park and drive all the way around (about a 4-hour drive, one-way) to the Box Canyon Trailhead at the end of Boulder River Road.

The second step is to call the backcountry office at Yellowstone National Park (307-344-7381) and ask about camping along Slough Creek within the park. The park has a policy of not giving out backcountry camping permits more than 48 hours in advance. If you plan to camp along Slough Creek in the park on the way out, you'll need one of these permits. You'll also need an exception to the 48-hour policy. Be sure to contact the park far enough in advance to get the permit before you leave. If you don't get a permit for one of the park's designated campsites along Slough Creek, you won't be able to camp in the park and you'll have at least 11 miles to cover on the last day of the trip. If you plan carefully, you might be able to pick up the permit and arrange shuttle transportation at the same time.

It's best to shuttle the vehicles early in the day and start hiking in the afternoon so you can spend the first night at the East Fork Boulder River. Either stay at the large camping area where the trail first crosses the river (at 3.5 miles) or at the second crossing 2 miles later, just after the junction with Trail 28, which goes north into the Lake Plateau. At this junction, go straight, staying on Trail 27. In about a quarter mile, the trail turns south and crosses the East Fork. There are also good campsites here, but no bridge.

After crossing the East Fork a second time, the trail narrows from a broad "two-lane" to a normal singletrack. It then heads gradually uphill for about 5 miles to the Slough Creek Divide.

The Slough Creek Divide is a wonderful place. It's well signed and is, surprisingly, the highest point of the trip: a mere 8,576 feet, significantly below timberline and unusually low for the Beartooths.

On the way up to the divide, be wary that you don't accidentally get on the side trail heading up to Wool Lake (not named on USGS topo map). Trail 27 meets the stream coming down from Lamb (not named on USGS topo map) and Blue Lakes, and it's easy to follow the side trail up the right side of the stream. Instead, stay on Trail 27, which crosses the stream at this point.

An excellent choice for a second campsite would be somewhere in the huge open park at the headwaters of the East Fork about a quarter mile before the divide. This differs from most campsites in the Beartooths, but it's no disappointment. Campers can spend lots of time marveling at the view across the lush meadow of Monument Peak and Haystack Peak. About halfway through the big meadow, the trail comes to a junction with Trail 104 leading northwest to the ghost town of Independence. This trail leads back to the end of the jeep road that continues on past the Box Canyon Trailhead. Bear left here, crossing the East Fork for the third and last time, and go straight (southeast) on Trail 104.

The next 10-mile section is not a good place for people deathly afraid of bears. When I hiked this route, I observed tracks, scat, and other bear signs everywhere, and I had an encounter with one grizzly at an uncomfortably close distance. This area obviously supports a healthy population of both grizzly and black bears.

You can also find another great campsite when the trail first hits Slough Creek. Keep in mind that this is bear country, so be extra careful with food and garbage.

From this divide the trail follows Slough Creek all the way to Slough Creek Campground in Yellowstone Park. The area just north of the park through Frenchy's Meadows and the Silver Tip Ranch (both private inholdings) can be confusing with a lot of major social trails.

Good campsites are common in the frequent meadows at least until the junction with Trail 309 that goes up Wounded Man Creek. Incidentally, this is not any relation to the Wounded Man Creek leaving the Lake Plateau and rushing down into the Stillwater River, the next major drainage east of Slough Creek. It would be interesting to know why we have two streams with the same name in the same area, but nobody seems to know. The dramatic fires of 1988 scorched the Slough Creek drainage all the way up to Wounded Man Creek, but nature has recovered nicely since then.

The side trail up Wounded Man Creek has not been maintained for many years and might be impossible to hike. The trails down from Horseshoe Basin and Lake Abundance get more regular maintenance, but still could be in rough shape. Explorers who want to take a side trip up any of these drainages should allow plenty of time for finding the trail and climbing over deadfall, but can expect to find quiet and utter solitude.

If you're on a four-night trip, for the third night out, push on to excellent campsites at Lake Abundance Creek and Bull Creek. Or camp anywhere along upper Slough Creek.

Just after Bull Creek the trail breaks out into vast Frenchy's Meadows, which has been cultivated in the past, as witnessed by old farm equipment rusting away here and there.

Many trails cross Frenchy's Meadows because of free-grazing stock, but try to stay more on the eastern half of the meadow as you progress south toward the guard station. Also, the west side of the meadow can be very wet and marshy and has several beaver pond crossings. At the south end of the meadow, you'll see the Slough Creek Guard Station and accompanying corrals.

About 3 miles farther down the trail is the Silver Tip Ranch, which is adjacent to the northern boundary of Yellowstone Park. Like Frenchy's Meadows, this is private land, so hurry through it. There's a gate at each end; be sure to leave the gates the way you found them. Rest assured, however, that you aren't trespassing. The Forest Service has a conservation easement that allows the public to cross both Frenchy's Meadows and the Silver Tip Ranch. In the past the trail followed an old wagon road through the middle of the ranch, but the Forest Service has rerouted the trail. When you reach the Silver Tip Ranch, the trail goes left (east) and skirts the fence line on the edge of the meadow before rejoining the wagon road. Part of the trail still crosses private land, so please be respectful of private property rights.

The park boundary is right at the south end of the ranch. The trail from the park boundary to the Slough Creek Trailhead is actually a two-lane wagon road, and it would be physically possible to drive all the way up Slough Creek to the Silver Tip Ranch from the Slough Creek Campground in the park. Motorized use, however, is strictly prohibited. The only vehicle allowed on this trail is a horse-drawn wagon operated by the owners of the Silver Tip Ranch.

A good choice for the fourth night out would be one of the designated campsites in Yellowstone Park—if you were able to get a permit. If you don't have a campsite reserved, then arrange your earlier campsites so you can camp somewhere between the Slough Creek Guard Station and the Silver Tip Ranch. Unfortunately, this leaves 11 miles or more out on the last day, but at least it's an easy 11 miles—an open, stream-grade, downhill walk along lower Slough Creek, world famous for its large cutthroat trout. Expect to see anglers fly casting the slow-moving waters of Slough Creek as it meanders through an expansive open valley.

OPTIONS

You can do this trip in reverse, but it involves slightly more elevation gain.

SIDE TRIPS

Take some time to explore the meadows around the Slough Creek Divide.

CAMPING

This route is lined with acceptable campsites, along the East Fork Boulder River near the beginning of the trip, in large meadows in the Slough Creek Divide area, and then all along Slough Creek to the vehicle campground in the park.

FISHING

Of all the 944 lakes in the Beartooths, a few lakes in the Slough Creek drainage may have been the only ones that originally contained fish. Both Heather and Peace Lakes, for example, contain indigenous Yellowstone cutthroat trout. There is no record of fish

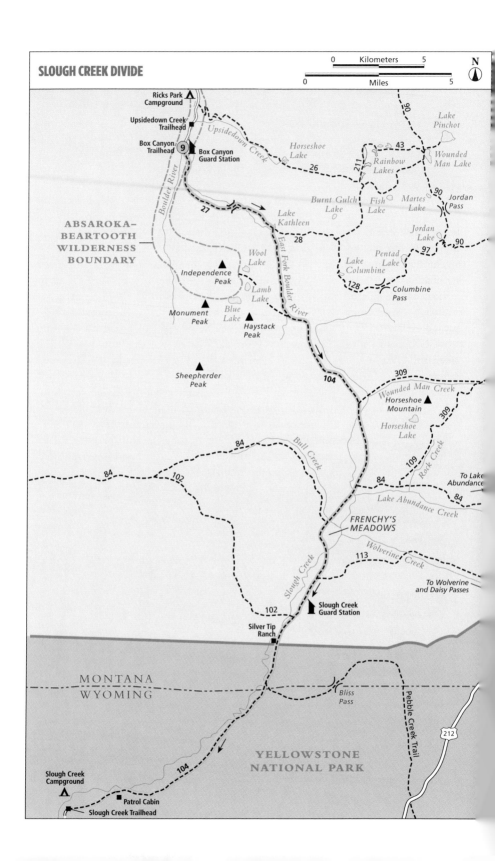

0   Kilometers   5

0   Miles   5

N

Ricks Park
Campground

Upsidedown Creek
Trailhead

Upsidedown Creek

Box Canyon
Trailhead   **9**

Box Canyon
Guard Station

*Lake
Pinchot*

90

*Horseshoe
Lake*

26

43

211

*Rainbow
Lakes*

*Wounded
Man Lake*

Boulder River

27

*Burnt Gulch
Lake*

*Lake
Kathleen*

*Fish
Lake*

*Martes
Lake*

90

*Jordan
Pass*

28

East Fork Boulder River

*Jordan
Lake*

90

**ABSAROKA–
BEARTOOTH
WILDERNESS
BOUNDARY**

*Wool
Lake*

*Independence
Peak*

*Lamb
Lake*

*Lake
Columbine*

*Pentad
Lake*

97

128

*Columbine
Pass*

*Monument
Peak*

*Blue
Lake*

*Haystack
Peak*

*Sheepherder
Peak*

104

309

Wounded Man Creek

*Horseshoe
Mountain*

309

*Horseshoe
Lake*

84

Bull Creek

Rock Creek

84

102

84

109

*To Lake
Abundance*

84

Lake Abundance Creek

**FRENCHY'S
MEADOWS**

113

Wolverine Creek

*To Wolverine
and Daisy Passes*

Slough Creek

102

Slough Creek
Guard Station

Silver Tip
Ranch

MONTANA
WYOMING

*Bliss
Pass*

Pebble Creek Trail

212

104

**YELLOWSTONE
NATIONAL PARK**

Slough Creek
Campground

Patrol Cabin

Slough Creek Trailhead

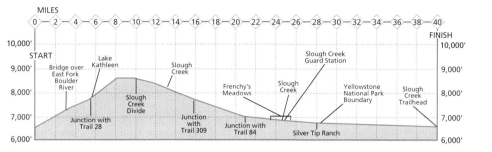

being planted in either lake, although there have been plants of Yellowstone cutthroats in Slough Creek.

This trail offers anglers a choice of cutthroat trout or cutthroat trout, with a possibility of an errant rainbow from the East Fork Boulder River side of the divide. Blue Lake is the only lake near the route, on the Boulder side, with fish—nice fat cutthroat trout.

Slough Creek is the premier cutthroat trout stream fishery in Montana, although a great deal of it is in Yellowstone Park. Anglers need a special fishing permit from Yellowstone National Park to fish Slough Creek in the park. Current park regulations call for catch-and-release fishing. Be sure to check both Montana and Yellowstone regulations before wetting a line.

MILES AND DIRECTIONS

0.0 Start at Box Canyon Trailhead.

3.5 East Fork Boulder River.

5.2 Junction with Trail 28; turn right.

8.2 Junction with unnumbered trail to Wool Lake; turn left.

9.5 Junction with Trail 104 to Independence Peak; turn left.

10.0 Slough Creek Divide.

11.8 Slough Creek.

15.7 Junction with Trail 309 up Wounded Man Creek; turn right.

21.1 Junction with Trail 84 up Lake Abundance Creek; turn right.

22.2 Junction with Trail 84 up Bull Creek; turn left.

24.9 Junction with Trail 113 up Wolverine Creek; turn right.

25.2 Slough Creek Guard Station.

26.2 Junction with Trail 102 up Tucker Creek; turn left.

28.0 Silver Tip Ranch.

28.4 Yellowstone National Park boundary.

31.4 Junction with trail up to Bliss Pass; turn right.

39.4 Arrive at Slough Creek Campground.

THE BEARTOOTH FRONT

The Beartooth Front is a huge rock massif facing north. In the shadow of the front, you find traditional ranching operations and a scattering of small towns. Several large streams have sliced notches through the front and provide access to normal folks on foot or hoof. Each spring the streams carry massive amounts of snowmelt down to the mighty Yellowstone River.

The trailheads covered in this section include, from west to east, the West Fork Stillwater River, Stillwater River, West Rosebud, and East Rosebud. You would be wise to use a high-clearance, four-wheel-drive vehicle to access the West Fork Stillwater Trailhead, but the other trailheads can be reached with any vehicle.

The West Fork Stillwater Trailhead receives much less use than trailheads to the east (Stillwater River) or to the west (Boulder River Road), but not because of a shortage of scenic attributes or excellent trails. To the contrary, the trail up the West Fork Stillwater River is definitely worth seeing. Perhaps one reason for this lower use is tougher access. Unlike the Boulder and the Stillwater (and most other major river drainages in Montana), the West Fork Stillwater River does not have an access road along its banks. Instead, travelers have to take a rough Forest Service gravel road over the ridge separating the West Fork Stillwater River and the main Stillwater River drainages to get to the West Fork Stillwater Trailhead. One interesting peculiarity of this trailhead is that the wilderness boundary has been extended downstream to the trailhead to include more of the river and its fragile habitat, mainly to protect this critical area from future development.

The Stillwater River Trailhead is one of the most accessible and heavily used access points to the Beartooths, and getting there is a treat. The route up the Stillwater River is one of the most scenic drives in Montana. The Stillwater River flows majestically through a landscape dominated by large ranches interspersed with small ranching communities like Fishtail, Nye, Beehive, Dean, and Moraine. Watch for bighorn sheep near the Stillwater Mine.

The Stillwater carries more water out of the Beartooths than any other stream, and it's certainly one of the most beautiful drainages. Nowadays, however, it is a little less wild than in the recent past. The north rim of the Beartooths, and especially the Stillwater River area, is highly mineralized. In recent years several controversial mining developments have sprung up in this area, including some large operations. The rapid growth of mines and the associated residential development have brought many more people into this formerly remote corner of Montana.

Located about 80 miles southwest of Billings, the West Rosebud is similar to the East Rosebud in that it has a gravel access road following beautiful West Rosebud Creek through traditional Montana ranching country, most of it undeveloped. The road may be rough in sections, but it's still suitable for two-wheel-drive vehicles. Besides, the scenery

Rainbow Lake campground. CASEY SCHNEIDER

is well worth the bumps. Travelers can see the narrow valley opening up in the front long before they arrive.

At the West Rosebud Trailhead, all hikes start on a trail in a power company work area and climb to a manmade dam on Mystic Lake. The dam raised the water level of the natural lake, making Mystic the deepest lake in the Beartooths (more than 200 feet). Plus, two delightful lakes—Emerald and West Rosebud—lie right at the trailhead. This area also resembles East Rosebud because of the little community at the trailhead. Instead of summer cabins, however, the structures at this trailhead house employees of the Mystic Dam Power Station.

The West Rosebud is the only major drainage in the Beartooths that's closed to horse traffic during the summer. This is due to hazardous rock fields and snowdrifts common on a section of trail just before Mystic Lake early in the season. Horses are allowed into the area, however, during the fall big-game hunting seasons starting in mid-September.

A short way up the trail, look for a plaque placed in a stone in memory of Mark E. Vonseggern, a Boy Scout from Columbus, Montana, who died in 1979 after a tragic slide down a snowbank near Mystic Lake. The plaque also offers that age-old (but never out-of-date) advice: "Be Prepared." This is especially true for weekend adventurers heading up to Froze-to-Death Plateau to climb Montana's highest mountain, Granite Peak. Granite isn't a difficult climb for experienced climbers, but many people going up the mountain are not experienced. Perhaps the plaque will remind them of that fact.

Many people who know the Beartooths say the East Rosebud is the most scenic valley of all. It's filled with lakes and waterfalls that would be major tourism attractions anywhere else. Here, there are so many that most don't even have names. The trout-filled lakes bring a smile to any angler's face, and climbers love the place because of the endless array of rock faces. Families and friends frequently choose The Beaten Path, Hike 20, for that long-planned wilderness adventure. Consequently, the East Rosebud Trailhead is probably the most heavily used trailhead in the Absaroka-Beartooth Wilderness.

Adding even more activity to the area is the small community of summer homes, called Alpine, right at the trailhead. The summer homes extend up both sides of the lower sections of East Rosebud Lake, closing off much of the lake to public use.

Actually, there are three trailheads at East Rosebud Lake. Phantom Creek Trail 18 (Slough Lake, Granite Peak, Rosebud to Rosebud) begins on the right (west) side of the road about a quarter mile before the lake. This is a popular route to Froze-to-Death Plateau and Granite Peak. About a half mile farther, as the road swings by Alpine and around the east side of the lake, turn left into East Rosebud Campground to reach the trailhead for Trail 14 to Sylvan Lake. Finally, Trail 16 up East Rosebud Creek (The Beaten Path and Elk Lake) begins at the end of the road about a quarter mile past the campground.

Note: In the spring of 2022, severe flooding greatly impacted many roads and trails on the Beartooth Front. Most trails and roads have been repaired or replaced, but some may still need repair when this guide comes out in 2024. I've made specific notes on each trail description impacted by the flooding using the most current information, but in several cases, hikers should double-check trail and road conditions before heading for the trailhead. The Sylvan Peak Mountain Shop in Red Lodge has a great website (www.sylvanpeak.com) with current trail conditions, and you can also check with the Beartooth Ranger District also in Red Lodge.

10 BREAKNECK PARK MEADOWS

Probably best for a long day hike, but could be a fairly difficult overnighter into an unusually large, gorgeous mountain meadow with a picture-perfect stream flowing through it.

Start: West Fork Stillwater Trailhead
Distance: 16 miles out and back
Difficulty: Difficult

Maps: USGS Picket Pin Mountain and Tumble Mountain; RMS Mount Douglas–Mount Wood; and at least 1 wilderness-wide map

FINDING THE TRAILHEAD

From I-90 at Columbus, drive 15 miles south on MT 78 to Absarokee. Continue south from town about 2 miles and turn right onto Nye Road (CR 419). Drive about 25 miles southwest, through Nye, to the Stillwater Mine (which is about 2 miles before the Stillwater River Trailhead and Woodbine Campground at road's end). Immediately after the mine, turn right (west) onto FR 846 (on the map) or FR 2846 (on the sign) at a well-marked intersection. From here it's a long, bumpy 8.6 miles to the trailhead with the first half mile through and above the Stillwater Mine. Initial Creek Campground is about a mile before the end of the road. Drive past the campground to the very end of the road. Ample parking for hikers (stock users have a separate trailhead about a half mile before the hikers' trailhead). Toilet. **GPS:** 45.39710 N, 109.96892 W

West Fork Stillwater leaving the Lake Plateau.

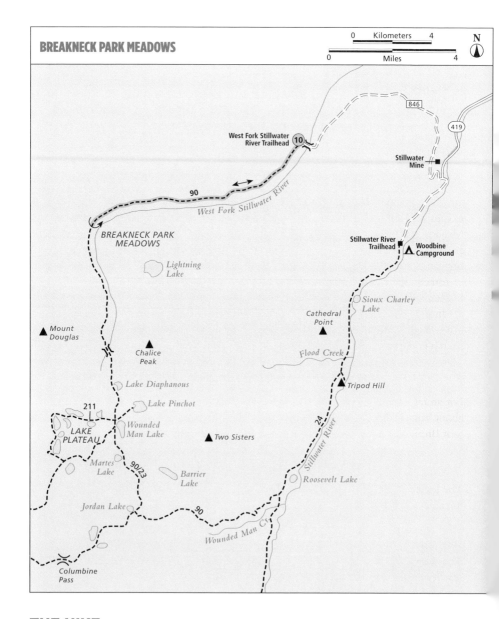

THE HIKE

Those who want to experience a remote and beautiful mountain river drainage without making it a weeklong trip should try an overnighter into Breakneck Park Meadows. The hike in and out can be done in a day, but at 16 miles, it's a bit long for a day hike.

You can start this hike at the trailhead, of course, but if you're camped at the Initial Creek Campground, you can also take a scenic trail directly from the campground for about a mile along the river to the official trailhead.

The well-maintained trail closely follows the West Fork Stillwater River most of the way, hugging the north and west bank. But just before Breakneck Park Meadows, it gradually climbs out of sight of the stream through several smaller meadows. Some of

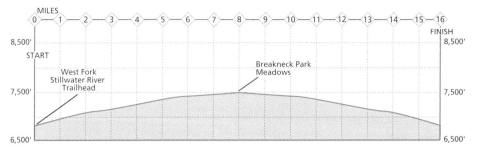

these clearings seem big enough to be a worthy destination, but there's no mistaking the expansive Breakneck Park Meadows when you get there. The trail hits Breakneck Park Meadows about a quarter mile above the West Fork Stillwater River. Take a break here, and if you're staying overnight, look around for that ideal campsite. Campers who want a fire can usually find enough wood nearby, but try for a low-impact fire.

You can also consider this a base camp for another long day hike up to explore the Lake Plateau instead lugging your big pack 8 more miles to reach the lake-filled wonderland.

Once settled in, most visitors just want to relax, fish, or watch for deer, moose, or elk—all abundant in the area. Even though it's an 8-mile return trip to the trailhead, this stretch goes fast because of the gradual gradient and excellent trail conditions.

SIDE TRIPS

For an interesting but difficult side trip, take the trail leaving Breakneck Park Meadows about halfway through and climb the 3 miles to Breakneck Plateau at the foot of 10,232-foot Breakneck Mountain.

CAMPING

The logical choice is Breakneck Park Meadows, but there are also numerous great camping areas along the stream on the way in.

FISHING

The West Fork of the Stillwater River harbors a mixed fishing opportunity. The lower reaches have brown, brook, and rainbow trout. The browns phase out upstream leaving rainbows and brookies. Cutthroat trout start to appear upstream, and the upper West Fork contains mostly cutthroats.

MILES AND DIRECTIONS

0.0   Start at West Fork Stillwater Trailhead.

3.4   Crescent Creek.

7.8   Divide Creek.

8.0   Breakneck Park Meadows.

16.0 Arrive back at West Fork Stillwater Trailhead.

11 LAKE PLATEAU NORTH

A long base-camp trip into the Lake Plateau that follows the beautiful, fish-filled West Fork Stillwater River most of the way.

Start: West Fork Stillwater Trailhead
Distance: 34-mile out-and-back base camp
Difficulty: Moderate but long

Maps: USGS Picket Pin Mountain and Tumble Mountain; RMS Mount Douglas–Mount Wood; and at least 1 wilderness-wide map

FINDING THE TRAILHEAD

From I-90 at Columbus, drive 15 miles south on MT 78 to Absarokee. Continue south from town about 2 miles and turn right onto Nye Road (CR 419). Drive about 25 miles southwest, through Nye, to the Stillwater Mine (which is about 2 miles before the Stillwater River Trailhead and Woodbine Campground at road's end). Immediately after the mine, turn right (west) onto FR 846 (on the map) or FR 2846 (on the sign) at a well-marked intersection. From here it's a long, bumpy 8.6 miles to the trailhead with the first half mile going through and above the Stillwater Mine. Initial Creek Campground is about a mile before the end of the road. Drive past the campground to the very end of the road. Ample parking for hikers (stock users have a separate trailhead about a half mile before the hiker's trailhead); toilet. **GPS:** 45.39710 N, 109.96892 W

RECOMMENDED ITINERARY

You'll want at least four nights for this trip, but planning for five nights gives you an extra day for exploring the Lake Plateau before heading back to your vehicle.

- First night: Breakneck Park Meadows
- Second night: Your base camp on the Lake Plateau
- Third night: Same campsite
- Fourth night: Same campsite
- Fifth night: Breakneck Park Meadows

THE HIKE

The West Fork Stillwater River provides the third major access route (along with the East Fork Boulder and Stillwater Rivers) into this popular high plateau. It's also the longest and most remote route, but it may be the easiest because it has no steep climbs.

Even though this trail might not be as popular as others in the Beartooths, it's in wonderful condition, well maintained, and easy to follow. If you're camped at the Initial Creek Campground, you can start directly from the campground and hike a scenic mile along the river to the official trailhead. From the trailhead, the route follows the West Fork Stillwater River for 16 miles to Lake Diaphanous.

Most backpackers will want to take two days to reach a base camp on Lake Plateau. Fortunately, the West Fork Stillwater River nicely accommodates this schedule with a

Many trails in the Absaroka-Beartooth involve some rock hopping.

perfect camping area at the halfway point, Breakneck Park Meadows. Although the trail into Breakneck Park Meadows is interrupted by several beautiful smaller meadows, the expansive Breakneck Park Meadows is exceptional and much larger. Campers can choose from many grand campsites with plenty of wood for a low-impact campfire.

After leaving Breakneck Park Meadows, the trail worsens slightly but is still in good shape. The stream gradient increases slightly, but no big climbs, the steepest grade being the mile after crossing the second bridge over the West Fork Stillwater River. Even this is much less of a climb than coming into the plateau from the east or west.

The trail continues along the west side of the river for just under 2 miles to the Lewis Creek, which crosses not Lewis Creek but a small branch of the West Fork Stillwater River. Sorry, no bridge. From here the trail climbs another 2 miles to the plateau and Lake Diaphanous. This small, high-altitude lake has an excellent campsite, but only one, so it might not be the best choice for your base camp. Lake Diaphanous lies above timberline, and the views are fantastic. Even though there are a few trees around the campsite, the wood supply is too scant for a campfire.

Most people prefer to go into the Lake Plateau for a base camp. Wounded Man Lake is another 0.8 mile down the trail, and there are many excellent campsites at nearby lakes. Take some extra time to find that five-star campsite. This means you should get an early start from your campsite at Breakneck Park Meadows, so you can reach the Lake Plateau early enough in the day to allow time to find your ideal base camp.

After spending a few enjoyable days on the Lake Plateau, return down the West Fork Stillwater River, a pleasant, gradual downhill all the way.

Hiking along Wounded Man Lake on the Lake Plateau.

OPTIONS

If you can arrange a shuttle or leave a vehicle at the Stillwater River Trailhead, you can make this a shuttle trip, which is described in detail in Hike 12, Stillwater to Stillwater. You could also exit the Lake Plateau down the Rainbow Lakes Valley or over Columbine Pass down to Box Canyon Trailhead at the end of the Boulder River Road, but this option would involve a long, time-consuming shuttle.

SIDE TRIPS

The side trip to Lightning Lake is enticing, but very difficult. There are two route options. Scramble up Lightning Creek, which joins the West Fork Stillwater River about 5 miles from the West Fork Stillwater Trailhead. Or leapfrog over Chalice Peak from Lake Diaphanous. Be wary of the trip up Lightning Creek. It's shorter, but very steep and difficult, definitely a Category H hill. Although the cross-country trip over Chalice Peak looks long and difficult, it really isn't that bad. If you visit Lightning Lake, you may experience one of your best days ever in the wilderness—but make sure you are in good shape, have good weather, and leave camp at or before daybreak so you don't get caught in the dark.

Refer to "Exploring the Lake Plateau" (page 62) for more side trips.

CAMPING

Breakneck Park Meadows offers a variety of good campsites, and you have a near-endless selection on the Lake Plateau.

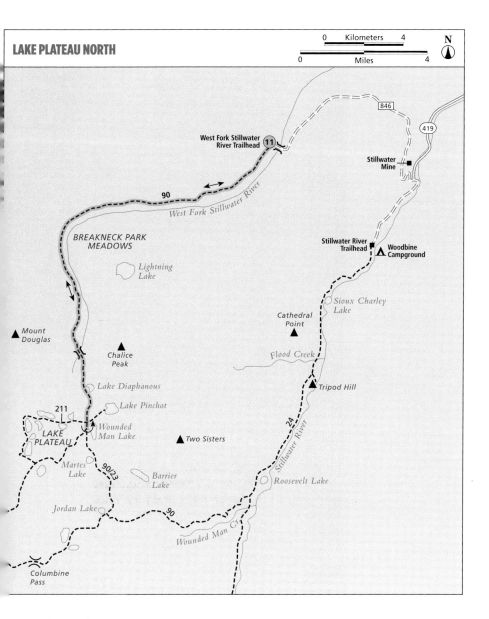

0   Kilometers   4

N

0   Miles   4

846

419

West Fork Stillwater
River Trailhead 11

Stillwater
Mine

West Fork Stillwater River

90

BREAKNECK PARK
MEADOWS

Stillwater River
Trailhead   Woodbine
Campground

Lightning
Lake

Sioux Charley
Lake

Cathedral
Point

Mount
Douglas

Chalice
Peak

Flood Creek

Lake Diaphanous

Tripod Hill

Lake Pinchot

211

Wounded
Man Lake

LAKE
PLATEAU

Two Sisters

24

Stillwater River

Martes
Lake

90/23

Barrier
Lake

Roosevelt Lake

Jordan Lake

90

Wounded Man Cr.

Columbine
Pass

FISHING

The West Fork of the Stillwater River harbors a mixed fishing opportunity. The lower reaches have brown, brook, and rainbow trout. The browns phase out upstream leaving rainbows and brookies. Cutthroat trout start to appear upstream, and the upper West Fork contains mostly cutthroats.

Lake Diaphanous is in the main Stillwater River drainage and supports some nice rainbows. Expect company, as this is a logical place to stop. From here it's straight downhill, southeast to Lake Pinchot for great camping and fishing for beautiful hybrids of golden, cutthroat, and rainbow descent. Flood Creek itself provides a pretty good alpine fishery

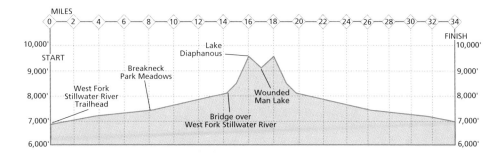

and would be worth a try. There are pure golden trout in Asteroid and some of the surrounding lakes, but getting there isn't easy.

The Lake Plateau offers a variety of fishing opportunities, mostly for rainbow and cutthroat trout, and most of the lakes along trails have fish. For solitude, get off the trails, but ask beforehand to learn which lakes hold fish before counting on trout for dinner.

Also refer to "Fishing the Lake Plateau" (page 68).

MILES AND DIRECTIONS

0.0 Start at West Fork Stillwater Trailhead.

8.0 Breakneck Park Meadows.

9.5 First bridge over the West Fork Stillwater River.

14.3 Lewis Creek Bridge over the West Fork Stillwater River.

16.2 Lake Diaphanous.

17.0 Wounded Man Lake.

34.0 Arrive back at West Fork Stillwater Trailhead.

12 STILLWATER TO STILLWATER

A long, point-to-point route through the Lake Plateau, mostly following closely the paths of two sparkling mountain rivers with the famed Lake Plateau in between.

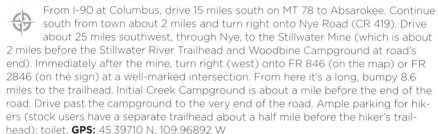

Start: West Fork Stillwater Trailhead
Distance: 38.7-mile shuttle
Difficulty: Moderate but long
Maps: USGS Cathedral Point, Little Park Mountain, Pinnacle Mountain, Picket Pin Mountain, and Tumble Mountain; RMS Mount Douglas–Mount Wood and Cooke City–Cutoff Mountain; and at least 1 wilderness-wide map

FINDING THE TRAILHEADS

From I-90 at Columbus, drive 15 miles south on MT 78 to Absarokee. Continue south from town about 2 miles and turn right onto Nye Road (CR 419). Drive about 25 miles southwest, through Nye, to the Stillwater Mine (which is about 2 miles before the Stillwater River Trailhead and Woodbine Campground at road's end). Immediately after the mine, turn right (west) onto FR 846 (on the map) or FR 2846 (on the sign) at a well-marked intersection. From here it's a long, bumpy 8.6 miles to the trailhead. Initial Creek Campground is about a mile before the end of the road. Drive past the campground to the very end of the road. Ample parking for hikers (stock users have a separate trailhead about a half mile before the hiker's trailhead); toilet. **GPS:** 45.39710 N, 109.96892 W

Leave a vehicle at the Stillwater River Trailhead, which is easy to find. In fact, you can't miss it. The distance between trailheads is short enough (about 10 miles) that you could also hide a mountain or gravel bicycle at the Stillwater Trailhead and ride back to the West Fork Stillwater Trailhead to retrieve your vehicle.

To reach the Stillwater River Trailhead, follow directions above to the Stillwater Mine. Stay on Nye Road, which eventually ends at the trailhead, about 2 miles past the mine. It's about 42 miles southwest of Columbus. Plenty of parking and toilet; Woodbine Campground near the trailhead. **GPS:** 45.35082 N, 109.90331 W

Note: The Stillwater/Sioux Charley Trailhead and Woodbine Campground areas had severe damage from the 2022 flood, but most damage should be repaired before this revision is released. The two exceptions might be the last few miles of this route where the flood washed out the trail in the gorge between Sioux Charley Lake and the trailhead. This section of trail might not be repaired, so you'll have to take the stock bypass trail the last few miles to the trailhead. Also, the trailhead parking lot was destroyed, but it is scheduled for repair in 2024. Until reconstruction is finished, parking will be along the road near the trailhead.

RECOMMENDED ITINERARY

The itinerary depends on how many nights you can spend in your Lake Plateau base camp—two nights minimum, I'd say, and more would be better.

- First night: Breakneck Park Meadows
- Second night: Your base camp on the Lake Plateau
- Third night: Same campsite
- Fourth night: Same campsite or move to Jordan Lake
- Fifth night: Along the Stillwater River

THE HIKE

If you can arrange a shuttle and want to see lots of wild country in one week, there's no use making the West Fork Stillwater River an out-and-back trip (Hike 11). Instead, just keep going through the Lake Plateau and out to civilization at the Stillwater River Trailhead and Woodbine Campground.

The trail along the West Fork Stillwater River is the easiest of the four access routes into the Lake Plateau. It's also the longest and most remote route, but it may be the easiest because it has no steep climbs.

Even though this trail might not be as heavily used as others in the Beartooths, it's still in great shape, well maintained, and easy to follow. It follows the West Fork Stillwater River for 16 miles to Lake Diaphanous. If you're camped at the Initial Creek Campground, you can add a scenic mile to your hike by starting directly from the campground and hiking along the river to the official trailhead.

Most backpackers will want to take two days to reach a base camp on Lake Plateau. Fortunately, the West Fork Stillwater River accommodates this schedule with a

Hiking Lake Plateau.

perfect camping area at the halfway point, Breakneck Park Meadows. Although the trail into Breakneck Park Meadows is interrupted by several beautiful smaller meadows, the expansive Breakneck Park Meadows is exceptional and much larger. Campers can choose from many grand campsites with plenty of wood for a low-impact campfire.

After leaving Breakneck Park Meadows, the trail worsens slightly but is still in good shape. The stream gradient increases slightly, but there are no big climbs, the steepest grade being the mile after crossing the second bridge over the West Fork Stillwater River. Even this is much less of a climb than coming into the plateau from the east or west.

The trail continues along the west side of the river for just under 2 miles to the Lewis Creek Bridge, which crosses not Lewis Creek but a small branch of the West Fork Stillwater River. From here the trail climbs another 2 miles to the plateau and Lake Diaphanous. This small, high-altitude lake has an excellent campsite, but only one, so it might not be the best choice for your base camp. Lake Diaphanous lies above timberline, and the views are fantastic. Even though there are a few trees around the campsite, the wood supply is too scant for a campfire.

Wounded Man Lake is another 0.8 mile down the trail, and there are many excellent campsites at nearby lakes. Take some extra time to find that five-star campsite. This means you should get an early start from your campsite at Breakneck Park Meadows, so you can reach the Lake Plateau early enough in the day to allow time to find your ideal base camp.

After spending a few enjoyable days on the Lake Plateau, head south from Wounded Man Lake on Trail 90 over Jordan Pass to Jordan Lake. Consider staying at Jordan Lake before heading down Wounded Man Creek, still on Trail 90. Jordan Lake gets lots of use, so even though it's a forested lake, camp softly and resist the temptation to have a campfire.

A good choice for the last night out would be the confluence of Wounded Man Creek and the Stillwater River or at a huge open area along the river about a mile farther down the trail.

When you hit the Stillwater River Trail 24, turn left (north) and follow it 10.2 miles to the Stillwater Trailhead, passing Sioux Charley Lake 3 miles before the end of the trail. It's a gradual, downhill grade the entire way.

OPTIONS

This trip can be done in reverse, but the climb up Wounded Man Creek is tougher than the more gentle grade of the West Stillwater.

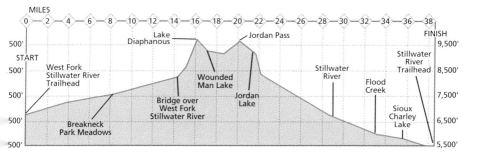

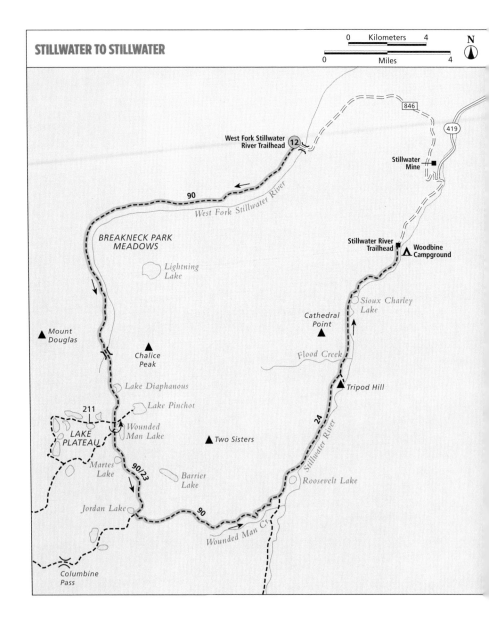

SIDE TRIPS

Refer to "Exploring the Lake Plateau" (page 62).

FISHING

This route offers many opportunities to sample the lakes of the Lake Plateau. There are rainbows in Lake Diaphanous, rainbows and cutthroats in Wounded Man Lake, and an interesting alpine fishery in the Flood Creek drainage.

In addition, the main Stillwater River has lots of pan-size trout for hungry hikers. There is a mixture of cutthroats, rainbows, and brookies to be had with minimal effort. Much of the slower water is dominated by brookies; please eat them—they taste great!

Also refer to "Fishing the Lake Plateau" (page 68).

MILES AND DIRECTIONS

0.0 Start at West Fork Stillwater Trailhead.

8.0 Breakneck Park Meadows.

9.5 First bridge over West Fork Stillwater River.

14.3 Lewis Creek Bridge over West Fork Stillwater River.

16.2 Lake Diaphanous.

17.0 Wounded Man Lake and junctions with Trail 211 and unofficial trail to Lake Pinchot; continue heading south on Trail 90 along the lakeshore.

17.3 Junction with Trail 43; turn left.

20.3 Jordan Pass.

21.5 Jordan Lake and junction with Trail 97; turn left.

28.5 Junction with Stillwater Trail 24; turn left.

32.3 Tripod Hill.

33.0 Flood Creek.

34.6 Sioux Charley Lake.

38.7 Arrive at Stillwater River Trailhead.

13 WOODBINE FALLS

A short day hike to an amazing waterfall.

Start: Woodbine Falls Trailhead in Woodbine Campground
Distance: 3 miles out and back
Difficulty: Easy

Maps: USGS Cathedral Point; RMS Mount Douglas–Mount Wood; and at least 1 wilderness-wide map

FINDING THE TRAILHEAD

From I-90 at Columbus, drive 15 miles south on MT 78 to Absarokee. Continue south 2 miles, turn west onto the paved Nye Road (CR 419), and go through Fishtail and Nye. Stay on this road, which eventually ends at the trailhead, about 2 miles past the Stillwater Mine to Woodbine Campground. It's about 42 miles southwest of Columbus. Plenty of parking and toilet. **GPS:** 45.35082 N, 109.90331 W

Note: The 2022 flood washed out the bridge over Woodbine Creek, and it might not be replaced in time for the 2024 hiking season. Hikers can still reach Woodbine Falls by carefully fording the creek just downstream from the trail or, even more carefully, crossing on a downed tree just upstream from the trail. Check with the Forest Service or the camp host at Woodbine Campground on the status of the bridge replacement.

THE HIKE

Woodbine Falls is one of the most heavily traveled trails in the Beartooths. The majority of people staying at Woodbine Campground probably take this hike since they can walk to the trailhead from their campsite.

From the trailhead, hike about a quarter mile to Woodbine Creek and cross the bridge. From here you hike up five or six nicely engineered switchbacks to an overlook where you can take in the majestic of Woodbine Falls. The trail is in great shape the entire way with the added touch of masonry on some switchbacks and at the overlook.

The earlier you can take this hike, the more majestic the falls. Snow usually departs this area earlier than the high country, so you probably can do this hike in June during the spring runoff.

Getting a good photo of the falls is difficult because of trees blocking part of the view, but it's still a very impressive view.

No camping on this route except for in the campground.

Spectacular and accessible Woodbine Falls.

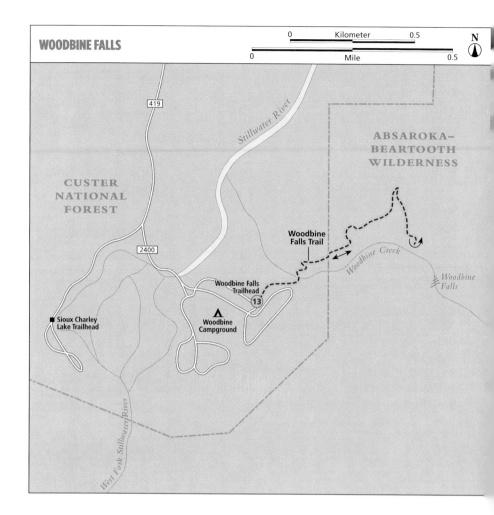

MILES AND DIRECTIONS

0.0 Start at Woodbine Falls Trailhead.

0.3 Woodbine Creek.

1.5 Woodbine Falls.

3.0 Arrive back at Woodbine Falls Trailhead.

14 SIOUX CHARLEY LAKE

A short, easy day hike or first overnighter along a wilderness river to a fish-filled mountain lake.

Start: Stillwater River Trailhead
Distance: 8 miles out and back
Difficulty: Easy

Maps: USGS Cathedral Point; RMS Mount Douglas–Mount Wood; and at least 1 wilderness-wide map

FINDING THE TRAILHEAD

From I-90 at Columbus, drive 15 miles south on MT 78 to Absarokee. Continue south 2 miles, turn west onto the paved Nye Road (CR 419), and go through Fishtail and Nye. Stay on this road, which eventually ends at the trailhead, about 2 miles past the Stillwater Mine. It's about 42 miles southwest of Columbus. Plenty of parking and toilet; Woodbine Campground near the trailhead. **GPS:** 45.35082 N, 109.90331 W

Note: This area was severely impacted by the 2022 flooding, but the Stillwater/Sioux Charley Trailhead reopened for the summer of 2023. The trailhead parking lot was destroyed but scheduled for reconstruction in 2024. Until it's finished, hikers can park along the road near the trailhead. The first part of the trail goes through a rocky gorge, and the flood washed away this section of trail, but hikers can take the stock bypass trail from the trailhead, which connects to the main trail just beyond the gorge. The distance

A fat brookie, just right for dinner.

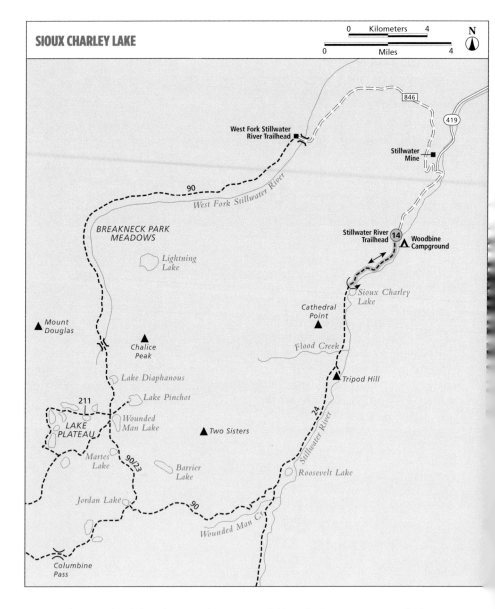

0   Kilometers   4

0   Miles   4

N

West Fork Stillwater
River Trailhead

846

419

Stillwater
Mine

90

West Fork Stillwater River

BREAKNECK PARK
MEADOWS

Stillwater River
Trailhead

14

Woodbine
Campground

Lightning
Lake

Sioux Charley
Lake

Cathedral
Point

Mount
Douglas

Chalice
Peak

Flood Creek

Lake Diaphanous

Tripod Hill

Lake Pinchot

211

24

LAKE
PLATEAU

Wounded
Man Lake

Two Sisters

Stillwater River

Martes
Lake

90/23

Barrier
Lake

Roosevelt Lake

Jordan Lake

90

Columbine
Pass

Wounded Man Cr.

is about the same, but hikers have to climb a steep hill on the bypass trail instead of enjoying the fairly flat section of trail through the gorge.

THE HIKE

This easy day trip into Sioux Charley Lake is one of the most popular day hikes in the Beartooths, so don't be surprised to see lots of people on the trail. From the trailhead it's 4 miles to the lake, all on an easy and gradual river grade.

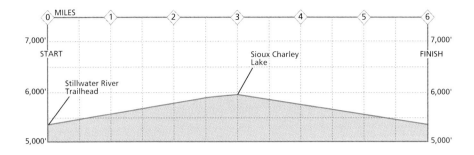

Soon after leaving the trailhead, the trail enters a narrow canyon where, right next to the trail, the Stillwater River tumbles over a series of cascades and rapids. Many a hiker has paused here to wonder why this stream was ever named the "still water."

After passing through the canyon, the trail winds through a heavy forest all the way to Sioux Charley Lake. Now the reason behind the river's name becomes clear. The lake is really just a large, slow-moving, or "still," section of the river. Farther upstream, the river slows into several similar still-water stretches.

Look across the lake to the east to see the northernmost reaches of the dramatic forest fires of 1988. The massive Storm Creek Fire burned all the way down the Stillwater River drainage to Sioux Charley Lake, almost completely through the Beartooths.

CAMPING

Although this is most often considered a day trip, you can spend the night at Sioux Charley Lake. The lake is heavily used, however, so be extra careful to leave zero impact. The area already shows the wear and tear of many past hikers.

FISHING

The Stillwater River can yield a lot of pan-size trout, a mix of rainbows and brookies, plus an occasional cutthroat. Brookies dominate the slower water, with rainbows and cutts liking the faster water. Since brook trout tend to overpopulate (to the detriment of other species), please eat them to help out the cutts and rainbows. Catch and release doesn't improve the brookies' size; it only limits the amount of food available per fish. Besides, they taste great! Sioux Charley Lake is one of the best places to catch these tasty morsels, and they can provide dinner for many large parties with no impact on the health of the population.

MILES AND DIRECTIONS

0.0   Start at Stillwater River Trailhead.

4.0   Sioux Charley Lake.

8.0   Arrive back at Stillwater River Trailhead.

15 LAKE PLATEAU EAST

A long base-camp trip, the least-used access route into the Lake Plateau.

Start: Stillwater River Trailhead
Distance: 43 miles out and back
Difficulty: Moderate but long
Maps: USGS Cathedral Point, Little Park Mountain, Pinnacle Mountain, and Tumble Mountain; RMS Mount Douglas–Mount Wood and Cooke City–Cutoff Mountain; and at least 1 wilderness-wide map

FINDING THE TRAILHEAD

From I-90 at Columbus, drive 15 miles south on MT 78 to Absarokee. Continue south 2 miles, turn west onto the paved Nye Road (CR 419), and go through Fishtail and Nye. Stay on this road, which eventually ends at the trailhead, about 2 miles past the Stillwater Mine. It's about 42 miles southwest of Columbus. Plenty of parking and toilet; Woodbine Campground near the trailhead. **GPS:** 45.35082 N, 109.90331 W

RECOMMENDED ITINERARY

Because of the terrain along this route, it's best to plan on two tough days to reach the plateau, even though this might be more mileage per day than you would prefer.

- First night: Along the Stillwater River, near junction with Trail 90
- Second night: Your base camp on the Lake Plateau
- Third night: Same campsite
- Fourth night: Same campsite
- Fifth night: Along the Stillwater River, near junction with Trail 24

Note: This area was severely impacted by the 2022 flooding, but the Stillwater/Sioux Charley Trailhead reopened for the summer of 2023. The trailhead parking lot was destroyed, but scheduled for reconstruction in 2024. Until it's finished, hikers can park along the road near the trailhead. The first part of the trail goes through a rocky gorge, and the flood washed away this section of trail, but hikers can take the stock bypass trail from the trailhead, which connects to the main trail just beyond the gorge. The distance is about the same, but hikers have to climb a steep hill on the bypass trail instead of enjoying the fairly flat section of trail through the gorge.

THE HIKE

The first 10.2 miles of the trail follow the Stillwater River, a magnificent mountain stream, appropriately named for its frequent "still" sections. With the exception of the first 3 miles into Sioux Charley Lake, the Stillwater area was badly burned by the 1988 fires. But the forest is rapidly coming back, and the valley is lush and moist all the way.

Lake Pinchot, the heart of the Lake Plateau.

Keep an eye open for the abundant white-tailed deer and moose, both common along the river.

From Sioux Charley Lake the trail runs south 2.5 miles to the base of well-named Cathedral Point and a bridge over Flood Creek. Just after the bridge a side trail heads off to the left (east) up to a scenic point, aptly named Tripod Hill. The overlook affords a full perspective of the grandeur of the Stillwater River drainage, and it's definitely worth the extra stroll.

Those who make good mileage on the first day can make it to the Lake Plateau for the second night out. Some backpackers might choose to spend two nights along the Stillwater before climbing the 7 miles up to Jordan Lake.

Turn right (west) onto Trail 90 going up Wounded Man Creek. It's a moderately steep climb for the first 6 miles, but the last mile is a lung-busting, Category 2 climb as the trail switchbacks 700 feet up to Jordan Lake.

To continue the hike from Jordan Lake, head north, still on Trail 90, for almost 5 miles over Jordan Pass, an easy climb, to Wounded Man Lake. Actually, the short climb just before Wounded Man Lake is more difficult than going up Jordan Pass.

When you reach the vicinity of Wounded Man Lake, start looking for your base camp. When you find one that's just right for you, spend at least two more days enjoying and exploring the Lake Plateau before retracing your steps back down the Stillwater to the trailhead.

Fishing Lake Pinchot.

Lake Plateau wildflower garden.

OPTIONS

Instead of retracing your steps down Wounded Man Creek and the Stillwater River, you could keep going and leave the Lake Plateau via the West Fork Stillwater River, Rainbow Creek, or Upsidedown Creek, but these options involve leaving a vehicle at another trailhead or arranging a pickup.

SIDE TRIPS

Really ambitious hikers can take a side trip up to Barrier Lake. Where the trail crosses the North Fork of Wounded Man Creek, scramble up the stream for about 1.25 miles. After about a quarter mile, the stream disappears, but you keep going. Barrier is a very unusual lake. It looks like a reservoir that has been drawn down and has a flat bench around it. Even though the map shows a fairly large stream (the North Fork of Wounded Man Creek) leaving Barrier Lake, the lake actually has no surface outlet. Instead, the stream flows underground for about a mile before suddenly bursting out of the rocks as a giant spring, and the North Fork of Wounded Man Creek is reborn. Notice that the North Fork has very cold water, almost painful to drink. You can also hike to Barrier Lake from the Lake Plateau.

For a great side trip from Jordan Lake, get up early in the morning and take Trail 97 from the south end of the lake over to Columbine Pass. Along the way the trail skirts Pentad and Favonius Lakes, and the scenery is magnificent, especially near the pass.

Also refer to "Exploring the Lake Plateau" (page 62) for more side trips.

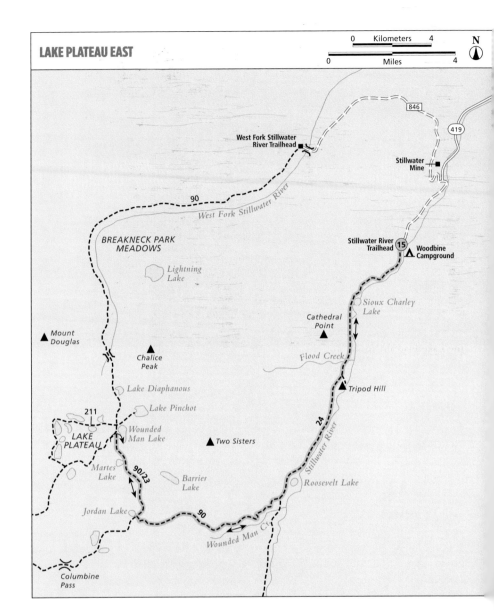

0   Kilometers   4

0   Miles   4

N

846

419

West Fork Stillwater
River Trailhead

Stillwater
Mine

90

West Fork Stillwater River

BREAKNECK PARK
MEADOWS

Stillwater River
Trailhead   15   Woodbine
Campground

*Lightning
Lake*

▲ Mount
Douglas

*Sioux Charley
Lake*

*Cathedral
Point*
▲

▲
*Chalice
Peak*

Flood Creek

Lake Diaphanous

▲ *Tripod Hill*

Lake Pinchot

211

24

LAKE
PLATEAU

*Wounded
Man Lake*

Stillwater River

▲ *Two Sisters*

*Martes
Lake*

90/23

*Barrier
Lake*

Roosevelt Lake

Jordan Lake

90

Wounded Man Cr.

*Columbine
Pass*

CAMPING

Camping is available anywhere along the Stillwater River. With an early start, travelers might make it to a great campsite on a smooth stretch of river about 1 mile before the junction with Trail 90 (about 10 miles from the trailhead). This is a slightly better camp-site than at Wounded Man Creek. Looking at the map, some people may want to head for Roosevelt Lake as a potential campsite. But this is really Roosevelt "marsh," and it doesn't have good campsites. Wood is abundant throughout the Stillwater for low-impact evening campfires.

Jordan Lake is a delightful place with several campsites on the south end just east of where the trail hits the lake. Together the sites make a camping area large enough to accommodate a large party or two or three small parties. The campsite is marginal for campfires, but if a fire is absolutely needed, there is an adequate supply of firewood in the area.

Once at Wounded Man Lake, spend some time selecting a good site for a base camp. There are many options, such as the Rainbow Lakes to the west or Lake Pinchot to the east. The best campsite at Wounded Man Lake is just southwest of the lake.

FISHING

This route offers less opportunity to sample lakes on the way to the Lake Plateau, but there's plenty of good fishing. Heading up along the main Stillwater River can provide a lot of great fishing for pan-size trout—a mixture of cutthroats, rainbows, and brookies that can be had without much effort. Brookies dominate the slower water, with cutthroats becoming more common as you get closer to the Wounded Man Creek drainage, which supports a mainly cutthroat trout fishery, although rainbows share Pentad and Favonius Lakes with cutts. Jordan Lake holds nice cutthroats that can be counted on to provide dinner.

Also refer to the fishing information for Sioux Charley Lake (Hike 14) and "Fishing the Lake Plateau" (page 68).

MILES AND DIRECTIONS

0.0 Start at Stillwater Trailhead.

4.0 Sioux Charley Lake.

5.5 Flood Creek.

6.2 Tripod Hill.

10.0 Junction with Trail 90; turn right.

10.2 Wounded Man Creek.

17.0 Jordan Lake and junction with Trail 97; turn right.

18.2 Jordan Pass.

21.5 Wounded Man Lake.

43.0 Arrive back at Stillwater Trailhead.

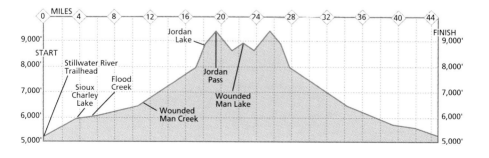

16 MYSTIC LAKE

A moderate day trip to the deepest lake in the Beartooths.

Start: West Rosebud Trailhead
Distance: 7 miles out and back
Difficulty: Moderate

Maps: USGS Granite Peak and Alpine; RMS Cooke City–Cutoff Mountain; and at least 1 wilderness-wide map

FINDING THE TRAILHEAD

From 1-90 at Columbus, drive 15 miles south on MT 78 through Absarokee. About 2 miles past Absarokee, turn right (west) onto CR 419. Drive through Fishtail and continue west and south about 1 mile, then turn left (south) along West Rosebud Road. About 6 miles later, take another left (southeast) at the sign for West Rosebud Lake (pavement ends). From here it's another 14.4 miles of bumpy gravel road to the trailhead—a total of 26 miles from Absarokee and 41 miles from Columbus. The road ends and the trail starts at the Mystic Dam Power Station. Ample parking (but sometimes packed) and toilet; two developed campgrounds on the way to the trailhead. **GPS:** 45.22782 N, 109.76183 W

THE HIKE

For those who aren't interested in strenuous mountain climbing or long arduous adventures, the Mystic Lake trail offers an excellent choice for an unhurried day into the wilderness. It also offers some spectacular scenery with the unusual twist of being able to observe the Mystic Lake Power Station. Besides being a popular day trip, the trail to Mystic Lake is also the first leg for the legions heading up to attempt an ascent of Granite Peak, so don't expect to have the trail to yourself. And you won't have to step over any horse apples on this trail. Horse use is prohibited on the section of trail between the power station and Mystic Lake during the hiking season but allowed during the fall hunting season.

From the trailhead follow West Rosebud Creek. After crossing a bridge over the creek, the trail follows a power line for a short way. After leaving behind these "signs of civilization," you switchback through open rock fields offering a great view of the West Rosebud valley, including West Rosebud and Emerald Lakes.

The climb doesn't seem that steep, but by the time the trail reaches the dam at the eastern end of Mystic Lake, it has ascended 1,200 feet in 3 miles, barely a Category 3 climb. Normally that would be considered a big climb, but for hikers who aren't in a hurry, it really doesn't seem like it.

When you finally break out over the ridge, you're treated to a sweeping view of Mystic Lake and Mystic Dam. Mystic Lake is a natural lake, but the dam increased its size and depth—now, at more than 200 feet, the deepest in the Beartooths.

The sandy beach along the east shore of the lake below is perhaps the largest in the Beartooths. This makes a good lunch spot for those who plan to turn back for the trailhead. But it's far better to set aside enough time to walk along the lake for a while. The trail is very scenic, flat, and well maintained. Plus, it's difficult to realize the full scope of

Mystic Lake from Froze-to-Death Plateau.

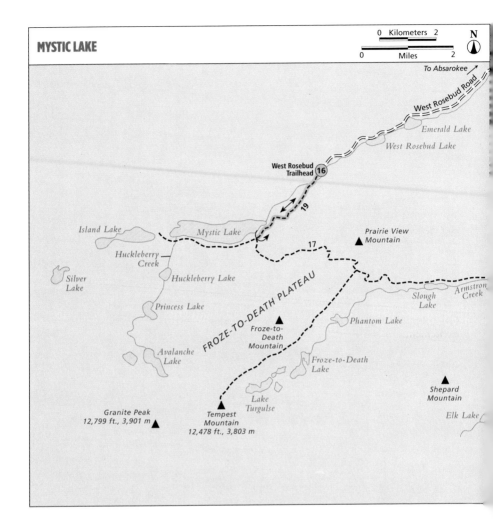

0   Kilometers   2

0   Miles   2

N

To Absarokee

West Rosebud Road

Emerald Lake

West Rosebud Lake

West Rosebud Trailhead **16**

19

Island Lake

Mystic Lake

Prairie View
▲ Mountain

17

Huckleberry
Creek

Silver
Lake

Huckleberry Lake

FROZE-TO-DEATH PLATEAU

Slough
Lake

Armstron
Creek

Princess Lake

Froze-to-
Death
Mountain

▲

Phantom Lake

Avalanche
Lake

Froze-to-Death
Lake

Shepard
Mountain

▲

Granite Peak
12,799 ft., 3,901 m ▲

Tempest
Mountain
12,478 ft., 3,803 m

▲

Lake
Turgulse

Elk Lake

Mystic Lake from the first overlook. This is a huge lake, and a walk along its shore is the best way to appreciate it.

Some people might think that the presence of the dam detracts from the wildness of the place, but the intrusion seems minimal, and, after all, the dam was here long before Congress designated the Absaroka-Beartooth Wilderness. Most visitors will have little difficulty enjoying this hike.

SIDE TRIPS

If you have some energy left when you reach Mystic Lake, hike along the shoreline for a mile or two before heading back. If you're very energetic, you could hike the steep hill up to Froze-to-Death Plateau.

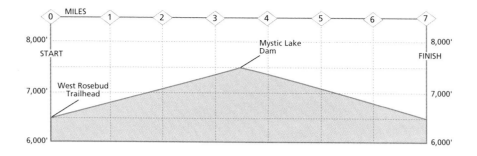

CAMPING

You can find several camp spots along Mystic's east shore, but the shoreline is heavily used and seems more suited to leisurely day hiking than camping.

FISHING

There are a lot of fish willing to be caught north of the trailhead at Emerald and West Rosebud Lakes. Both lakes support hefty fish, with brown trout, cutthroat trout, and whitefish all common. Rainbows are stocked in both lakes to provide additional excitement.

Mystic Lake supports a rainbow trout fishery that is fantastic when the fish are feeding and frustrating when they aren't. The steeply graded stream up to Mystic doesn't provide much fish habitat, so save your efforts for the lake.

MILES AND DIRECTIONS

0.0 Start at West Rosebud Trailhead.

3.0 Mystic Lake Dam.

3.5 Mystic Lake and junction with Phantom Creek Trail 17.

7.0 Arrive back at West Rosebud Trailhead.

17 GRANITE PEAK

A long, steep, strenuous backpack to a traditional launching point for ascents of Montana's highest mountain, Granite Peak—strictly for experienced, well-conditioned hikers.

Start: West Rosebud Trailhead
Distance: 21 miles out and back, plus the climb up Granite Peak
Difficulty: Very difficult

Maps: USGS Granite Peak and Alpine; RMS Cooke City–Cutoff Mountain and Alpine–Mount Maurice; and at least 1 wilderness-wide map

FINDING THE TRAILHEAD

From I-90 at Columbus, drive 15 miles south on MT 78 through Absarokee. About 2 miles past Absarokee, turn right (west) onto CR 419. Drive through Fishtail and continue west and south about 1 mile, then turn left (south) along West Rosebud Road. About 6 miles later, take another left (southeast) at the sign for West Rosebud Lake (pavement ends). From here it's another 14.4 miles of bumpy gravel road to the trailhead—a total of 26 miles from Absarokee and 41 miles from Columbus. The road ends and the trail starts at the Mystic Dam Power Station. Ample parking (often packed) and toilet; two campgrounds on the way to the trailhead.
GPS: 45.22782 N, 109.76183 W

THE HIKE

Of the two trailheads used for this hike (West Rosebud and Phantom Creek), the West Rosebud is more popular, mainly because it's slightly shorter and cuts 400 feet of elevation gain off the approach to Granite Peak. The trails from both trailheads lead to the same place—the saddle between Prairie View Mountain and Froze-to-Death Mountain. And whether coming from the east or west, the trails are for rugged individuals. Just reaching the saddle where the two trails meet is a climb of 3,500 feet from West Rosebud Trailhead or 3,900 feet from Phantom Creek Trailhead near East Rosebud Lake.

Once at the saddle, turn southwest and follow a series of cairns around the north side of Froze-to-Death Mountain. The destination is an 11,600-foot plateau on the west edge of Tempest Mountain, 1.6 miles north of Granite Peak. You can camp here, but it must be a strict zero-impact camp.

In past years climbers have built rock shelters (rock walls about 3 feet high) on the west edge of Tempest Mountain to protect themselves from the strong winds that frequently blast the area.

By the time you reach Tempest Mountain, you have covered more than 10 miles and gained more than 5,000 feet. You crossed timberline many miles earlier, and now you see only rock, ice, and sky. No plants or grasses can survive the climate and elevation at the plateau, with the exception of a few hardy lichens and an occasional mountain goat.

Such a forbidding place has a few advantages. Strong winds usually keep mosquitoes at lower elevations, and there's no danger of seeing a bear or getting heatstroke. And, of course, the high altitude grants superb views in all directions.

One of the disadvantages is no protection from the elements. Check the forecast carefully, and forget about trying to climb Granite in bad weather, which can happen any

Yes, Froze-to-Death Plateau might be more suited for mountain goats than hikers. Expect to see them there. NATIONAL PARK SERVICE

summer day up here. Definitely be prepared for the worst. Hint: They don't call it Froze-to-Death Plateau for nothing.

Along the west edge of the plateau leading up to Tempest, the view of Granite Peak is awesome. Granite buttresses rise almost vertically from Huckleberry Creek Canyon to form a broad wall nearly a half mile wide. The north face is heavily etched with fissures running almost straight up between the buttresses. Granite Glacier clings to the center of the wall. At the top a series of pinnacles builds from the west side up to the peak.

To those skilled in technical climbing, Granite is an easy ascent in good weather, but for those with little experience, it's challenging if not dangerous. Probably the best advice is to go with someone who has the experience and proper equipment. Especially important is a good climbing rope for crossing several precipitous spots. The easiest approach is across the ridge that connects Granite to Tempest and then up the east side.

Check with the Forest Service for more information before attempting this climb, and get a copy of the agency's special brochure for people interested in climbing Granite Peak. In recent years not one summer has passed without mishaps and close calls, mostly due to bad judgment and inexperience. One sobering concern is the extreme difficulty of rescuing an injured person from Granite Peak.

People have tried this hike and climb at almost all times of the year, but August and early September are the most logical choices. Even then, prepare for sudden storms with subzero windchills and snow. And the thunderstorms around Granite Peak are legendary. Be ready with warm, waterproof, and windproof clothing and preferably a tent that can withstand a very strong wind.

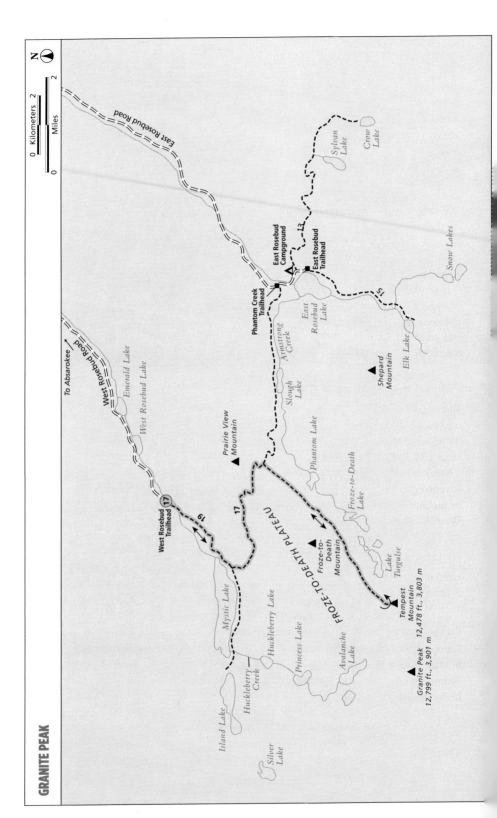

GRANITE PEAK

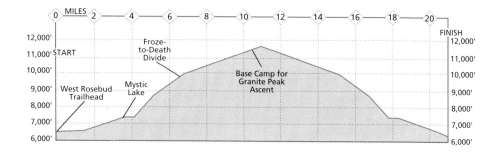

Whether or not you climb Granite, take the time to walk up to the top of Tempest. To the north and 2,000 feet below are Turgulse and Froze-to-Death Lakes. On a clear day you can see perhaps 100 miles out onto the Great Plains. And if you move a little east toward Mount Peal, you can look southwest over Granite Peak's shoulder to Mount Villard and Glacier Peak, both over 12,000 feet.

It should be no surprise that there is little wildlife at this altitude. Nearer the saddle, where grass and other hardy alpine plants eke out an existence, mountain goats are common. An occasional golden eagle soars through this country looking for marmots and pikas. Down near the trailheads, a few mule deer and black bears make their summer homes.

OPTIONS

Those who come in from the Phantom Creek Trailhead may wish to take an alternate way back. From the east edge of the plateau to the west–northwest of Turgulse Lake, it's possible to descend into the bowl that holds Turgulse and hike past Froze-to-Death Lake and Phantom Lake. Then cross the hill to rejoin the trail above Slough Lake. There's no trail on this route, but the adventurous among us will enjoy it. And high adventure is what this trip is all about in the first place. If you have arranged a shuttle or pickup, you can go out the East Rosebud instead of retracing your steps back to the West Rosebud.

SIDE TRIPS

Even if you elect to retrace your steps back to the West Rosebud, you might want to dip over to Turgulse and Froze-to-Death Lakes.

CAMPING

Camping on the Froze-to-Death Plateau or Tempest Mountain is for hardy, well-prepared backpackers only. There's no problem finding a place to camp; the trick is keeping your tent from blowing away. This entire area is way above timberline and gets heavy use, so please adhere strictly to zero-impact camping ethics.

FISHING

There's no fishing on this route with the exception of Mystic Lake.

MILE AND DIRECTIONS

0.0 Start at West Rosebud Trailhead.

3.0 Mystic Lake Dam.

3.5 Junction with Phantom Creek Trail 17.

6.4 Froze-to-Death Divide.

10.5 Tempest Mountain.

21.0 Arrive back at West Rosebud Trailhead.

18 ROSEBUD TO ROSEBUD

A fantastic but long and difficult day trip requiring a time-consuming shuttle.

Start: West Rosebud Trailhead
Distance: 13-mile shuttle
Difficulty: Difficult

Maps: USGS Granite Peak and Alpine; RMS Cooke City–Cutoff Mountain and Alpine–Mount Maurice; and at least 1 wilderness-wide map

FINDING THE TRAILHEADS

From 1-90 at Columbus, drive 15 miles south on MT 78 through Absarokee. About 2 miles past Absarokee, turn right (west) onto CR 419. Drive through Fishtail and continue west and south about 1 mile, then turn left (south) along West Rosebud Road. About 6 miles later, take another left (southeast) at the sign for West Rosebud Lake (pavement ends). From here it's another 14.4 miles of bumpy gravel road to the trailhead—a total of 26 miles from Absarokee and 41 miles from Columbus. The road ends and the trail starts at the Mystic Dam Power Station. Ample parking and toilet; two developed campgrounds on the way to the trailhead. **GPS:** 45.22782 N, 109.76183 W

To reach the Phantom Creek Trailhead: From I-90 at Columbus, go south 29 miles on MT 78 to Roscoe. Drive through this small ranching community, being careful not to stop at the Grizzly Bar—until the return trip, of course, when you'll be really ready for their famous Grizzly Burger. At the north end of Roscoe, the road turns to gravel and goes about 14.5 miles to the East Rosebud Trailhead. About 7 miles from Roscoe, the road crosses East Rosebud Creek and forks. Take a sharp right and continue south along the creek. The road is mostly gravel, except for a 4-mile paved section near the end. Phantom Creek Trail 17 begins on the right (west) side of the road about a quarter mile before East Rosebud Lake. Ample parking and toilet; large vehicle campground nearby. **GPS:** 45.205611 N, 109.642111 W

THE HIKE

If you aren't a peak bagger but you're in good shape and want to see lots of sensational scenery in one long day, consider arranging a shuttle from West Rosebud Trailhead to Phantom Creek Trailhead. Even better, talk some friends into a "trade keys" hike. This hike is a perfect choice for such a plan. One party starts at West Rosebud and the other at East Rosebud (Phantom Creek Trailhead); meet on top of Froze-to-Death Plateau for lunch, then trade keys and drive each other's vehicle home.

The trading keys plan can be risky on long trips where folks want to stop to fish, climb, or partake of other activities that might lead them off the trail. In this case, though, most of the trip is above timberline and on a well-maintained trail. It's almost impossible to miss each other. Whoever gets to the top of the plateau first should just relax and wait for the other party.

Be sure to pick a day with a good weather forecast. And roll out of bed early. This is a 13-mile day hike with lots of elevation gain—3,668 feet from West Rosebud and 3,932 feet from East Rosebud. Weather can be completely unpredictable at this elevation, but

Mystic Lake from Froze-to-Death Plateau.

normally the morning is better weather for hiking. Thunderstorms commonly roll over the plateau in midafternoon.

It would be difficult to argue which approach to the plateau is more scenic—definitely a win-win situation. It's about the same distance to an ideal rendezvous site on the top of Froze-to-Death Plateau. The trail is in terrific shape the entire way.

OPTIONS

This long day hike can be launched from either end with no major difference in difficulty.

SIDE TRIPS

Since this is a long, strenuous day hike, there probably won't be much time or energy for side trips, but a stroll along the shoreline of Mystic Lake is most pleasant. Ditto for a walk on Froze-to-Death Plateau, assuming, of course, that thunderheads aren't threatening.

ROSEBUD TO ROSEBUD

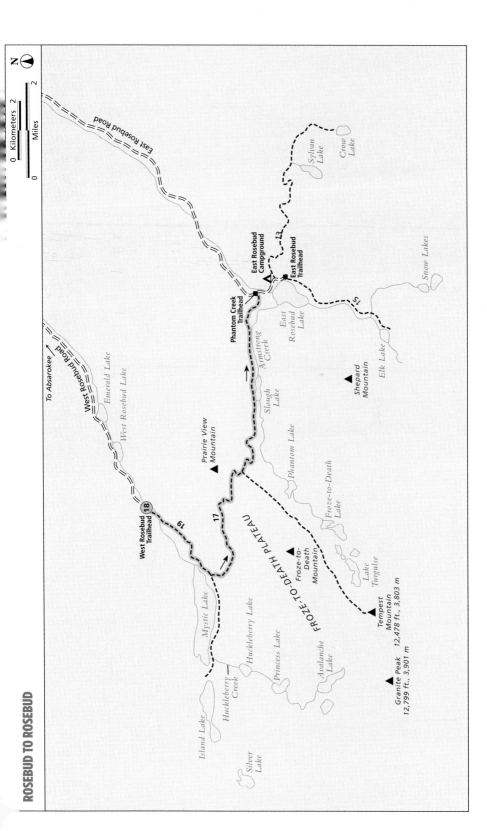

East Rosebud Road

West Rosebud Road

To Absarokee

N

0   Kilometers   2
0   Miles   2

West Rosebud Trailhead 18

Mystic Lake

Island Lake

Huckleberry Creek

Huckleberry Lake

Princess Lake

Silver Lake

Avalanche Lake

FROZE-TO-DEATH PLATEAU

19

17

Prairie View Mountain

Emerald Lake

West Rosebud Lake

Phantom Creek Trailhead

Armstrong Creek

Slough Lake

Phantom Lake

Froze-to-Death Mountain

Froze-to-Death Lake

Lake Turgulse

Tempest Mountain
12,478 ft., 3,803 m

Granite Peak
12,799 ft., 3,901 m

East Rosebud Campground

East Rosebud Trailhead

13

15

East Rosebud Lake

Shepard Mountain

Elk Lake

Snow Lakes

Sylvan Lake

Crow Lake

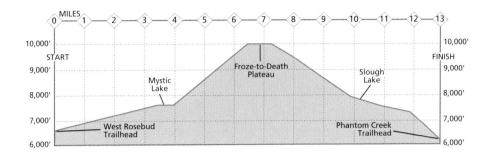

CAMPING

This trip really doesn't offer much for overnight campsites. But camping is available at the upper end of Slough Lake on the East Rosebud side and along the east shore of Mystic Lake on the West Rosebud side. Those who camp should practice strict zero-impact camping techniques, as this area receives heavy use (mainly because of the fanatical interest in climbing Granite Peak).

FISHING

If doing this as a day hike, there won't be much time to get in any relaxed fishing. The rainbows are generally willing in Mystic Lake, as are the brookies along the lower stretches of Phantom Creek.

MILES AND DIRECTIONS

0.0 Start at West Rosebud Trailhead.

3.0 Mystic Lake Dam.

3.5 Junction with Phantom Creek Trail 17.

6.4 Froze-to-Death Plateau.

10.2 Slough Lake.

13.0 Arrive at Phantom Creek Trailhead.

19 ISLAND LAKE

One of the easiest-to-reach base camps in the Beartooths with numerous options for side trips.

Start: West Rosebud Trailhead
Distance: 12 miles out and back
Difficulty: Moderate but with some difficult side trips (optional)

Maps: USGS Granite Peak; RMS Cooke City–Cutoff Mountain; and at least 1 wilderness-wide map

FINDING THE TRAILHEAD

From 1-90 at Columbus, drive 15 miles south on MT 78 through Absarokee. About 2 miles past Absarokee, turn right (west) onto CR 419. Drive through Fishtail and continue west and south about 1 mile, then turn left (south) along West Rosebud Road. About 6 miles later, take another left (southeast) at the sign for West Rosebud Lake (pavement ends). From here it's another 14.4 miles of bumpy gravel road to the trailhead—a total of 26 miles from Absarokee and 41 miles from Columbus. The road ends and the trail starts at the Mystic Dam Power Station. Ample parking (often packed) and toilet; two developed campgrounds on the way to the trailhead. **GPS:** 45.22782 N, 109.76183 W

THE HIKE

The West Rosebud Trailhead seems to have one disadvantage—or advantage, depending on your point of view. It's mostly suited for "just passing through."

The first three trips from this trailhead offer either day hikes or trips that pass through the West Rosebud drainage to other destinations. Island Lake, however, affords a great chance to stay a few days and enjoy the many wonders of the Upper West Rosebud valley. It's especially well-suited for hikers who like to set up a base camp.

From the trailhead follow West Rosebud Creek. After crossing a bridge over the creek, the trail follows a power line for a short way. After leaving behind these "signs of civilization," you switchback through open rock fields offering a great view of the West Rosebud valley, including West Rosebud and Emerald Lakes.

The climb doesn't seem that steep, but by the time the trail reaches the dam at the eastern end of Mystic Lake, it has ascended 1,200 feet in 3 miles, barely a Category 3 climb. Normally that would be considered a big climb, but for hikers who aren't in a hurry, it really doesn't seem like it.

When you finally break out over the ridge, you're treated to a sweeping view of Mystic Lake and Mystic Dam. Mystic Lake is a natural lake, but the dam increased its size and depth—now, at more than 200 feet, the deepest in the Beartooths. The sandy beach along the east shore of the lake below is perhaps the largest in the Beartooths—and a good lunch spot.

After taking a break here, start hiking along the east shoreline of the lake on a very scenic, flat, well-maintained trail, going right at the junction with the Phantom Creek Trail that climbs up to the Froze-to-Death Plateau. From the junction it's 2.5 picturesque miles to the head of the lake and then another 0.5 mile to Island Lake. Just before the end of the lake, the trail crosses Huckleberry Creek, which tumbles down from several lakes in the western shadow of Granite Peak. This is a big stream, but fortunately the Forest Service has built a sturdy bridge over it.

If you're staying overnight or setting up a multiday base camp at Island Lake, you must cross West Rosebud Creek to get to the choice campsites on the west side of the stream, and there's no bridge. In August or September, this won't be a big problem. You can cross easily on a logjam at the outlet of Island Lake. Early in the year at high water, however, this crossing could be more difficult and dangerous. Lots of water comes down West Rosebud Creek. The Forest Service doesn't maintain the trail beyond a point just before crossing West Rosebud Creek or above Island Lake.

OPTIONS

This route works well as a base camp, but you can also make this an enjoyable moderate day hike.

SIDE TRIPS

The trail continues on beyond Island Lake to Silver Lake, which also offers base-camp opportunities. But the trail to Silver Lake is muddy and brushy, and the campsites aren't as nice as those at Island Lake. Instead, consider visiting Silver Lake on a day trip from your Island Lake base camp. Another good possibility is a hike up Huckleberry Creek to Princess Lake and, for the well-conditioned, on to Avalanche Lake.

Two more potential side trips include a long trek to Grasshopper Glacier and a climb up to a series of lakes—Nugget, Beckworth, Frenco, Nemidji, and Weeluma—just west

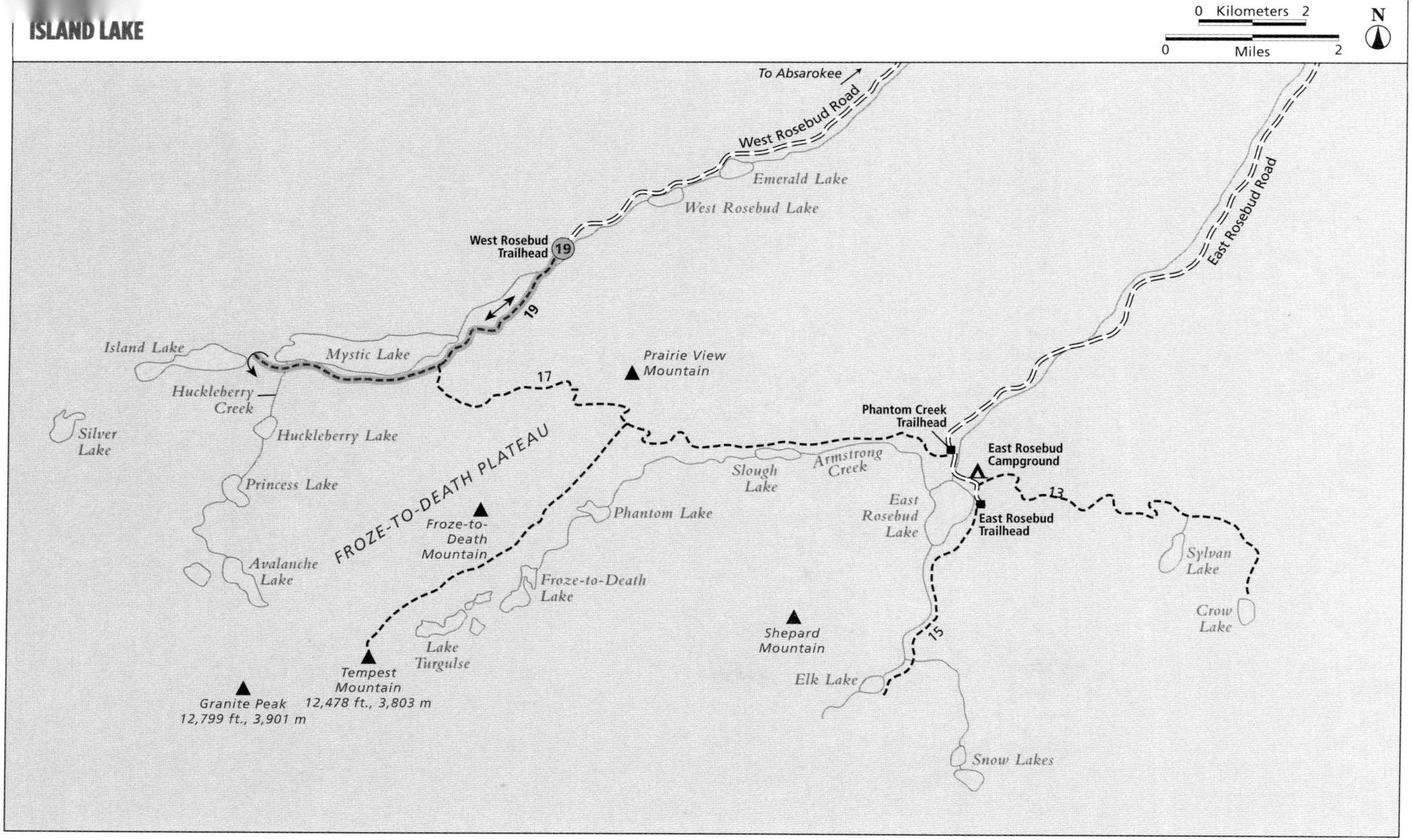

ISLAND LAKE

N

0 Kilometers 2
0 Miles 2

To Absarokee

West Rosebud Road

East Rosebud Road

Emerald Lake

West Rosebud Lake

Prairie View
Mountain

West Rosebud
Trailhead 19

19

17

FROZE-TO-DEATH PLATEAU

Mystic Lake

Huckleberry
Creek

Huckleberry Lake

Princess Lake

Avalanche
Lake

Island Lake

Silver
Lake

Froze-to-
Death
Mountain

Lake
Tirgulse

Tempest
Mountain
12,478 ft., 3,803 m

Granite Peak 12,799 ft., 3,901 m

Froze-to-Death
Lake

Phantom Lake

Slough
Lake

Armstrong
Creek

Phantom Creek
Trailhead

East Rosebud
Campground

East Rosebud
Trailhead

East
Rosebud
Lake

13

15

Shepard
Mountain

Elk Lake

Snow Lakes

Sylvan
Lake

Crow
Lake

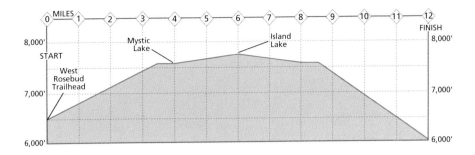

of Island Lake. Only those in good shape and savvy in wilderness skills should attempt these side trips.

Refer to the list of side trips in "Where to Go from Island Lake" (page 120).

CAMPING

Just after crossing West Rosebud Creek, you'll find a huge flat area where many large parties could camp and still not bother each other.

FISHING

Starting at Island Lake, anglers will begin to find an occasional cutthroat trout mixed in with the rainbow population. These have migrated down from Weeluma, Nemidji, Nugget, Beckworth, and Frenco Lakes, all pure cutthroat fisheries. Silver Lake sports some nice-size hybrid trout that are hard to catch, but worth the effort.

While many people use Trail 17 to access Granite Peak, a lesser-used alternative is up Huckleberry Creek. Huckleberry Lake supports a healthy rainbow population, while Avalanche and the Storm Lakes above are stocked with willing cutthroats that grow above average in size and weight. Mountain goats frequent this basin, and although this route is a steeper approach to Granite Peak, the added aspect of great fishing may make the climb worth it.

MILES AND DIRECTIONS

0.0 Start at West Rosebud Trailhead.

3.0 Mystic Lake Dam.

3.5 Junction with Phantom Creek Trail 17.

5.7 Huckleberry Creek.

6.0 Island Lake.

12.0 Arrive back at West Rosebud Trailhead.

20 **THE BEATEN PATH**

The most popular trans-Beartooth route and perhaps the best opportunity to really experience the austerity, breadth, and diversity of the Beartooths.

Start: East Rosebud Trailhead
Distance: 26-mile shuttle
Difficulty: Long and strenuous but not technically difficult or dangerous

Maps: USGS Alpine, Castle Mountain, and Fossil Lake; RMS Cooke City–Cutoff Mountain and Alpine-Mount Maurice; and at least 1 wilderness-wide map

FINDING THE TRAILHEADS

From I-90 at Columbus, go south 29 miles on MT 78 to Roscoe. Drive through this small ranching community, being careful not to stop at the Grizzly Bar—until the return trip, of course, when you'll be really ready for their famous Grizzly Burger. At the north end of Roscoe, the road turns to gravel and goes about 14.5 miles to the East Rosebud Trailhead. About 7 miles from Roscoe, the road crosses East Rosebud Creek and forks. Take a sharp right and continue south along the creek. From here the road is gravel, except for a 4-mile paved section near the end. Just before the lake, you pass the Phantom Creek Trailhead on your right (west). Keep going to the lake, cross East Rosebud Creek Bridge, and continue to the end of the road where you will find a huge parking area, which is often full. Ample parking and toilet. Room for large horse trailers. Large vehicle campground nearby. **GPS:** 45.19727 N, 109.63520 W

To leave a vehicle at the Clarks Fork Trailhead, drive 3.4 miles east from Cooke City or 58.1 miles west from Red Lodge and turn north on the well-marked road to the hiking trailhead. Don't turn onto FR 306, which is about a quarter mile west of the hiking trailhead, and goes only to the stock trailhead. Huge trailhead with plenty of parking, toilet, picnic area, and interpretive displays. **GPS:** 45.01762 N, 109.86935 W

RECOMMENDED ITINERARY

Twenty-six miles is not a bragging distance, and a strong hiker could do the entire trip in a day. You could even run it in a few hours as some people do each year, but instead, take your time and make this the best backpacking vacation of your life by taking at least four days.

If you get a late start, you might want to stay the first night at little Elk Lake, but most hikers go at least as far as Rainbow Lake before pitching a tent. For the second night, you have a choice of hundreds of campsites. Pick a good one and stay two nights or more, spending the extra days experiencing the heart of the Beartooth Plateau around Fossil Lake.

You can hike all the way out to the Clarks Fork Trailhead from Fossil Lake in one day, but if you prefer a less demanding schedule, there are also many campsites along the way. Russell Lake is a logical choice, but everybody else has that idea too, so this lake is always crowded and shows signs of overuse. Strive for an alternate campsite.

- First night: Rainbow Lake
- Second night: Somewhere around Fossil Lake
- Third night: Same campsite
- Fourth night: Russell, Fox, or Rock Island Lake

Note: The 2022 flood washed out several sections of the last 3 miles of the East Rosebud Road, including the 2-mile bridge over East Rosebud Creek, but the road was repaired and reopened in 2023. The second major problem is The Beaten Path trail, which was severely damaged by the flood. The flood washed out the upper end of Elk Lake, destroyed large sections of the trail between East Rosebud Lake and Rimrock Lake, and washed away the all-important Rimrock Lake Bridge. The trail to Elk Lake has been repaired, but the section between Elk Lake and Rimrock Lake might not be repaired in time for the 2024 hiking season. A bigger problem is the missing bridge at Rimrock Lake. Fording East Rosebud Creek can be very dangerous, especially before late August or early September. Hikers, especially those inexperienced fording fast-moving streams, probably should wait until the bridge is replaced before trying to hike over to the Clarks Fork Trailhead. This bridge probably won't be replaced until 2025 or later.

THE HIKE

Many people who know the Beartooths say the East Rosebud is the most scenic valley of all. It isn't a national park, they say, but could be. It's definitely more scenic than most national parks. To further emphasize the scenic grandeur of the drainage, East Rosebud Creek has been officially designated a Wild and Scenic River.

The valley is filled with lakes and waterfalls that would be major tourism attractions anywhere else. Here, there are so many that most don't even have names. The cutthroat-filled lakes bring a smile to any angler's face, and climbers love the place because of the endless array of rock faces. Families and friends frequently choose The Beaten Path for that long-planned wilderness adventure. Consequently, the East Rosebud Trailhead may be the most heavily used in the wilderness.

Adding even more use to the area is the small community of summer homes called Alpine right at the trailhead. The summer homes extend up both sides of the lower sections of East Rosebud Lake, closing off much of the lake to public use.

Actually, doing this trip in reverse, starting at the Clarks Fork Trailhead, involves slightly less elevation gain, but I have also done it from the East Rosebud.

This backpacking trip showcases all the beauty, austerity, emptiness, and majesty of the Beartooths. It's a great introduction to the region's richness, diversity, and starkness, traveling through the lowest bottomlands and the highest plateaus. Along the way the route skirts dozens of trout-filled lakes and stunning waterfalls. It penetrates rich forests and wanders the treeless, lichen-covered Beartooth Plateau. This trail embodies the true essence of the Beartooths.

This is the land of rushing water, waterfalls, and frothy, cascading streams. There's no such scenery in Yellowstone National Park. Nonetheless, we should all be elated to have the park so near, because it sucks up most of the visitors and leaves places like the East Rosebud for us.

On The Beaten Path above Rimrock Lake. KIM SCHNEIDER

Still, this trail receives heavy use compared to other routes in the Absaroka-Beartooth, especially camping areas at Elk Lake, Rainbow Lake, Dewey Lake, and Russell Lake. To hikers accustomed to fighting through swarms of people in national parks or popular roadless areas on the east or west coasts, the East Rosebud might not seem crowded, but for hikers used to hiking in Montana forests, yes, it may seem crowded. For uninterrupted solitude, and to really enjoy and experience the Beartooths, however, get off The Beaten Path. This route has dozens of options for off-trail adventures, which is one reason the Beartooths can swallow up hundreds of people and seem nearly abandoned.

Don't take this trip lightly. This route description suggests four nights out, but avid explorers could stay two weeks and not see anything twice.

It's also hard to make good time on this trail. There are simply too many distractions—too many scenic vistas, too many hungry trout, too many fields of juicy berries. Plan on traveling about a mile per hour slower than normal.

Dewey Lake, a popular and scenic campsite for Beaten Path hikers.

Also, be sure to plan this trip carefully. The first big issue is transportation. The best option is to arrange with another group of hikers to do the trip at the same time, starting at opposite ends of the trail, meeting at a campsite midway, spending a day or two together, trading keys, and then heading out to drive each other's vehicle home. More time-consuming options involve leaving a vehicle at one end of the trip and driving around to the other trailhead or arranging to be picked up.

The entire 26 miles of trail is well maintained and easy to follow, so even a beginning backpacker can master it with ease. However, getting off The Beaten Path requires advanced wilderness skills.

The well-traveled first 3 miles into Elk Lake go by quickly. Expect to see lots of people on this popular stretch of trail. But every step of the way beyond Elk Lake is a step deeper into the wilderness, and it really feels like it. Elk Lake has a few campsites, but Rainbow Lake (7 miles in) is a better choice for the first night out if you have enough daylight to get there.

Just after Elk Lake the trail passes through an area where wild berries are as abundant as anywhere in the Beartooths, so browsers beware. Progress can slow to glacial speed. For about a mile a kaleidoscope of berries beckons from trailside, with huge crops of huckleberries, thimbleberries, and wild raspberries, all nicely ripe in mid-August.

After finally making it through this berry paradise, you break out of the forest and climb about 800 feet through a monstrous rock field to Rimrock Lake, the steepest pitch of the entire route. For a mile or so below the lake, East Rosebud Creek is little more than a long series of cascades. Apparently a big rockslide formed a natural dam and backed up Rimrock Lake. Take a rest on the rock field and look at the trail to marvel at how it was constructed. Building a trail here was no small feat, especially negotiating the steep slopes around Rimrock Lake.

The trail crosses East Rosebud Creek on a sturdy wooden bridge at the outlet of Rimrock Lake. Then it skirts above the west side of the lake, the tread expertly etched out of the rock face. After the climb to get here, camping at Rimrock Lake might seem like a good idea, but good luck finding a decent campsite. It's better to push on for another mile to Rainbow Lake for the first night out.

Both Rimrock and Rainbow Lakes display a beautiful blue-green color (often called "glacier milk") indicative of a glacier-fed lake. Camping at Rainbow Lake affords a great view of Whirlpool Creek as it falls into the lake after tumbling down from Sundance Glacier on 12,408-foot Castle Rock Mountain.

The terrain at the upper end of Rainbow Lake flattens out and offers plenty of good campsites. You won't have it to yourself, but the huge camping area provides ample solitude for all campers. Horse campers also use this place, but the Forest Service requires horses to stay above the trail, leaving several excellent campsites below the trail for backpackers only.

After the great scenery at Rimrock and Rainbow Lakes, you might think that it can't get much better. Guess again. Plan on lots of camera stops on the trip from Rainbow Lake to Fossil Lake. Also watch for the mountain goats that inhabit this section of the East Rosebud drainage.

The falls on Whirlpool Creek was impressive, but not nearly as awe inspiring as the two falls from Martin Lake dropping into well-named Lake at Falls.

Another mile or so up the trail, be prepared for perhaps the most astounding sight of the trip, massive Impasse Falls, which plunges about 100 feet into Duggan Lake right beside the trail. Travelers get great views of the torrent from both below and above as the trail switchbacks up beside the falls.

From Impasse Falls the trail goes by two more large, unnamed waterfalls before arriving at Twin Outlets Lake. And the short stretch between Twin Outlets Lake and Dewey Lake features another series of waterfalls.

With all this scenery on the second day of this trip, it's hard to hold a steady pace, but don't be too distracted. It's 9 miles from Rainbow Lake to Fossil Lake. With four nights out, you have two options for the second night's camp—camp somewhere along the trail or push on to Fossil Lake and stay two nights there.

From the standpoint of available campsites, it's slightly better to forge on to Fossil Lake. Even though the scenery is great along this stretch, there aren't many good campsites. If you decide to camp before Fossil Lake, look for sites at Big Park Lake, Twin Outlets Lake, or Dewey Lake and along the stream above Big Park Lake. Lake at Falls and Duggan Lake offer virtually no campsites.

Twin Outlets Lake is just below timberline, and it's the last place along this trail where the Forest Service allows campfires, but not at the lake itself, only up to the outlet of the lake and downstream from there. Campfires are prohibited beyond the outlet of Twin Outlets Lake including in the Fossil Lake area, which is at about 10,000 feet in elevation. Not having a campfire should take nothing away from the grand experience of spending a few nights in the absolute core of the Beartooths.

One more choice for the second campsite is Echo Lake, which entails a 1-mile side trip. The trail breaks off to the west from the main trail above Big Park Lake and just before the bridge across Granite Creek. This isn't an official trail, but it's easy to follow. Watch for mountain goats on the slopes on the south side of Echo Lake.

Impasse Falls and Duggan Lake, a memorable highlight of every Beaten Path adventure.

If you're worried about bad weather, you might be smart to pick a campsite at or before Dewey Lake, which is your last partially protected spot before emerging onto the vast Beartooth Plateau.

Count on spending at least one night in the Fossil Lake area. Arriving fairly early on the third day allows extra time to search for that flawless, dream campsite. You can also find choice campsites just past Fossil Lake at Windy, Bald Knob, or Mermaid Lakes.

The Fossil Lake area is the beating heart of a great wilderness, and much of the spirit of this top-of-the-world environment seems to flow from it, just as East Rosebud Creek does. You'll really be missing something if you hurriedly pass through it.

From a base camp here, a multitude of remarkable day trips await. Always keep a close eye on the weather, though, and head back to camp if a storm rolls in—as they often do in this high-elevation paradise. Try to rise early and cruise around in the mornings instead of the afternoons, which is when thunderstorms rip through the Beartooths on an almost daily basis. Plan on spending a full day just to walk the perimeter of Fossil Lake.

About halfway along the trail around octopus-like Fossil Lake, a huge cairn marks the divide between two drainages (East Rosebud Creek and the Clarks Fork of the Yellowstone River) and the boundary between Custer and Gallatin National Forests (recently merged). Fossil Lake drains into the East Rosebud, and Windy Lake empties into the Clarks Fork. On Forest Service maps the trail numbers change from Trail 15 to Trail

Climbing up to Rimrock Lake.

567. This is also the logical place for cross-country hikers to break off the main trail and head over to Windy Lake, which can be seen off to the west. Windy Lake might be called Fizzle Lake on some maps, just as several other lakes in this area have different names on different maps. That's reason enough to bring along a complete selection of maps.

Leaving Fossil Lake the trail goes by Skull, Bald Knob, and Ouzel Lakes before dipping below timberline on the way to Russell Lake. Russell is nicely located for the last night out. Camp at either the upper or lower end of the lake. To reach the campsite at the lower end, you must ford the stream, which gets seriously large as it slowly leaves the lake. Unfortunately, Russell Lake receives heavy use and shows it, so you might want to camp elsewhere. Other choices for the last night out would be Fox or Rock Island Lake, both a short detour to the left off The Beaten Path.

The trail from Russell Lake to the Clarks Fork Trailhead might be the least attractive section, but most people would still rate it quite highly. For 6 miles it passes through a dense lodgepole forest. The 1988 fires burned the section around Kersey Lake.

With luck you'll come out on a hot day. Besides being the most scenic trailhead in the Beartooths, the Clarks Fork Trailhead has the best swimming hole. Wearing a five-day accumulation of sweat and grime, most hikers feel an overpowering temptation to jump in. Don't fight it; just do it.

OPTIONS

Starting at the Clarks Fork Trailhead (8,036 feet) involves less elevation gain. However, since the north end is more accessible and scenic, hikers usually start from the East Rosebud Trailhead (6,208 feet). Either way, the uphill climb isn't really severe; it's more of a gradual ascent most of the way.

SIDE TRIPS

Refer to "Getting Off the Beaten Path," above.

CAMPING

Choosing a campsite is a big issue on this trail, mainly because of the heavy use this route receives. Several camping areas such as Elk and Russell Lakes show signs of serious overuse. Other lakes, such as Rimrock Lake, Lake at Falls, and Duggan, may look like logical camping areas on the map but offer few, if any, decent campsites. On the other side of the coin, if you get off the trail a mile or so, you can frequently find a good campsite that looks as though it has never been used—and it will be up to you to leave it that way. Also, be sure to check current regulations for camping and campfires at the information board at the trailhead.

FISHING

The Montana Department of Fish, Wildlife & Parks (FWP) knows this is the most popular trail in the Beartooths and tries hard to complement this popularity with a great fishery.

East Rosebud Lake houses a mixed bag of brown trout, brookies, rainbows, and cutthroat trout. The steep terrain keeps the browns from moving far upstream, but brookies, rainbows, cutthroats, and even a few goldens survive in various places upstream in East Rosebud Creek. Goldens were stocked in several lakes along this trail in the 1950s, but they have readily crossbred with both rainbows and cutthroats. Unless you really know trout, the golden trout characteristics are difficult to see.

With the exception of Cairn and Billy Lakes, there are no brook trout above Elk Lake in this drainage. Rainbows dominate in Rimrock and Rainbow Lakes, and cutthroat trout dominate in the lakes above Rainbow Lake. Because of its popularity, Fossil Lake is stocked frequently with cutts to keep the fishing hot, although they can be hard to find because they tend to school.

If you camp at Elk Lake, you might have time for a side trip up to Snow Lakes. These lakes hold some nice rainbows, but the tough climb up the east side of Snow Creek keeps all but the most determined anglers away.

Anglers who camp near Big Park Lake might want to reserve an entire day for climbing (and it truly is a climb) into and out of Scat and Martin Lakes. FWP is trying to establish a pure golden trout fishery there, and it may be worth the climb.

Cairn Lake would also provide a worthwhile side trip for those camping near Dewey Lake. Cairn and Billy Lakes both have brook trout well above average in size. The trout don't reproduce well here, allowing those remaining to grow larger. FWP closely monitors these lakes—a downstream migration of brook trout would seriously harm the cutthroat/rainbow fishery down below. If you catch brookies below Billy Lake, notify FWP.

Entering the Clarks Fork drainage near Fossil Lake, the fishing gets even better. There are a great many lakes in this drainage, and the trail goes through the heart of this incredible fishery. Because of the easy access for horses, most of the lakes along the trail were stocked with brook trout in the first half of the twentieth century. The brookies tend to be on the smaller side but provide some great fishing and an easy meal.

Just off the trail, Leo Lake, Lake of the Winds, and Lake of the Clouds host cutthroat trout, while Gallery Lake has rainbows. Fox Lake is one of those places where few people stop, but many more should. It sports larger than average brookies, nice rainbows, and an occasional grayling that works its way down from Cliff Lake.

As an experiment, FWP has stocked lake trout in Kersey Lake to prey on the brook trout population. It is hoped that by reducing the number of brookies, the remaining ones will grow larger. At last check this seems to be working.

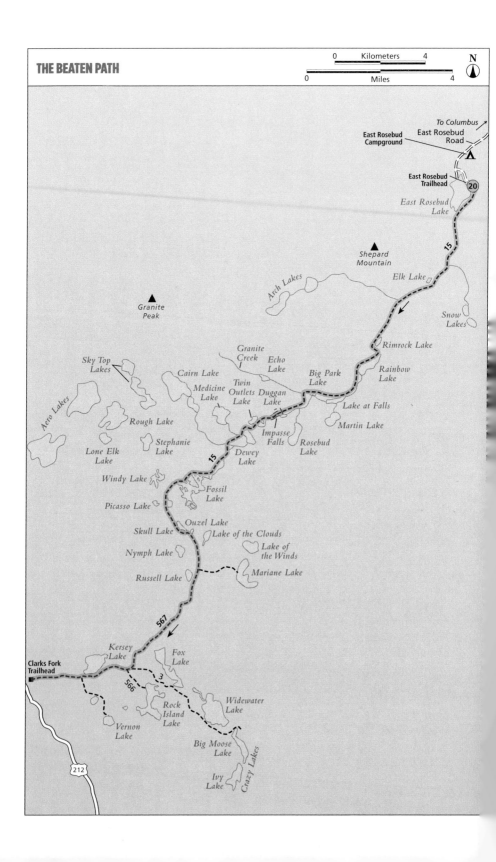

0   Kilometers   4

0   Miles   4

N

To Columbus

East Rosebud
Campground

East Rosebud
Road

East Rosebud
Trailhead

20

East Rosebud
Lake

15

Shepard
Mountain

Arch Lakes

Elk Lake

Snow
Lakes

Granite
Peak

Rimrock Lake

Granite
Creek

Echo
Lake

Big Park
Lake

Rainbow
Lake

Sky Top
Lakes

Cairn Lake

Medicine
Lake

Twin
Outlets
Lake

Duggan
Lake

Lake at Falls

Aero Lakes

Rough Lake

Martin Lake

Stephanie
Lake

Impasse
Falls

Rosebud
Lake

Lone Elk
Lake

Dewey
Lake

15

Windy Lake

Fossil
Lake

Picasso Lake

Ouzel Lake

Skull Lake

Lake of the Clouds

Lake of
the Winds

Nymph Lake

Russell Lake

Mariane Lake

567

Kersey
Lake

Fox
Lake

Clarks Fork
Trailhead

3

566

Rock
Island
Lake

Widewater
Lake

Vernon
Lake

Big Moose
Lake

Crazy Lakes

212

Ivy
Lake

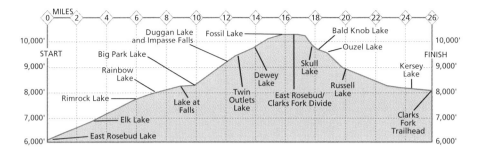

MILES AND DIRECTIONS

0.0 Start at East Rosebud Trailhead.

3.0 Elk Lake.

6.0 Rimrock Lake.

7.0 Rainbow Lake.

9.0 Lake at Falls.

9.9 Big Park Lake.

10.2 Junction with trail to Echo Lake; turn left.

11.8 Duggan Lake.

12.0 Impasse Falls.

12.8 Twin Outlets Lake.

14.0 Dewey Lake.

16.0 Fossil Lake.

16.8 East Rosebud/Clarks Fork Divide.

16.8 Gallatin/Custer National Forest boundary.

17.1 Windy Lake.

17.8 Skull Lake.

18.4 Bald Knob Lake.

18.8 Ouzel Lake.

20.0 Russell Lake.

22.0 Junction with trail 575 to Fox Lake; turn right.

22.2 Junction with Crazy Lakes Trail No. 3; turn right.

23.0 Junction with Trail 566 to Rock Island Lake; turn right.

24.5 Kersey Lake.

24.7 Junction with trail to Vernon Lake; turn right.

25.2 Junction with trail to Curl Lake; turn left.

25.5 Junction with stock trail/jeep road 306; turn left.

26.0 Arrive at Clarks Fork Trailhead, US 212.

21 **ELK LAKE**

A fairly easy day trip and possible candidate for an easy overnighter.

Start: East Rosebud Trailhead
Distance: 6 miles out and back
Difficulty: Easy

Maps: USGS Alpine; RMS Alpine–
Mount Maurice; and at least 1
wilderness-wide map

FINDING THE TRAILHEAD

From I-90 at Columbus, go south 29 miles on MT 78 to Roscoe. Drive through this small ranching community, being careful not to stop at the Grizzly Bar— until the return trip, of course, when you'll be really ready for their famous Grizzly Burger. At the north end of Roscoe, the road turns to gravel and goes about 14.5 miles to the East Rosebud Trailhead. About 7 miles from Roscoe, the road crosses East Rosebud Creek and forks. Take a sharp right and continue south along the creek. From here the road is gravel, except for a 4-mile paved section near the end. Just before the lake, you pass the Phantom Creek Trailhead on your right (west). Keep going to the lake, cross East Rosebud Creek Bridge, and continue to the end of the road where you will find a huge parking area, which is often full. Ample parking, toilet, and room for large horse trailers with large vehicle campground at trailhead.
GPS: 45.19727 N, 109.63520 W

Note: The 2022 flood washed out several sections of the last 3 miles of the East Rosebud Road, including the 2-mile bridge over East Rosebud Creek, but the road reopened in 2023. The trail to Elk Lake was also severely damaged by the flood, but this section of trail was also repaired in 2023. The flood also washed away the upper end of Elk Lake.

THE HIKE

This route covers the first 3 miles of the popular trans-Beartooth trail from the East Rosebud Trailhead to the Clarks Fork Trailhead, often called The Beaten Path (Hike 20). The trail goes through thick, partially burned forest all the way to Elk Lake and is well maintained and well traveled. Expect to see lots of people.

From the trail there are several great views of 10,979-foot Shepard Mountain to the west and East Rosebud Creek as it tumbles down from the Beartooth Plateau. Elk Lake is nestled in a forested pocket just below the point where the trail starts to traverse rockier,

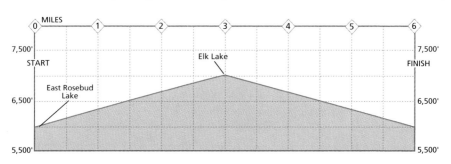

A nice East Rosebud cutthroat, common throughout the drainage.

steeper, more open terrain. As a destination, it's best suited for day trips. The upper end of the lake has a pleasant but well-used spot for lunch.

In 1999 a forest fire burned through the drainage above Elk Lake.

CAMPING

Even though Elk Lake offers limited camping, a fair number of people spend the night here, mainly those who started too late in the day on their trans-Beartooth adventure and didn't have time to reach Rainbow Lake. The main camping area at the inlet shows signs of overuse, but you can find other campsites along the eastern shore.

FISHING

Elk Lake has both cutthroat and brook trout, with the brookies providing the best chance for a fish dinner. Anglers day hiking to Elk Lake should plan a couple of stops to fish in the creek. At the trailhead, East Rosebud Lake holds some large brown trout, along with a mixed bag of brookies, rainbows, and cutthroats.

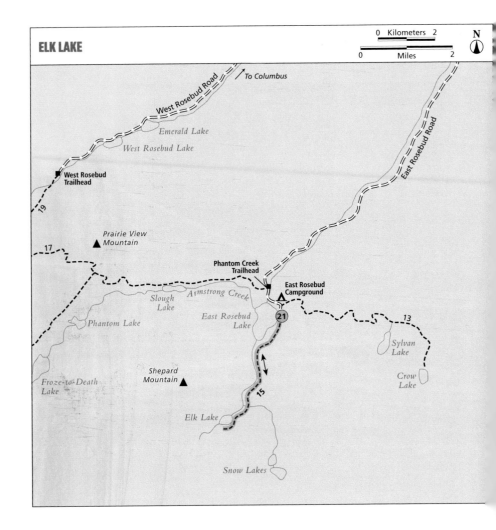

ELK LAKE

0 Kilometers 2
0 Miles 2

N

To Columbus

West Rosebud Road

Emerald Lake

West Rosebud Lake

West Rosebud Trailhead

East Rosebud Road

19

Prairie View Mountain

17

Phantom Creek Trailhead

East Rosebud Campground

Slough Lake

Armstrong Creek

East Rosebud Lake

21

13

Phantom Lake

Sylvan Lake

Shepard Mountain

Froze-to-Death Lake

Crow Lake

15

Elk Lake

Snow Lakes

MILES AND DIRECTIONS

0.0 Start at East Rosebud Trailhead.

3.0 Elk Lake.

6.0 Arrive back at East Rosebud Trailhead.

22 SYLVAN LAKE

A long, hard day trip or moderate overnighter to one of the few easily accessible golden trout fisheries in the Beartooths.

Start: Sylvan Lake Trailhead, at the north end of East Rosebud Campground
Distance: 10 miles out and back

Difficulty: Moderate
Maps: USGS Alpine and Sylvan Peak; RMS Alpine–Mount Maurice; and at least 1 wilderness-wide map

FINDING THE TRAILHEAD

From I-90 at Columbus, go south 29 miles on MT 78 to Roscoe. Drive through this small ranching community, being careful not to stop at the Grizzly Bar—until the return trip, of course, when you'll be really ready for their famous Grizzly Burger. At the north end of Roscoe, the road turns to gravel and goes about 14.5 miles to the East Rosebud Trailhead. About 7 miles from Roscoe, the road crosses East Rosebud Creek and forks. Take a sharp right and continue south along the creek. From here the road is gravel, except for a 4-mile paved section near the end. Just before the lake, you pass the Phantom Creek Trailhead on your right (west). Keep going to the lake and cross East Rosebud Creek Bridge. Just before reaching the huge parking lot for the East Rosebud Trailhead, take a sharp left into the campground and drive to the far end to the Sylvan Lake Trailhead. Limited parking and no toilet, but toilets in the campground and at the East Rosebud Trailhead. **GPS:** 45.20054 N, 109.63260 W

THE HIKE

The true beauty of Sylvan Lake lies beneath the surface. There swim the gorgeous, multicolored golden trout in abundance. Biologists call the Sylvan Lake golden trout population one of the purest in the Beartooths, and they use the lake as a source of fish to plant in other lakes. Even for the non-angler, however, this lake is worth the uphill trek.

Start up Trail 13 right from the East Rosebud Campground and gradually switchback up the steep slopes of the East Rosebud Plateau. It's 5 miles to the lake, almost completely uphill, but, of course, the return trip is all downhill. The trail is heavily used and well maintained. It's also expertly designed so the climb doesn't seem so steep. The top of the ridge offers a fantastic view ("I climbed that!") of the East Rosebud drainage, including East Rosebud Lake about 2,400 feet below.

On the ridge the trail markers fade into a series of cairns for a few hundred yards, so be alert to stay on the trail. Also, don't miss the junction where the spur trail heads up to Sylvan Lake and Trail 13 continues on to Crow Lake. The junction is well marked, but inattentive hikers could end up at the wrong lake.

SIDE TRIPS

An overnight stay at Sylvan Lake allows time for the short side trip over to Crow Lake, which probably surpasses Sylvan Lake for beauty, at least above the surface. Here, below the surface, the brook trout aren't as beautiful as the golden trout of Sylvan Lake but are still mighty nice and larger than those in a lot of lakes in the Beartooths.

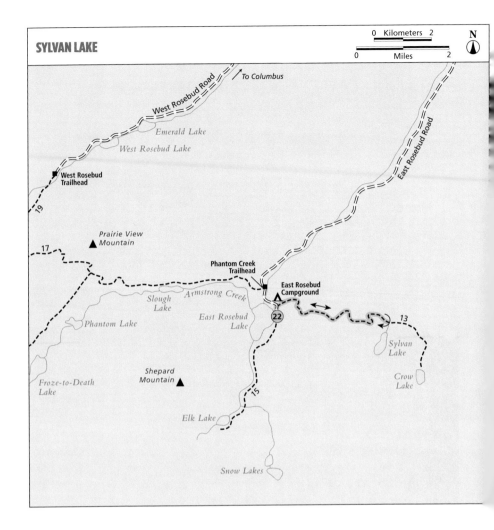

CAMPING

Even though it's a 10-mile round trip, Sylvan Lake is more suited for day trips. There is one campsite on a small plateau to the right just before the trail breaks over the last ridge into the lake basin. Camp here, however, and people will be walking by the front door of your tent. There are no good campsites right at the lake. Sylvan Lake is at timberline, so please refrain from building a campfire.

FISHING

Anglers truly intent on pursuing the golden trout of Sylvan Lake might plan to spend the night. Goldens are shy and more easily caught in the morning and evening. The golden trout of Sylvan Lake reproduce readily, so don't worry about taking a few home, even if it's just to put one of these beauties on the wall. Anglers who make the trek to Crow Lake will find that the brook trout there are larger than average and much easier to catch than the goldens at Sylvan.

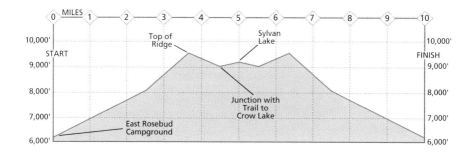

MILES AND DIRECTIONS

0.0 Start at Sylvan Lake Trailhead.

3.5 Top of ridge.

4.6 Junction with trail to Crow Lake; turn right.

5.0 Sylvan Lake.

10.0 Arrive back at Sylvan Lake Trailhead.

Fishing beneath unnamed waterfalls.

23 SLOUGH LAKE

A leisurely day trip with a terrific view of the upper Phantom Creek drainage leading to Froze-to-Death Plateau.

Start: Phantom Creek Trailhead
Distance: 4 miles out and back
Difficulty: Easy

Maps: USGS Alpine; RMS Alpine–Mount Maurice; and at least 1 wilderness-wide map

FINDING THE TRAILHEAD

From I-90 at Columbus, go south 29 miles on MT 78 to Roscoe. Drive through this small ranching community, being careful not to stop at the Grizzly Bar—until the return trip, of course, when you'll be really ready for their famous Grizzly Burger. At the north end of Roscoe, the road turns to gravel and goes about 14.5 miles to the East Rosebud Trailhead. About 7 miles from Roscoe, the road crosses East Rosebud Creek and forks. Take a sharp right and continue south along the creek. The road is mostly gravel, except for a 4-mile paved section near the end. Phantom Creek Trail 17 begins on the right (west) side of the road about a quarter mile before East Rosebud Lake. Ample parking and toilet with large vehicle campground nearby. **GPS:** 45.205611 N, 109.642111 W

THE HIKE

This trail is perfectly suited for that leisurely, quiet day in the wilderness amid some great scenery.

Trail 17 climbs, with gradual switchbacks, along Armstrong Creek (yes, it probably should be called the Armstrong Creek Trailhead) for about 2.5 miles before it breaks out of the forest into a great panorama highlighted by Hole-in-the-Wall Mountain to the south. Look ahead to see how the trail climbs up to Froze-to-Death Plateau.

The trail reaches Slough Lake (no relation to the Slough Creek that drains south from Boulder River country to the west) about a half mile after the forest opens up. This is a gorgeous, glacier-carved cirque, and Slough Lake sits in the midst of it like a little pearl. Actually, there are two small lakes, and the second lake has a campsite, for hikers interested in an easy overnighter.

Even though this trail receives heavy use, few people stop at Slough Lake. Most rush to the top of Froze-to-Death Plateau to climb Granite Peak. Too bad for them; they missed a great place to sit on a sunny day and soak in the spirit of the wilderness.

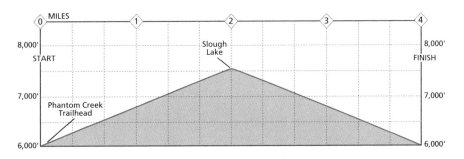

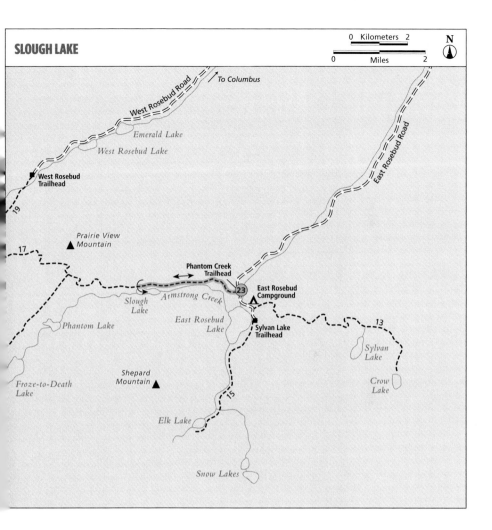

SLOUGH LAKE

0 Kilometers 2

0 Miles 2

N

To Columbus

West Rosebud Road

Emerald Lake

West Rosebud Lake

West Rosebud Trailhead

19

East Rosebud Road

Prairie View Mountain

17

Phantom Creek Trailhead

East Rosebud Campground

23

Slough Lake

Armstrong Creek

Phantom Lake

East Rosebud Lake

Sylvan Lake Trailhead

13

Sylvan Lake

Froze-to-Death Lake

Shepard Mountain

15

Crow Lake

Elk Lake

Snow Lakes

CAMPING

There are a couple of campsites on the north shore of Armstrong Creek near the trail and one campsite at the upper end of the second lake, so this can be an easy overnighter.

FISHING

Slough Lake provides a good source of willing brookies for dinner or for fun.

MILES AND DIRECTIONS

0.0 Start at Phantom Creek Trailhead.

2.0 Slough Lake.

4.0 Arrive back at Phantom Creek Trailhead.

RED LODGE AREA

The area between Red Lodge and Beartooth Pass has several trailheads, mostly along the West Fork of Rock Creek, but also in the Lake Fork of Rock Creek and the main fork of Rock Creek below Beartooth Pass. The trails in this area provide a nice variety ranging from short, easy, flat hikes to long, strenuous off-trail adventures. Many lakes and other scenic areas can be reached within a few miles of a trailhead. The climbs to some lakes are often steep but usually short.

The West Fork of Rock Creek Road, known locally as the West Fork Road and officially as FR 2071, actually has five trailheads along with three vehicle campgrounds and a sprinkling of residential developments. Since the West Fork Road starts right in Red Lodge, the lower valley feels like the town's backyard wilderness.

The West Fork Road is paved for the first 7 miles up to Basin Creek Campground. All West Fork trailheads are well signed and can be reached with any vehicle, with the possible exception of the Silver Run Trailhead, which is difficult to reach without a high-clearance, four-wheel-drive vehicle. This is a heavily used area, both for day trips and extended backcountry excursions. Fortunately, the area offers a wide range of trail choices, and visitors tend to disperse. Trails rarely feel crowded.

To access the West Fork trailheads, turn west onto the West Fork Road (FR 2071), which leaves US 212 on the south edge of Red Lodge and is marked with a ski area sign. After 3 miles the road bends left and heads up the West Fork. Calculating from Red Lodge, the mileage to the trailheads in the West Fork is as follows:

Silver Run—4.5 miles

Basin Creek—7 miles

Timberline Lake—11 miles

West Fork and Senia Creek—13 miles

The Lake Fork of Rock Creek area is similar to the West Fork. Both drainages are easily accessible from Red Lodge and receive lots of use. The high level of use in the Lake Fork may be more noticeable because everybody uses the same trail. In the West Fork, multiple trailheads tend to disperse the use.

The Rock Creek area is the last stop before driving up the world-famous switchbacks to the top of Beartooth Pass and into Wyoming. The two trailheads (Glacier Lake and Hellroaring) are accessed from the Forest Service campgrounds at the base

The off-trail route to Moon Lake, a popular side trip when going to Glacier Lake.

of Beartooth Pass. Day hikers can camp at one of the three vehicle campgrounds and go to Hellroaring Plateau and Glacier Lake on one-day outings. Regrettably, both the Hellroaring Plateau and Glacier Lake roads have deteriorated badly in recent years and require a high-clearance, four-wheel-drive vehicle to reach the trailheads. Even with such a vehicle, it might be difficult to reach the Hellroaring Plateau. That road has deteriorated to a point where you might need am ATV to drive on it.

Mileage to trailheads as calculated from Red Lodge:

Lake Fork—9 miles
Hellroaring Plateau—11 miles
Glacier Lake—11 miles

Note: The 2022 floods caused lots of damage to the trails and roads around Red Lodge, but most of it has been repaired or will be by the time this revision is released.

24 BASIN CREEK LAKES

An easy day hike well suited for families on a designated National Recreation Trail.

Start: Basin Creek Trailhead
Distance: 5 miles to lower lake and 8 miles to upper lake, out and back
Difficulty: Easy

Maps: USGS Bare Mountain; RMS Alpine–Mount Maurice; and at least 1 wilderness-wide map

FINDING THE TRAILHEAD

From I-90 at Laurel, drive south on US 212 about 45 miles to the south side of Red Lodge. Watch for the big sign for the Red Lodge Mountain Ski Resort and take a right (west) onto West Fork Road (also called Ski Run Road and FR 71). When the road forks at 3 miles, take the left fork, staying on the paved West Fork Road and not the gravel road continuing up to the ski resort. The road is paved until you reach Basin Creek Campground, where it turns into a good gravel road. The trailhead is on your left just before the campground. Fairly large parking lot with toilet and vehicle camping at nearby Basin Creek and Cascade Campgrounds. **GPS:** 45.15922 N, 109.38926 W

THE HIKE

The Forest Service has designated Basin Creek Lakes as a National Recreation Trail, so, not surprisingly, it's popular. It's so popular, in fact, that this is one of the few trails in the Beartooths restricted to hiking only—no horses are allowed until mid-September when the big-game hunting seasons get under way.

Technically, Trail 61 to Basin Creek Lakes doesn't pass through the Absaroka-Beartooth Wilderness, but it's a wilderness trip by all other definitions. The trail is well maintained, easy to follow, and ideal for family day trips for anyone who can handle a gradual but steady uphill gradient. The route crosses Basin Creek on a bridge.

About a half mile up the trail, listen for Basin Creek Falls tumbling down from above. Where the trail takes a sharp right, hikers can scramble up a short, undeveloped spur trail to get a closer look at the falls, which is well worth the short detour. The rest of the trail is hazard-free, but this short climb up to see the falls might be too hazardous for small children.

The trail passes through thick forest all the way to the lakes with the exception of a short burned section near the trailhead. With so much of the Beartooths burned by recent fires, this peaceful walk in the woods can be a real treat. You can still see the remains of logging activity from the early 1900s along the way—and how nature has mostly reclaimed the disturbed landscape.

Lower Basin Creek Lake is one of those forest-lined mountain ponds with darkish, warm water that tends to be half covered by lily pads. Upper Basin Creek Lake is larger, deeper, and nestled in a picturesque mountain cirque.

BASIN CREEK LAKES

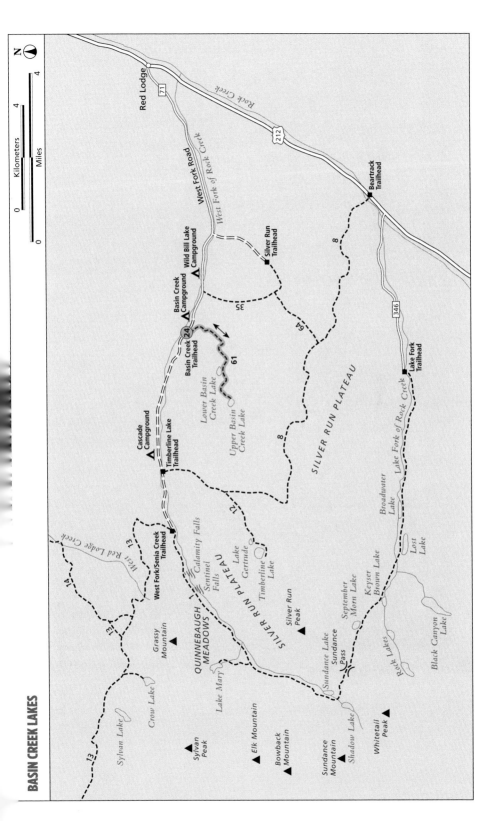

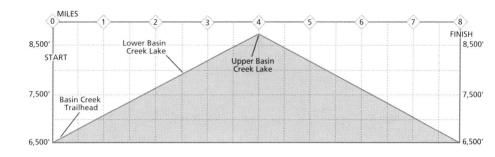

CAMPING

Although better suited as a destination for day trips, the upper lake also offers a few potential campsites. You might find enough firewood for a low-impact campfire.

FISHING

While both of these lakes once supported brook trout populations, the lower lake suffered a freeze-out a few years back and currently has no fish. Since the brook trout in the stream and lake above will eventually work their way back down to Lower Basin, there is no immediate need to restock. Brook trout fishing in Upper Basin Creek Lake is excellent.

MILES AND DIRECTIONS

0.0   Start at Basin Creek Trailhead.

0.5   Basin Creek Falls.

2.5   Lower Basin Creek Lake.

4.0   Upper Basin Creek Lake.

8.0   Arrive back at Basin Creek Trailhead.

25 TIMBERLINE LAKE

A moderately long day trip or easy overnighter to an idyllic mountain lake.

Start: Timberline Lake Trailhead
Distance: 9 miles out and back
Difficulty: Easy

Maps: USGS Sylvan Peak and Bare Mountain; RMS Alpine–Mount Maurice; and at least 1 wilderness-wide map

FINDING THE TRAILHEAD

From I-90 at Laurel, drive south on US 212 about 45 miles to the south side of Red Lodge. Watch for the big sign for the Red Lodge Mountain Ski Resort and take a right (west) onto West Fork Road (also called Ski Run Road and FR 71). When the road forks at 3 miles, take the left fork, staying on the paved West Fork Road and not the gravel road continuing up to the ski resort. The road is paved until you reach Basin Creek Campground, where it turns into a good gravel road. Go 4 more miles and turn left (south) into the Timberline Lake Trailhead (11 miles total from Red Lodge). Fairly large parking lot (but too small for horse trailers) with toilet. **GPS:** 45.17180 N, 109.46017 W

Timberline Lake.

The Silver Run Basin above Timberline Lake.

THE HIKE

Similar to the nearby trail up Basin Creek, the trail to Timberline Lake passes through a forested environment. Unlike Basin Creek, much of this route burned when the 2008 Cascade Fire swept through the upper West Fork Valley. As with almost all trails in this section of the Absaroka-Beartooth Wilderness, this one is well maintained and marked.

The corridor to Timberline Lake was excluded from the Absaroka-Beartooth Wilderness. However, Lake Gertrude and Timberline Lake lie within the wilderness boundary.

It's a short 3 miles to the junction with Silver Run Lakes Trail 18, which veers off to the left and heads up to Silver Run Plateau. Turn right and continue along Timberline Creek. If you cross the stream here, you took a wrong turn.

After another mile or so, look for Lake Gertrude off to the right. This is a good spot to pause for a rest while enjoying the lake, which also marks the boundary of the Absaroka-Beartooth Wilderness. Don't burn too much daylight here, however. Timberline Lake is only 0.5 mile farther, and you'll want to leave time to explore this high-altitude basin.

The view from Timberline Lake is fantastic, especially to the south toward Timberline Glacier and 12,500-foot Silver Run Peak.

SIDE TRIPS

Adventuresome hikers might want to try a side trip up to the glacier.

CAMPING

For an overnight trip it's possible to camp near the inlet of Lake Gertrude, but most people will probably enjoy the night out more by going the extra half mile to Timberline Lake. At Timberline Lake, camp on the moraine on the east side of the lake or near the inlet.

TIMBERLINE LAKE

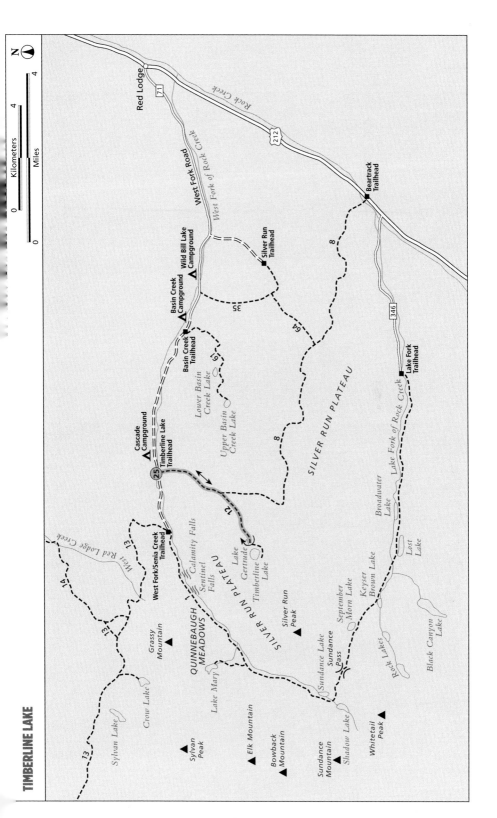

N

Kilometers
0   4

Miles
0   4

Red Lodge

71

Rock Creek

212

West Fork of Rock Creek

West Fork Road

Beartrack Trailhead

8

Wild Bill Lake Campground

Basin Creek Campground

Silver Run Trailhead

346

Basin Creek Trailhead

35

64

8

Cascade Campground

Timberline Lake Trailhead

25

Lower Basin Creek Lake

6

Upper Basin Creek Lake

SILVER RUN PLATEAU

Lake Fork of Rock Creek

Lake Fork Trailhead

West Fork/Senia Creek Trailhead

West Red Lodge Creek

13

Calamity Falls

Sentinel Falls

12

Timberline Lake

Gertrude Lake

Broadwater Lake

QUINNEBAUGH MEADOWS

SILVER RUN PLATEAU

Silver Run Peak

Sundance Lake

September Morn Lake

Keyser Brown Lake

Lost Lake

Grassy Mountain

Lake Mary

Sundance Pass

Rock Lakes

Black Canyon Lake

Sylvan Lake

Crow Lake

13

Sylvan Peak

Elk Mountain

Bowback Mountain

Sundance Mountain

Shadow Lake

Whitetail Peak

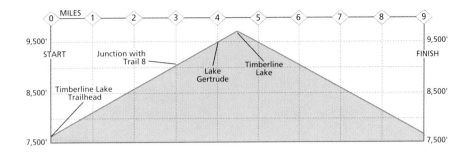

FISHING

Both lakes along this trail have healthy populations of brook trout. The fish aren't large but can probably be counted on to provide dinner. The small outlet ponds below Timberline Lake may prove an easier place to catch fish than the lake itself.

MILES AND DIRECTIONS

0.0   Start at Timberline Lake Trailhead.

3.0   Junction with Silver Run Lakes Trail 18; turn right.

4.0   Lake Gertrude.

4.5   Timberline Lake.

9.0   Arrive back at Timberline Lake Trailhead.

Arctic gentian, one of the rarest flowers in the Beartooths, often seen on Silver Run Plateau.

26 SILVER RUN PLATEAU

A long, challenging trek over an extraordinarily scenic high plateau for experienced hikers only.

Start: Timberline Lake Trailhead
Distance: 14.5-mile shuttle
Difficulty: Difficult
Maps: USGS Sylvan Peak, Black Pyramid Mountain, and Bare

Mountain; RMS Alpine–Mount Maurice; and at least 1 wilderness-wide map

FINDING THE TRAILHEADS

From I-90 at Laurel, drive south on US 212 about 45 miles to the south side of Red Lodge. Watch for the big sign for the Red Lodge Mountain Ski Resort and take a right (west) onto West Fork Road (also called Ski Run Road and FR 71). When the road forks at 3 miles, take the left fork, staying on the paved West Fork Road and not the gravel road continuing up to the ski resort. The road is paved until you reach Basin Creek Campground, where it turns into a good gravel road. Go 4 more miles and turn left (south) into the Timberline Lake Trailhead (11 miles total from Red Lodge). Fairly large parking lot (but too small for horse trailers) with toilet. **GPS:** 45.17180 N, 109.46017 W

The turnoff to Silver Run Trail 64 (the end of this hike) is marked on the south side of West Fork Road, about 2 miles past the turnoff to the ski resort. You can make it over this 2-mile spur road up to the trailhead in any vehicle, barely, but it gets steep and rocky in a few places, so a high-clearance vehicle is better. Limited parking and toilet. **GPS:** 45.13543 N, 109.35170 W

If you decide not to leave a vehicle or bicycle at the trailhead for Trail 64, you can leave it at the parking area off West Fork Road just after crossing the West Fork of Rock Creek (ample parking and toilet), but this will add 2.1 miles to your hike because you'll have to walk down the jeep road to your vehicle.

THE HIKE

This is unconditionally one of the most remarkable and unusual trails in the Beartooths—or anywhere else. It doesn't feature an endless string of lakes as many Beartooth trails do, but hikers might be too busy enjoying the trip to notice. Only the midsection of this trail is actually within the Absaroka-Beartooth Wilderness, but the entire trip seems exceptionally wild. The 2008 Cascade Fire scorched the first few miles of this route.

Weather is always critical in the Beartooths, but good weather is essential for this hike. Double-check the weather report before leaving home, and don't go unless you have a good forecast. Take an extra water bottle, as water is scarce, especially in late summer.

Another big issue on this hike is transportation because it's a problematic shuttle. Arrange to be picked up or leave a vehicle (or bicycle) at the end of the trail to get back to your vehicle at the Timberline Lake Trailhead.

For some reason that will always be a mystery to me, this route doesn't get much use. I've hiked it three times (so far) and haven't yet seen another hiker up on the plateau. The scenic cluster of small lakes in the Silver Run Basin isn't much of a fishery, so that might be one reason for the light use. Another might be the difficulty—it's definitely

Hiking above the clouds on Silver Run Plateau.

a route for well-conditioned, experienced hikers only. But whatever the reason, I have to counter with "Ya don't know what you're missing," as the scenery equals or exceeds anything, anywhere in the Beartooths.

This is not, however, a good backpacking route, but those backpackers who choose to spend a night or two in the Silver Run Basin won't be disappointed because it's definitely a room with a view.

As you hike this route, you pass through four strikingly distinct environs. You start with a climb on a fairly rocky trail through a lodgepole forest, now nothing but a forest of ghostly snags as it recovers from the massive Cascade Fire of 2008. Then you emerge from the wildflower-carpeted burn into the postcard panorama called the Silver Run Basin, followed by 6 remarkable miles of high-altitude splendor on the Silver Run Plateau. Finally, you finish up with a steep downhill plunge through what most might consider a typical mature forest, primarily lodgepole and Douglas fir.

From the trailhead Timberline Trail 12 ascends 3 miles through the big burn and offers a great study on how a landscape quickly recovers from a forest fire—including, for your enjoyment, a robust growth of huckleberries, raspberries, and just about every other berry. At 3 miles turn left onto Silver Run Lakes Trail 18 and ford Timberline Creek (no bridge). Shortly after that ford and another over Silver Run Creek (again, no bridge), you emerge from the burn into the gorgeous Silver Run Basin, dotted with small lakes and all in the backdrop of mighty Silver Run Peak, which, at 12,542 feet, casts a mighty big shadow. You'll also find mature stands of healthy whitebark pine, which, in the era of the pine beetle, you really don't see much anymore. Fortunately, the severe winter temperatures at this elevation keep the beetle at bay.

You have a lot of time to relish the scenery of the Silver Run Basin as you gradually switchback up the basin's east side until you step out onto the unique Silver Run Plateau. Up to this point the trail has been distinct and easy to follow, but once on the plateau, it becomes mostly a series of cairns with no visible trail in most places. Other trails in the Beartooths have short stretches of cairns, but in this case the cairns last for about 6 miles. The cairns are well placed, large, and easy to see.

The entire Silver Run Plateau is at or above 10,000 feet and affords a fresh perspective on the Beartooths. It's trackless, treeless, bugless, waterless, and almost peopleless. The rare

Taking a break to enjoy Silver Run Plateau.

exception is that determined devil, the horsefly, that can follow you anywhere, defying all the laws of nature, up to 10,500 feet and many miles from the nearest horse, looking for a mouthful of soft meat from behind your knee. The plateau actually has a few charming spring- and snowmelt-fed rivulets where you can filter water, but depending on the year and time of year, they can be dry.

Most of your off-trail trek over the plateau is above 10,000 feet, topping out at about 10,650 feet. You can see many of the highest peaks of the Beartooths on the horizon, and below you, a truly fascinating carpet of plant life such as aged willows that top out at about 10 inches in height and perhaps my favorite wildflower, the rare Arctic gentian. This is the only place I've ever seen this lovely pale-green flower.

After following cairns for about 6 miles, watch for the junction with Silver Run Trail 64 at the 11-mile point. Beartrack Trail 8 continues straight into the Lake Fork of Rock Creek. You turn left (north) onto Silver Run Trail 64 and head down Silver Run Creek into the West Fork of Rock Creek.

The last time I hiked this route, this junction was unsigned and easy to miss, but the Forest Service has recently marked the junction, so you shouldn't miss it. When you look carefully, you can see cairns in both directions, another signal that you're at the junction.

After this junction you still have another half mile or so of your fantastic journey over the Silver Run Plateau until you finally slip below 10,000 feet and then drop off the edge of the plateau.

Trail 64 drops rapidly (from 9,400 feet to 7,100 feet in less than 4 miles!) into Silver Run Creek, so steeply that doing this trip in reverse would seem unwise. Stay on this trail for 3.5 miles to the trailhead, bearing right after 2 miles at the junction with the Ingles Creek Trail. On the way down you might see a few "stock driveway" signs nailed on trees, which are also signs of a much different past. Decades ago the Forest Service allowed heavy sheep grazing on the Silver Run Plateau, but fortunately, that grazing allotment has been abandoned, mainly because of potential damage to this fragile and unique environment. Some things do, it seems, get better with time.

SILVER RUN PLATEAU

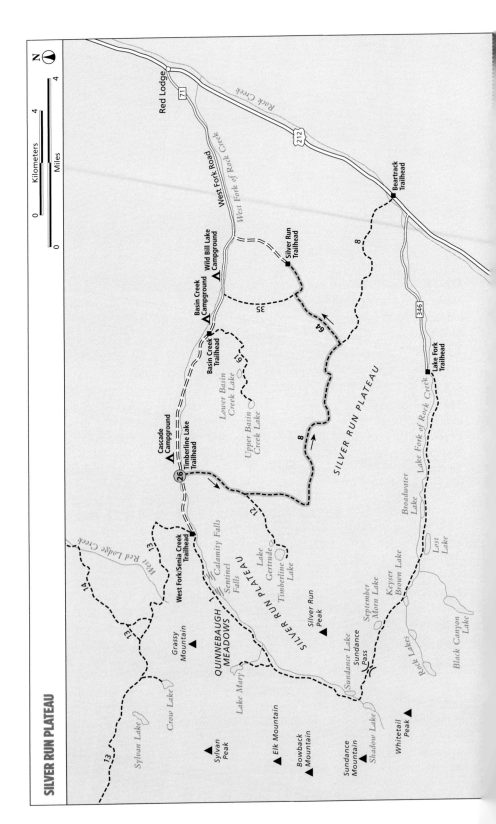

N

Kilometers
0   4

Miles
0   4

Red Lodge

71

Rock Creek

West Fork Road

West Fork of Rock Creek

212

Beartrack
Trailhead

8

346

Wild Bill Lake
Campground

Basin Creek
Campground

Silver Run
Trailhead

35

6A

Lake Fork of Rock Creek

Lake Fork
Trailhead

Cascade
Campground

Timberline Lake
Trailhead

Basin Creek
Trailhead

6

Lower Basin
Creek Lake

Upper Basin
Creek Lake

8

8

SILVER RUN PLATEAU

26

West Red Lodge Creek

West Fork/Senia Creek
Trailhead

Calamity Falls

Sentinel
Falls

13

1A

QUINNEBAUGH
MEADOWS

13

2

Gertrude
Lake

Timberline
Lake

Broadwater
Lake

Lost
Lake

Grassy
Mountain

SILVER RUN PLATEAU

Silver Run
Peak

Keyser
Brown Lake

Lake Mary

Crow Lake

Elk Mountain

Sundance Lake

Sundance
Pass

September
Morn Lake

Black Canyon
Lake

13

Sylvan Lake

Sylvan
Peak

Bowback
Mountain

Sundance
Mountain

Shadow Lake

Whitetail
Peak

Rock Lakes

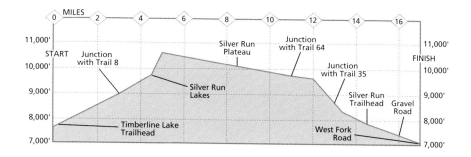

SIDE TRIPS
An exceptionally ambitious and fit hiker could try a climb to the summit of Silver Run Peak.

OPTIONS
Doing this shuttle hike in reverse is possible but more difficult. You can also stay on Trail 8 instead of turning north onto Trail 64 and drop down to the Beartrack Trailhead at US 212. This route is also steep and difficult to follow in places—and about a mile longer. The shuttle would be much longer, though.

CAMPING
This route isn't well suited for backpacking, but if you prefer to stay overnight, you won't have trouble finding a five-star campsite in the Silver Run Basin. The basin isn't centrally located on the route, but you could stay an extra day and spend it exploring the plateau. You can also camp on the plateau, but be prepared for a dry camp and cross your fingers for two consecutive days of good weather. Wherever you camp, follow strict zero-impact practices to keep this area as pristine as it presently is. No campfires or fire rings, please.

FISHING
The only fishery along this route is Silver Run Lakes. Only one of the five small lakes, the southernmost lake, contains brookies.

MILES AND DIRECTIONS

0.0   Start at Timberline Lake Trailhead.

3.0   Junction with Beartrack Trail 8; turn left.

4.4   Silver Run Basin.

5.1   Trail becomes a string of cairns.

11.0   Junction with Silver Run Trail 64; turn left.

13.0   Junction with Ingles Creek Trail 35; turn right.

14.5   Arrive at Silver Run Trailhead.

27 QUINNEBAUGH MEADOWS

A moderate day hike, easy overnighter, or base-camp trip to an unusually large and beautiful mountain meadow.

Start: West Fork Trailhead
Distance: 10 miles out and back
Difficulty: Moderate

Maps: USGS Sylvan Peak and Bare Mountain; RMS Alpine–Mount Maurice; and at least 1 wilderness-wide map

FINDING THE TRAILHEAD

From I-90 at Laurel, drive south on US 212 about 45 miles to the south side of Red Lodge. Watch for the big sign for the Red Lodge Mountain Ski Resort and take a right (west) onto West Fork Road (also called Ski Run Road and FR 71). When the road forks at 3 miles, take the left fork, staying on the paved West Fork Road and not the gravel road continuing up to the ski resort. The road is paved until you reach Basin Creek Campground, where it turns into a good gravel road. From here you have about 6 more miles of gravel to the end of the road and the West Fork Trailhead. Fairly large parking lot and toilet. **GPS:** 45.16835 N, 109.59605 W

Camping at Quinnebaugh Meadows.

WHERE TO GO FROM QUINNEBAUGH MEADOWS

Anybody who ventures off the trail in this area (or anywhere, for that matter) should be proficient with compass and topo map and GPS. The following destinations are ranked for difficulty as follows: Human (easy for almost everyone, including children), Semi-human (moderately difficult), or Animal (don't try it unless you're very fit and wilderness-wise). Also refer to more detailed rating information in "How to Use This Guide" (page 4).

Destination	Difficulty
Lake Mary	Human
Crow Lake	Animal
Sundance Lake	Human
Sundance Pass	Human
Dude Lake	Animal
Shadow Lake	Human
Kookoo Lake	Animal
Ship Lake Basin	Animal
Marker Lake	Animal

THE HIKE

This trail, like most others in this region, is well maintained and marked. It closely follows the West Fork of Rock Creek, not climbing any more than the stream drops in elevation as it powers its way out of the Beartooths. The first 2 miles pass through a forest burned by the 2008 Cascade Fire, which gradually thins out and greens up as you progress up the drainage. In a few places the forest opens up into small meadows with rewarding vistas of Elk Mountain and Bowback Mountain on the southern horizon near the terminus of the West Fork valley.

The trail passes close by Calamity Falls and Sentinel Falls. These cascades are reminders that the West Fork is not only a peaceful stream meandering out of the wilderness, but that it can also be a powerful force. Short spur trails lead to both falls for better views.

The West Fork broadens and slows as the trail nears Quinnebaugh Meadows. Look for the sign for Lake Mary just after breaking out into the enormous mountain meadow.

An extra dimension of Quinnebaugh Meadows is its attractiveness as a base camp. This site is perfect for someone who wants to camp in a lovely wilderness setting but doesn't want to carry a heavy pack very far—or up any big climbs. It's a moderate 5 miles to reach the meadows, and that's 5 miles closer to many interesting destinations, mostly off-trail excursions. Strong hikers might be tempted to go 2 or 3 more miles past Quinnebaugh Meadows before setting up a base camp, but the drainage above Quinnebaugh Meadows doesn't have many good campsites.

From this base camp, avid hikers could spend a week exploring the surrounding wilderness, taking a new route each day. Whether you're an angler, a climber, or simply out to see lots of really grand country, you won't be disappointed.

SIDE TRIPS

Lake Mary is the obvious side trip, but there are several other possibilities. Refer to "Where to Go from Quinnebaugh Meadows," above.

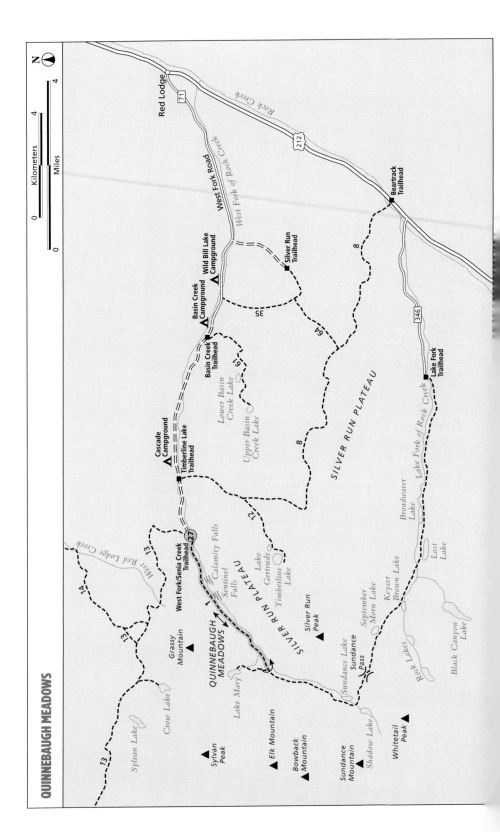

QUINNEBAUGH MEADOWS

N

0   Kilometers   4

0   Miles   4

Red Lodge

71

Rock Creek

West Fork Road

212

West Fork of Rock Creek

Beartrack Trailhead

Wild Bill Lake Campground

Basin Creek Campground

Silver Run Trailhead

Cascade Campground

Basin Creek Trailhead

35

64

Timberline Lake Trailhead

Lower Basin Creek Lake

Upper Basin Creek Lake

346

8

8

Lake Fork Trailhead

SILVER RUN PLATEAU

West Red Lodge Creek

West Fork/Senia Creek Trailhead

27

Calamity Falls

Sentinel Falls

Gertrude Lake

2

Lake Fork of Rock Creek

Broadwater Lake

Lost Lake

13

14

15

Grassy Mountain

Crow Lake

Sylvan Lake

QUINNEBAUGH MEADOWS

Lake Mary

Sylvan Peak

Elk Mountain

Bowback Mountain

SILVER RUN PLATEAU

Timberline Lake

Silver Run Peak

Sundance Lake

Sundance Pass

September Morn Lake

Keyser Brown Lake

Rock Lakes

Black Canyon Lake

Sundance Mountain

Shadow Lake

Whitetail Peak

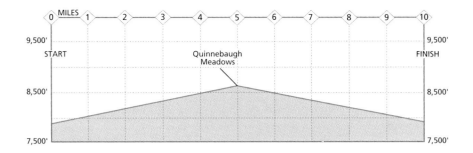

CAMPING

Set up camp almost anywhere in Quinnebaugh Meadows. It would, in fact, be difficult to find a bad campsite. You might find enough wood for a low-impact campfire. This is a popular place, so expect company. Fortunately, the meadow is large enough to accommodate several parties, including backcountry horseback riders.

FISHING

Although the West Fork of Rock Creek is not a highly productive fishery, anglers can find a few trout in many stretches of this stream, including the stretch through Quinnebaugh Meadows. The best fishing, however, is found in various basin lakes 1,000 feet higher in elevation. With the exception of Lake Mary, none of these lakes are easy to access, but for anglers, all of them may be worth the trip.

A crude trail leads to Senal and Dude Lakes between two bridges over the creek that drains them. It's a difficult side trip, but there are nice brookies and cutts in Senal and pure cutts in Dude. Cutthroats are stocked in Dude on an eight-year cycle.

Ship Lake Basin contains six lakes, all of which hold fish. The highest lake in Montana with fish is Marker Lake, and it has nice, aggressive cutthroats stocked on an eight-year cycle, as are Bowback, Kookoo, and Triangle Lakes. Ship Lake has easy-to-catch brookies, if the local cutts have stumped you.

On the West Fork, Shadow, Sundance, and Silt Lakes are stocked with cutthroat trout, but these don't grow as well as those in the lakes above.

Many hikers use Sundance Pass as access to the Lake Fork of Rock Creek, where the first lake encountered is September Morn Lake, which has an abundance of brookies.

MILES AND DIRECTIONS

0.0   Start at West Fork Trailhead.

1.3   Calamity Falls.

1.8   Sentinel Falls.

5.0   Quinnebaugh Meadows.

10.0 Arrive back at West Fork Trailhead.

28 LAKE MARY

A steep climb to a gorgeous mountain lake, well suited for a weekend trip and with a special view of the entire West Fork of Rock Creek valley.

Start: West Fork Trailhead
Distance: 12 miles out and back
Difficulty: Moderate for the first 5 miles, very steep for the last mile

Maps: USGS Sylvan Peak and Bare Mountain; RMS Alpine–Mount Maurice; and at least 1 wilderness-wide map

FINDING THE TRAILHEAD

From I-90 at Laurel, drive south on US 212 about 45 miles to the south side of Red Lodge. Watch for the big sign for the Red Lodge Mountain Ski Resort and take a right (west) onto West Fork Road (also called Ski Run Road and FR 71). When the road forks at 3 miles, take the left fork, staying on the paved West Fork Road and not the gravel road continuing up to the ski resort. The road is paved until you reach Basin Creek Campground, where it turns into a good gravel road. From here you have about 6 more miles of gravel to the end of the road and the West Fork Trailhead. Fairly large parking lot with toilet. **GPS:** 45.16835 N, 109.59605 W

THE HIKE

Most of this route passes through a forest burned by the 2008 Cascade Fire, which gradually thins out as you progress up the drainage. In a few places the forest opens up into small meadows with rewarding vistas of Elk Mountain and Bowback Mountain on the southern horizon near the terminus of the West Fork valley.

The trail passes close by Calamity Falls and Sentinel Falls. These cascades are reminders that the West Fork is not only a peaceful stream meandering out of the wilderness, but that it can also be a powerful force. Short spur trails lead to both falls for better views.

The West Fork broadens and slows as the trail nears Quinnebaugh Meadows. Look for the sign for Lake Mary just after breaking out into the enormous mountain meadow.

At Quinnebaugh Meadows, enjoy a nice long rest and relish the picturesque openness of the meadow. Then take a deep breath and psych yourself up before starting the ascent. The trail is well constructed, with frequent switchbacks to minimize the grade, but it's still a grind. It climbs 1,200 feet in only 1 mile, a Category H hill, one of the toughest in the Beartooths. Even though Lake Mary sits at 9,900 feet, the trail doesn't break out of the forest until just before the lake. The good news is that Lake Mary is worth the effort.

OPTIONS

If the climb is too intimidating with a pack, there is the option of pitching camp in Quinnebaugh Meadows and hiking up to the lake with just a day pack.

You can also make a loop out of this trip by bushwhacking over to Crow Lake and out to the Senia Creek Trailhead, but if you decide to take this loop option, you would be smart to start at Senia Creek and hike down the Category H hill to the West Fork.

Fishing on Lake Mary.

SIDE TRIPS

If you have some extra time, you can climb up onto the saddle between Lake Mary and Crow Lake.

CAMPING

There are campsites on either side of Lake Mary, which is actually two lakes. Especially agile hikers can cross the shallow section separating the lakes with some precarious rock-hopping. Since Lake Mary is above timberline, please refrain from building campfires.

FISHING

The West Fork of Rock Creek is characterized by beautiful cascades and sparkling pools, all of which are exceptionally photogenic, but most of which provide few fish. The very cold water, restricted sunlight, and rapid current make life difficult for fish. Cutthroat trout are more able to cope with these factors, although anglers will also find a few brook trout.

Lake Mary harbors a nice population of brook trout, comparable to those found else-where in the Beartooths. Count on them for dinner.

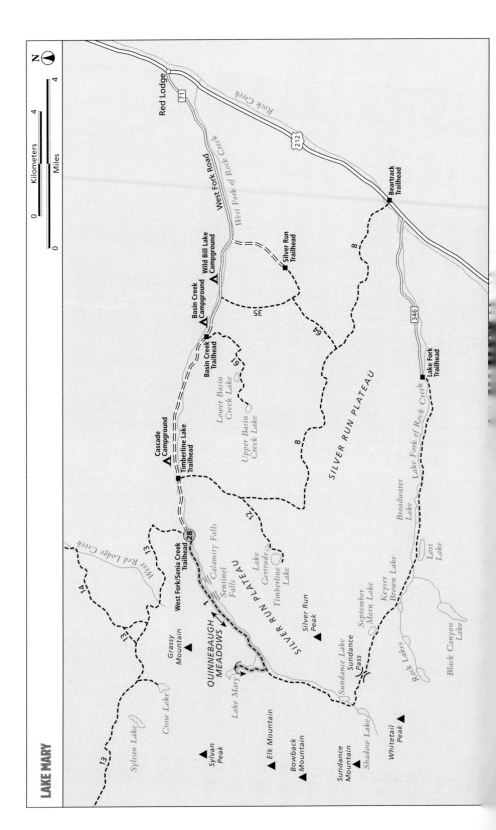

LAKE MARY

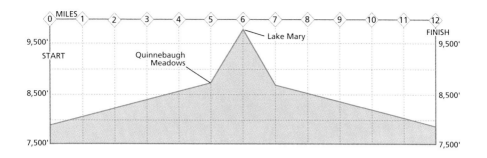

MILES AND DIRECTIONS

0.0 Start at West Fork Trailhead.

1.3 Calamity Falls.

1.8 Sentinel Falls.

5.0 Quinnebaugh Meadows.

5.1 Junction with Lake Mary Trail; turn right.

6.0 Lake Mary.

12.0 Arrive back at West Fork Trailhead.

29 CROW LAKE

A long day trip or overnighter into a remote, seldom-visited mountain lake.

Start: West Fork/Senia Creek Trailhead
Distance: 17 miles out and back
Difficulty: Moderate, except for the difficult trip to Lake Mary (optional)

Maps: USGS Sylvan Peak and Bare Mountain; RMS Alpine–Mount Maurice; and at least 1 wilderness-wide map

FINDING THE TRAILHEAD

From I-90 at Laurel, drive south on US 212 about 45 miles to the south side of Red Lodge. Watch for the big sign for the Red Lodge Mountain Ski Resort and take a right (west) onto West Fork Road (also called Ski Run Road and FR 71). When the road forks at 3 miles, take the left fork, staying on the paved West Fork Road and not the gravel road continuing up to the ski resort. The road is paved until you reach Basin Creek Campground, where it turns into a good gravel road. From here you have about 6 more miles of gravel to the end of the road and the West Fork Trailhead. Fairly large parking lot; toilet. **GPS:** 45.16835 N, 109.59605 W

It can be confusing. After the dramatic 2008 Cascade Fire, the Forest Service moved the Senia Creek Trailhead to the end of West Fork Road. Previously the trail started at a small trailhead on the north side of West Fork Road about a mile before the end of the road. At the end of the road, for some unknown reason, there is no sign for the Senia Creek Trailhead. To find it, hike about 0.1 mile up the West Fork Trail until you see the Senia Creek trail junction.

THE HIKE

When you get to the end of the West Fork Road, you won't see any sign saying you're at the Senia Creek Trailhead, but rest assured you're at the right trailhead. After the big fire in 2008, the Forest Service abandoned the old trailhead a mile back down the road along with the first mile or so of the trail, combined the Senia Creek and West Fork Trailheads, and rebuilt the first part of the trail. Don't fret if you don't see a sign at the end of the road, although the Forest Service plans to put one there in the future. After you hike up the trail about 200 feet, you'll see a junction where Senia Creek Trail 13 to Crow Lake starts.

The Forest Service also rebuilt the first part of Trail 13. Now it isn't quite as steep, but it is 1.5 miles longer, which adds 3 miles to the total distance.

Before heading up the trail to Crow Lake, make sure your water bottles are full. It's a long, steep 4 miles until they can be refilled.

From the trailhead the route switchbacks up to the Red Lodge Creek Plateau, climbing about 1,800 feet in 2.6 miles, a steep Category 1 climb. At this point (above 9,500 feet) the trail breaks out of the timber onto the plateau. The first part of this trail is a grind, but after catching your breath, you'll find the scenic vistas from this high-altitude plateau a fitting reward.

The trail up to the plateau is well defined, but after about a half mile on the plateau, it starts to fade away in places. Stay alert and follow cairns to stay on the route. Try to stay on the trail to protect the fragile vegetation clinging to existence in this austere environment.

After about a mile on the plateau, the trail reaches its highest point on this trip (9,980 feet) just before descending about 500 feet into West Red Lodge Creek. This is a great place to stop for a lengthy rest and to refill water bottles.

About a quarter mile after crossing the creek, there's a well-signed junction with a trail cutting off to the northwest and joining Trail 14 down West Red Lodge Creek. Turn left (west), staying on Trail 13.

After the junction Trail 13 descends over the course of 1.8 miles to Hellroaring Creek. The first half mile or so is still above timberline. Just off the plateau and into the timber, watch for a glimpse of Crow Lake to the southwest. The trail soon crosses Hellroaring Creek and meets the trail to Crow Lake. Trail 13 keeps on heading west to Sylvan Lake. To get to Crow Lake, turn left (south) and follow the trail along the stream (no trail number) nearly a mile up to the lake.

Crow Lake doesn't get as many visitors as some lakes in the Beartooths, but that's changing. In the past few years, the lake has seen more use, especially from backcountry horseback riders. There is, of course, a good reason for the newfound popularity. Crow Lake is well worth the trip. It lies in a beautiful forested pocket with several unnamed crags to the south, giving the lake a panoramic backdrop.

OPTIONS

You can also reach Crow Lake from the East Rosebud Trailhead. It's about the same distance, and both routes start with big hills.

For a little adventure and to avoid backtracking, you can make a loop out of this trip by going over the ridge south of Crow Lake and dropping into Lake Mary. Then follow Trail 1 along the West Fork back to the West Fork/Senia Creek Trailhead at the end of the road.

The off-trail section (about 2 miles) between Crow Lake and Lake Mary covers some rough country and should only be attempted by those capable of navigating with compass and topo map and GPS. Be wary of what looks like the easiest route from the lake, a low pass to the right. Instead, check the topo map carefully before leaving Crow Lake, and you'll see the best route is to the east over a ridge that looks more difficult than the other route but really isn't. The last half mile into the Lake Mary basin goes through a pile of oversize rocks, so go slowly and carefully.

Taking the off-trail loop option allows you to spend your second night at Lake Mary, leaving an easy 6 miles for the last day.

SIDE TRIPS

A base camp at Crow Lake allows hikers to day hike to Sylvan Lake, about 1.8 miles west on Trail 13. Head back down along Hellroaring Creek to the junction with Trail 13, turn left (west), and go about 1 mile. Just after crossing the outlet stream, the trail up to Sylvan Lake takes off to the left (south).

CROW LAKE

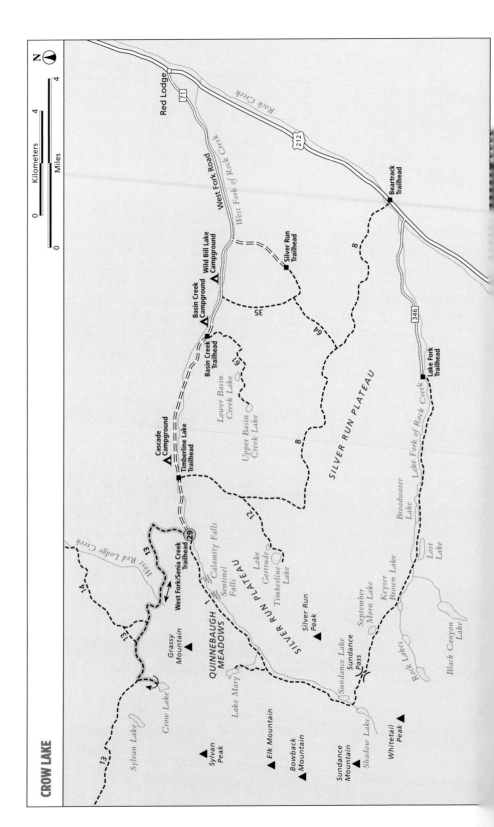

N

Kilometers
0   4

Miles
0   4

Red Lodge

71

Rock Creek

212

West Fork Road

West Fork of Rock Creek

Wild Bill Lake Campground

Basin Creek Campground

Silver Run Trailhead

35

64

Basin Creek Trailhead

61

Lower Basin Creek Lake

Upper Basin Creek Lake

8

8

SILVER RUN PLATEAU

Lake Fork of Rock Creek

346

Lake Fork Trailhead

Beartrack Trailhead

8

Cascade Campground

Timberline Lake Trailhead

West Fork/Senia Creek Trailhead

29

Calamity Falls

West Red Lodge Creek

13

71

Sentinel Falls

Lake Gertrude

Timberline Lake

Silver Run Peak

72

Broadwater Lake

Lost Lake

QUINNEBAUGH MEADOWS

Grassy Mountain

Lake Mary

Elk Mountain

SILVER RUN PLATEAU

Sundance Lake

Sundance Pass

September Morn Lake

Keyser Brown Lake

Black Canyon Lake

4

13

Sylvan Lake

Crow Lake

Sylvan Peak

Bowback Mountain

Sundance Mountain

Shadow Lake

Whitetail Peak

Rock Lakes

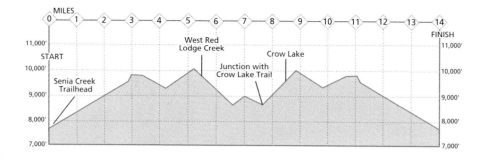

CAMPING

There are campsites at the outlet of Crow Lake, but those who still have some energy might want to carefully cross the stream at the outlet and follow an angler's trail along the east side of the lake to a selection of better campsites on the west side of the inlet.

FISHING

Crow Lake is not as popular as some lakes, and the brook trout found here are larger than average. Also make a fishing expedition over to Sylvan Lake. It holds a thriving golden trout population.

MILES AND DIRECTIONS

0.0   Start at West Fork (now combined with Senia Creek) Trailhead.

0.2   Junction with newly built Trail 13; turn right.

5.5   Junction with cutoff to Trail 14 down West Red Lodge Creek; turn left.

7.6   Junction with Crow Lake Trail (no number); turn left.

8.5   Crow Lake.

17.0   Arrive back at West Fork Trailhead.

30 SUNDANCE PASS

A fairly rugged, two- or three-day backpacking trip for experienced hikers through spectacular mountain scenery, especially the view from Sundance Pass.

Start: Lake Fork Trailhead
Distance: 21-mile (not counting side trips) shuttle
Difficulty: Difficult

Maps: USGS Black Pyramid Mountain, Silver Run Peak, and Sylvan Peak; RMS Alpine–Mount Maurice; and at least 1 wilderness-wide map

FINDING THE TRAILHEADS

From Red Lodge drive southwest for 9 miles on US 212. Turn right (west) at the well-marked road up the Lake Fork of Rock Creek. The 2-mile paved road leads to a turnaround and the trailhead. Huge trailhead area with plenty of parking and room for horse trailers (even this large lot gets full on busy weekends); toilet. **GPS:** 45.07915 N, 109.41104 W

To reach the West Fork Trailhead: From the south side of Red Lodge, watch for the big sign for the Red Lodge Mountain Ski Resort and take a right (west) onto West Fork Road (also called Ski Run Road and FR 71). When the road forks at 3 miles, take the left fork, staying on the paved West Fork Road and not the gravel road continuing up to the ski resort. The road is paved until you reach Basin Creek Campground, where it turns into a good gravel road. From here you have about 6 more miles of gravel to the end of the road and the West Fork Trailhead. Large parking lot with toilet. **GPS:** 45.16835 N, 109.59605 W

RECOMMENDED ITINERARY

A three-day trip staying one night in the Lake Fork of Rock Creek (September Morn or Keyser Brown Lake) and another in the West Fork of Rock Creek (Quinnebaugh Meadows).

THE HIKE

This well-maintained and heavily used trail is not only one of the most scenic in the Beartooths, but it's also only a short drive from the Billings area.

This trail offers absolutely spectacular scenery. From Sundance Pass, for example, vistas include 12,000-foot mountains, such as 12,548-foot Whitetail Peak, and the Beartooth Plateau, a huge mass of contiguous land above 10,000 feet. Hikers are also treated to views of glaciers and obvious results of glaciation, exposed Precambrian rock, and waterfalls. Watch for mountain goats, deer, golden eagles, and gyrfalcons. Goats are also frequently seen from First and Second Rock Lakes.

This is a fairly difficult, 21-mile shuttle trip that ends at the end of the West Fork Road (FR 71). Arrange to be picked up at the trailhead at the end of West Fork Road or leave a vehicle there. An alternative is to have another party start at the other end of the trail, meet up on Sundance Pass, and trade vehicle keys.

Looking up at Sundance Pass from the base camp.

Since lingering snowbanks don't give up Sundance Pass until mid-July, wait until then to take this trip. This delay also avoids the peak season for mosquitoes and no-see-ums, which can be quite bad in this area, especially on the West Fork side.

Although nicely suited to a three-day/two-night trip, the route also offers many scenic side trips. If you have an extra day or two, you'll be well rewarded by spending the extra time exploring the area.

The main route passes by three lakes—Keyser Brown, September Morn, and Sundance—but several others can be reached with short side trips. One of these is Lost Lake, which is a quarter-mile climb from the main trail. This is a very heavily used lake, and it shows. There are campsites here, but consider staying somewhere else that hasn't been trampled so much. The trail to Lost Lake leaves the main trail on the left, 5 miles from the trailhead or about 200 yards before the bridge over the Lake Fork of Rock Creek.

Another lake-bound trail departs from the main trail immediately before the same bridge. The unofficial trail to Black Canyon Lake scrambles uphill to the left also. Black Canyon Lake lies just below Grasshopper Glacier. The undeveloped trail to Black Canyon Lake is a rough but short hike of about 1.5 miles one-way. Part of the route traverses rock talus with no trail, and there is a steep climb near the lake. The hike to Black Canyon is probably too tough for small children or poorly conditioned hikers. There is almost no place to camp at this high, rugged lake, and it's often very windy at Black Canyon during midday.

The main trail continues west along the Lake Fork another mile or so to Keyser Brown Lake, about 6.5 miles from the trailhead. To do this trip in three days and two nights, plan to start early and spend the first night at September Morn Lake (better camping areas than at Keyser Brown Lake). Please consider doing without a campfire.

Keyser Brown Lake isn't right on the trail. It's about a quarter mile to the left (southwest), so watch carefully for the side trail. It's an official, signed trail. The lake itself comes into view from the main trail, but if you can see it, you've missed the junction and need to backtrack about 200 yards to the trail to the lake. An anglers' trail leads south from the far end of Keyser Brown to First and Second Rock Lakes. This side trip involves some difficult boulder-hopping. Continue 2 miles up the main trail to September Morn Lake.

Get a good night's sleep and a hearty breakfast before starting the second day. From Keyser Brown it's a 1,660-foot, Category 2 climb to the top of Sundance Pass. The scenery is so incredible, however, that hikers might not notice how much work it is getting to the top. To the north and east stretch the twin lobes of the Silver Run Plateau, rising to their apex at 12,500-foot Silver Run Peak. Directly south of the pass, 11,647-foot Mount Lockhart partially shields the pyramid of 12,548-foot Whitetail Peak. Remember to carry extra water on this stretch—it's scarce on the pass.

Coming down from Sundance Pass into the West Fork won't take long. A series of switchbacks drops about 1,000 feet in about a mile to a bridge over the headwaters of the West Fork.

Although there are campsites in a meadow about a quarter mile down the trail from the Sundance Bridge, Quinnebaugh Meadows is the best choice for the second night out. It offers plenty of excellent campsites, and you can probably find enough downed wood for a campfire. It's a long 9.5 miles from Keyser Brown to Quinnebaugh Meadows, but there aren't many good campsites between September Morn Lake and Quinnebaugh Meadows.

Camping at the meadows leaves an easy 5 miles for the last day out. It might also allow enough time for a side trip up to Lake Mary or Dude Lake. Dude Lake is about a mile west via a rough, steep trail from Quinnebaugh Meadows. And there's a steep but good trail from Quinnebaugh Meadows to Lake Mary. Some people use the saddle to the north of Lake Mary as a cross-country route to Crow, Sylvan, and East Rosebud Lakes.

The final day of hiking follows the trail along the north bank of the West Fork all the way to the trailhead. Sentinel and Calamity Falls both offer good places to drop the pack and relax.

OPTIONS

This trip also works well in reverse with no major difference in difficulty. Starting from the West Fork results in about 600 feet less overall elevation gain. Sundance Pass is a longer, but less precipitous climb from the west side than the east side.

SIDE TRIPS

This hike offers an abundant variety of side trips, including Lost Lake (Human), Black Canyon Lake (Animal), Rock Lakes (Semihuman), Whitetail Peak (Animal), Sundance Mountain (Animal), Sundance Lake (Human), Marker Lake (Animal), Ship Lake Basin (Animal), Kookoo Lake (Animal), Shadow Lake (Human), Dude Lake (Animal), Lake Mary (Human), and Crow Lake (Animal). Refer to Quinnebaugh Meadows (Hike 27) for more suggested side trips.

CAMPING

Enough good on-trail and off-trail campsites can be found in both drainages, but since this area gets heavy use, please make sure you have zero-impact campsites.

FISHING

The lakes found along the Lake Fork provide some of the easiest fishing in the Beartooths. Anglers will find plenty of hungry brookies in September Morn, Keyser Brown, and First and Second Rock Lakes. Overnight campers can count on these lakes to supply dinner. Keyser Brown and Second Rock Lakes also support healthy cutthroat fisheries.

For those with something other than brook trout on their mind, Lost Lake supports a few cutthroat trout of surprisingly large size. Grayling also have been planted in Lost Lake, and they grow large as well.

The scramble up to Black Canyon Lake rewards anglers with plenty of cutthroats near the glacial moraine that blocks the outlet. While this lake once grew exceptionally large fish, a probable change in food organisms, caused by the fish themselves, now keeps them in the slightly above-average range. This lake offers the best chance for catching a 15-inch or larger trout in the Lake Fork drainage.

From the crest of Sundance Pass, look to the lakes in the high basin across the West Fork to the northwest. Ship Lake is the largest of these. There are plenty of fish in these waters for hikers who don't mind climbing up the other side of the valley after coming down Sundance Pass.

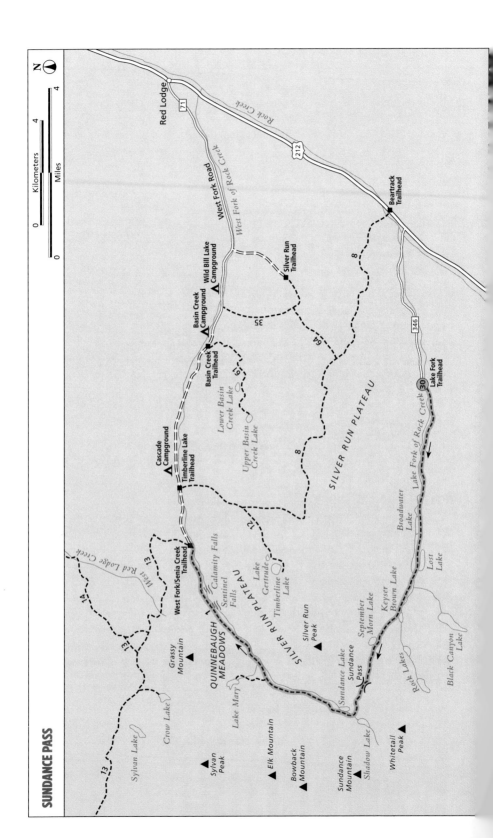

SUNDANCE PASS

N

| 0 | Kilometers | 4 |
| 0 | Miles | 4 |

Red Lodge

71

West Fork Road

West Fork of Rock Creek

Rock Creek

212

Beartrack Trailhead

8

346

Lake Fork Trailhead

30

Wild Bill Lake Campground

Basin Creek Campground

Silver Run Trailhead

35

64

Basin Creek Trailhead

69

Lower Basin Creek Lake

Upper Basin Creek Lake

8

SILVER RUN PLATEAU

Cascade Campground

Timberline Lake Trailhead

2

Lake Fork of Rock Creek

Broadwater Lake

Lost Lake

West Fork/Senia Creek Trailhead

13

West Red Lodge Creek

14

13

Sylvan Lake

Crow Lake

Grassy Mountain

Sylvan Peak

QUINNEBAUGH MEADOWS

Lake Mary

Elk Mountain

Bowback Mountain

Calamity Falls

Sentinel Falls

SILVER RUN PLATEAU

Gertrude Lake

Timberline Lake

Silver Run Peak

Sundance Lake

Sundance Pass

September Morn Lake

Keyser Brown Lake

Rock Lakes

Black Canyon Lake

Sundance Mountain

Shadow Lake

Whitetail Peak

13

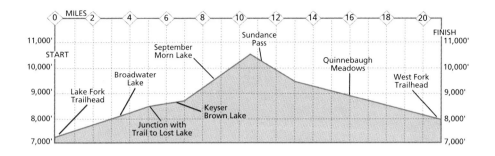

MILES AND DIRECTIONS

0.0 Start at Lake Fork Trailhead.

3.5 Broadwater Lake.

5.0 Trail to Lost Lake; turn right.

5.2 Trail to Black Canyon Lake; turn right.

6.5 Trail to Keyser Brown Lake; turn right.

8.5 September Morn Lake.

11.3 Sundance Pass.

13.0 West Fork of Rock Creek.

13.5 Sundance Lake.

15.9 Junction with trail to Lake Mary; turn right.

16.0 Quinnebaugh Meadows.

21.0 Arrive at West Fork Trailhead.

31 BROADWATER LAKE

An easy day trip to a small in-stream lake.

Start: Lake Fork Trailhead
Distance: 7 miles out and back
Difficulty: Easy

Maps: USGS Black Pyramid Mountain; RMS Alpine–Mount Maurice; and at least 1 wilderness-wide map

FINDING THE TRAILHEAD

From Red Lodge drive southwest for 9 miles on US 212. Turn right (west) at the well-marked road up the Lake Fork of Rock Creek. The 2-mile paved road leads to a turnaround and the trailhead. Huge trailhead area with plenty of parking and room for horse trailers (even this large lot gets full on busy weekends) with toilet. **GPS:** 45.07915 N, 109.41104 W

Lake Fork of Rock Creek.

BROADWATER LAKE

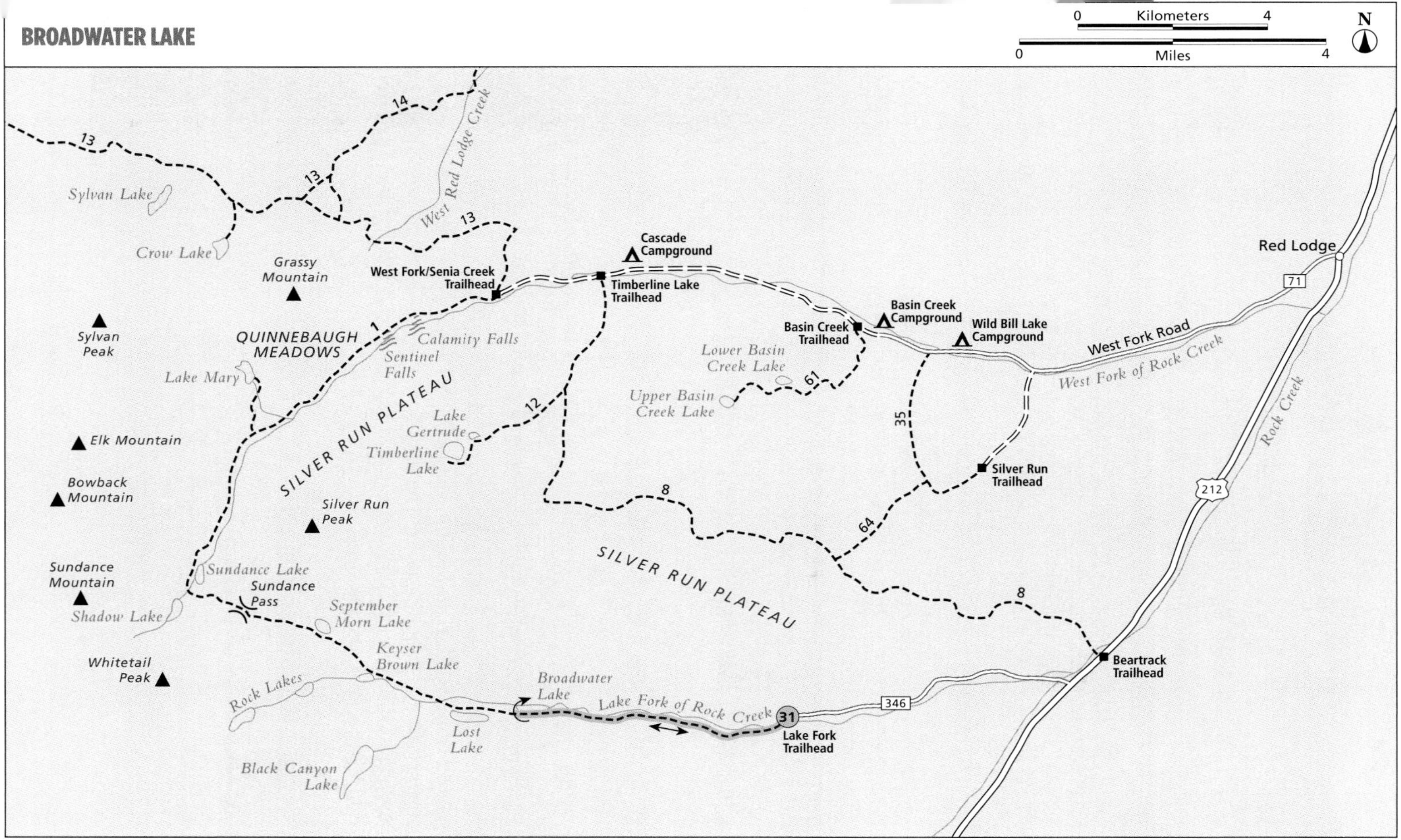

N

Kilometers
0   4

Miles
0   4

Red Lodge

71

Rock Creek

212

Beartrack
Trailhead

West Fork Road

West Fork of Rock Creek

Wild Bill Lake
Campground

Basin Creek
Campground

Silver Run
Trailhead

35

6A

8

346

Basin Creek
Trailhead

6

Lower Basin
Creek Lake

Upper Basin
Creek Lake

Cascade
Campground

Timberline Lake
Trailhead

SILVER RUN PLATEAU

8

Lake Fork
Trailhead

31

Lake Fork of Rock Creek

Broadwater
Lake

Lost
Lake

West Red Lodge Creek

13

1A

3

Grassy
Mountain

QUINNEBAUGH
MEADOWS

Calamity Falls

Sentinel
Falls

SILVER RUN PLATEAU

2

13

West Fork/Senia Creek
Trailhead

Gertrude
Lake

Timberline
Lake

Silver Run
Peak

Sundance Lake

Sundance
Pass

September
Morn Lake

Keyser
Brown Lake

Black Canyon
Lake

Rock Lakes

Sylvan Lake

Crow Lake

Lake Mary

Sylvan
Peak

Elk Mountain

Bowback
Mountain

Sundance
Mountain

Shadow Lake

Whitetail
Peak

13

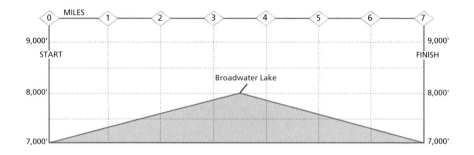

THE HIKE

From the trailhead immediately cross a bridge over the Lake Fork of Rock Creek, turn right (west), and head upstream along the Lake Fork. The trail stays close to the stream all the way and is easy to follow, well maintained, hazard-free, and usually dry. Plus, there are no steep hills, and the trail stays on the south side of the stream the entire way to Broadwater Lake with one easy stream crossing.

All of these advantages make this trip near-perfect for an easy day hike with children. Perhaps the best part of the trip into Broadwater Lake is constantly being near a clean, natural mountain stream. Hikers can stop at dozens of places and just sit back against a tree, relax, and soak in the sound of the rushing water. Along the way watch for water ouzels playing in the blue-green waters of the Lake Fork and expect to see lots of wildflowers along the stream.

Broadwater Lake is beautiful, but not well named. It's not really a lake at all, but a long "glide" where the stream widens and slows for a few moments before continuing to hurry out of the mountains.

CAMPING

There aren't really any good campsites in the area, so consider this a nice day trip.

FISHING

Like the West Fork the Lake Fork of Rock Creek is exceptionally photogenic, but it supports fewer fish than you might expect. The cold water, restricted sunlight, and fast current make life tough for trout. The Lake Fork supports low numbers of both cut-throat and brook trout. Fish concentrate in the slower sections of the stream, of which Broadwater Lake is a good example.

MILES AND DIRECTIONS

0.0 Start at Lake Fork Trailhead.

3.5 Broadwater Lake.

7.0 Arrive back at Lake Fork Trailhead.

32 HELLROARING PLATEAU

A short, mostly off-trail trip into a high-elevation basin filled with lakes; best suited for day hiking, but can be an overnighter.

Start: Hellroaring Plateau Trailhead
Distance: 4 to 8 miles (depending on how much exploring you do) out and back with loop option
Difficulty: Moderate to difficult if you go into the basin; easy if you stay on the plateau

Maps: USGS Black Pyramid Mountain; RMS Alpine–Mount Maurice; and at least 1 wilderness-wide map

FINDING THE TRAILHEAD

A big part of this hiking adventure is the adventure you get driving to the trailhead, a 2-hour drive each way. Drive south from Red Lodge on US 212 for 10.9 miles. Watch for a well-marked turnoff on the right (west) to three Forest Service campgrounds. Stay on this paved road for 0.9 mile until you cross a bridge near the entrance to Limberpine Campground. Immediately after the bridge the pavement ends and you reach a fork in the road. For the Hellroaring Plateau, turn right (north then sharply southwest). It's a very rough 7 miles to the end of the road and the trailhead on the edge of the Hellroaring Plateau. There's only one fork in the road, about a half mile before the trailhead, where you go left. You definitely need at least a high-clearance, four-wheel-drive vehicle to get to this trailhead, but the road has deteriorated so badly that an ATV would be better. Snow usually blocks this gravel road until at least early July. This road isn't for fainthearted drivers or horse trailers. Ample parking but no toilet. **GPS:** 45.03783 N, 109.45190 W

Note: The 2022 floods washed out a bridge on the Hellroaring Road, so the trailhead is not accessible with a vehicle. There is no timetable for replacing the bridge, so this road could be a great hiking and biking trail for several years. ATVs can use the road, but only go as far as where the bridge used to be, and there is very limited parking here.

THE HIKE

From the trailhead follow an old, closed-off jeep road (Trail 11) about a mile along the Hellroaring Plateau. Lower Hellroaring Lakes are soon visible in the valley off to the right (north). You're better off continuing along the plateau instead of going down to the lakes from this point. If you drop off the plateau too early, the terrain gets very steep and you have to fight through a maze of alpine willows and small streams. Instead, continue along the plateau for another half mile or so. The scenery is worth it. Wander over to the south edge of the plateau on the left to see the main fork of Rock Creek.

At about the 1.5-mile mark and just before a huge snowbank on the right (northwest), head down to the lakes. Take a close look at the topo map or set a waypoint before dropping off the plateau, and keep the map handy until you climb back out of the basin.

The climb down to the lakes is more gradual from this point. Watch for game or social trails on the way down, but be prepared for essentially off-trail hiking. Once at the lakes the hiking is much easier. There are fairly well-defined anglers' trails between the lakes.

Hellroaring Plateau lakes are full of brookies for dinner.

This is a heavenly basin filled with lakes, mostly above 10,000 feet. Hairpin Lake, for example, is definitely worth seeing. It has a series of beautiful bays, and a waterfall plunges into the lake from the northwest. There are plenty of grand places to explore, and all within a short distance.

After a few hours exploring the basin, climb back up to the plateau and hike back to your vehicle.

While exploring the basin, watch the weather. It's all too easy—and dangerous—to get caught on the plateau by one of the severe thunderstorms that often roll through here in the afternoon.

OPTIONS

To make a short loop out of the trip, hike down to the lower lakes and then up to the plateau. Bear in mind that the climb back to the plateau from the lower basin will be brutal. It's much easier to retrace your steps up the valley and then take the more gradual climb to the plateau just east of the large snowbank. Another short loop can be made by

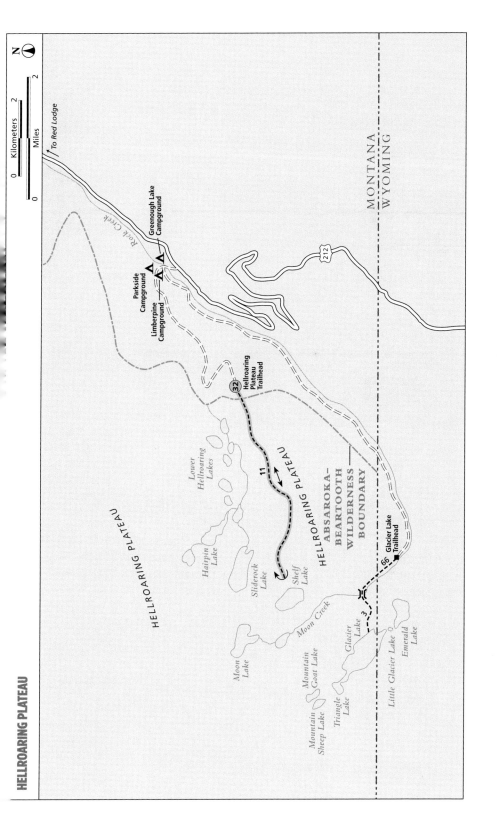

N

Kilometers

0   2   2

Miles

0   2

To Red Lodge

Rock Creek

Greenough Lake
Campground

Parkside
Campground

Limberpine
Campground

MONTANA
WYOMING

212

Hellroaring
Plateau
Trailhead

32

HELLROARING PLATEAU

Lower
Hellroaring
Lakes

11

Hairpin
Lake

HELLROARING PLATEAU

Sliderock
Lake

Shelf
Lake

HELLROARING–
ABSAROKA–
BEARTOOTH
WILDERNESS
BOUNDARY

Glacier Lake
Trailhead

66

Moon Creek

3

Glacier
Lake

Little Glacier Lake

Emerald
Lake

Moon
Lake

Mountain
Goat Lake

Triangle
Lake

Mountain
Sheep Lake

heading west to Sliderock Lake and then climbing back to the plateau on the west side of the snowbank.

SIDE TRIPS

The entire purpose of this hike is side trips. Simply get out your topo map and find a vantage point to decide where to go.

CAMPING

The basin is best suited for an extended day hike, but a few people stay overnight. The best choice for a campsite is around one of the lower lakes where there are more level spots and trees to break the wind. This is alpine country, so please don't burn up the aesthetic wood supply.

FISHING

There are thirteen Hellroaring Lakes in the basin, and most offer fishing opportunities. Three lakes are fishless, and please leave them that way. If you're prepared for mosquitoes, the lower lakes are the perfect place to take your son or daughter for his or her first mountain backpacking and fishing trip. Each small lake has its own personality, and most support brook trout and cutthroat trout, both of which are willing to be caught. The trees here provide cover from the wind and a visual break from the rocky terrain above. When you're tired of catching the numerous smaller trout in the lower lakes, head up the drainage. Hairpin Lake has nice-size cutts. On the way back out, make the side trip to Sliderock Lake for some of the healthiest brook trout anywhere in the Beartooths.

The author and his favorite hiking partner, his wife Marnie, amid Hellroaring Lakes.

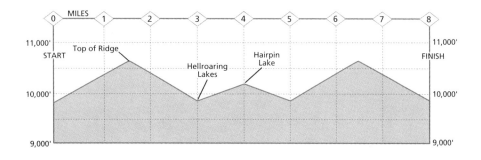

33 GLACIER LAKE

A steep but short day trip or overnighter to a high-elevation lake basin.

Start: Glacier Lake Trailhead
Distance: 4 miles (plus side trips) out and back
Difficulty: Moderately strenuous but short to Glacier Lake; some side trips and exploring can be difficult

Maps: USGS Beartooth Butte and Silver Run Peak; RMS Alpine–Mount Maurice; and at least 1 wilderness-wide map

FINDING THE TRAILHEAD

Drive south from Red Lodge on US 212 for 10.9 miles. Watch for a well-marked turnoff on the right (west) to three Forest Service campgrounds. Stay on this paved road for 0.9 mile until you cross a bridge near the entrance to Limberpine Campground. Immediately after the bridge the pavement ends and you reach a fork in the road. For Glacier Lake turn left (southwest). It's a long, slow, bumpy 8 miles to the trailhead, but there's no chance of making a wrong turn because there are no forks or spur roads. The Forest Service has recently improved this road, so you can make it to the trailhead in any vehicle, but you might want an all-wheel-drive for the last half mile. Snow usually blocks this gravel road until at least early July. The small parking area is frequently full, so be careful not to take more than one space. Toilet and a National Weather Service precipitation gauge. There are undeveloped camping areas and one developed campground along the road on the way up with three developed campgrounds at the start of the road to Glacier Lake. **GPS:** 45.00343 N, 109.51465 W

THE HIKE

Although this route could be done as an overnighter, the Glacier Lake area seems better suited to a long day of exploring, fishing, photographing, and simply enjoying majestic high-elevation vistas. It's easily accessible by a 2-mile trail. The Forest Service has restricted stock use on this trail due to hazardous conditions for horses.

The trail to Glacier Lake is short but very steep. The trailhead is at 8,680 feet and the lake is at 9,702 feet, but the route actually climbs more than the difference (1,022 feet) in the 2 miles to Glacier Lake. That's because there's a ridge in the middle that's about 800 feet higher than the lake, making the first part of the trail a Category 1 climb.

After climbing for about a half mile, the trail crosses Moon Creek on a bridge. After Moon Creek the trail gets even steeper—and the higher it goes, the better the scenery. Shortly after crossing Moon Creek, a faint, unofficial trail veers off to the north to Moon Lake and Shelf Lake. Turn left (west) and stay on what is obviously the main trail. For most of the way, the trail is rough and rock-studded, but it remains easy to follow and without hazards.

Once atop the ridge you cross some rock shelves on the way down to massive Glacier Lake. Even though the lake sits at 9,702 feet (above timberline), some large trees stand along the shoreline.

The trail reaches the lake at a small dam built long ago to increase the depth of Glacier Lake. A faint trail heads off to the right and goes about halfway around the lake. After

Moon Lake.

passing a large point jutting out into the lake, the trail degenerates into a series of boulder fields and talus slopes.

Bearing right along the north shore of the lake affords views of Triangle Lake and access to Mountain Sheep Lake and Mountain Goat Lake at the head of the basin. Bearing left and across the dam around the south shore of the lake leads directly to Little Glacier Lake, a small jewel just barely separated from Glacier Lake. Continuing south on this trail over a small ridge treats wanderers to the sight of lovely Emerald Lake.

If you're fishing, be sure to keep track of which state you're in, and make sure you have the right license. The state line goes right through Glacier Lake. Little Glacier and Emerald Lakes are in Wyoming.

Because of topography, Glacier Lake tends to become remarkably windy during mid-day, so try to arrive early to catch the scenery before the winds start ripping through this valley. Emerald Lake is usually not quite as windy.

SIDE TRIPS
Mountain Goat and Mountain Sheep Lakes can be reached with a reasonable effort, but Moon and Shelf Lakes are strenuous side trips.

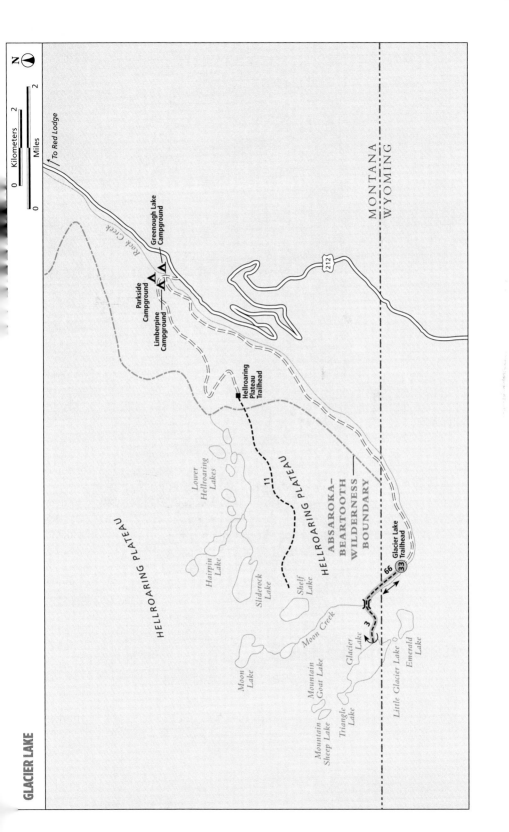

GLACIER LAKE

N

0   Kilometers   2

0   Miles   2

To Red Lodge

Rock Creek

Greenough Lake
Campground

Parkside
Campground

Limberpine
Campground

212

MONTANA
WYOMING

Hellroaring
Plateau
Trailhead

HELLROARING PLATEAU

Lower
Hellroaring
Lakes

11

HELLROARING PLATEAU

ABSAROKA–
BEARTOOTH
WILDERNESS
BOUNDARY

Hairpin
Lake

Sliderock
Lake

Shelf
Lake

66

33   Glacier Lake
     Trailhead

Moon
Lake

Mountain
Goat Lake

Moon Creek

3

Glacier
Lake

Little Glacier Lake

Emerald
Lake

Mountain
Sheep Lake

Triangle
Lake

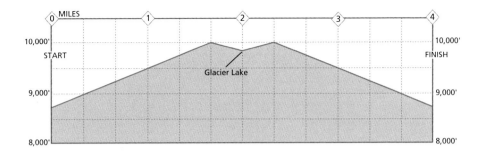

CAMPING

All of the potential campsites along the north shore of Glacier Lake are cramped, marginal, and too close to the lake. For those planning to stay overnight, check out the north side of Emerald Lake. The south side of the lake is spectacularly steep. This is high alpine country, so please resist the temptation to have a campfire and leave zero impact of your visit.

FISHING

The ice-cold, swift-running water and high canyon walls make Rock Creek extremely attractive to look at, but these conditions also make life hard for fish. Rock Creek is home to small populations of cutthroat and brook trout. Fish concentrate in slower water, so look for good holding places out of the current. The main fork of Rock Creek winds in and out of Wyoming and Montana, so anglers need to know which state they're in and have the appropriate license.

Glacier Lake supports cutthroat and brook trout, both of which grow to above-average size. The fish tend to school, with cutthroats working rocky shorelines, so anglers should work the shoreline as well. When water levels are high, water flows between Glacier and Little Glacier Lakes, so the fishery is the same in both. But the fish are easier to find in Little Glacier. Emerald Lake supports both cutts and brookies as well, though slightly smaller than those in Glacier Lake. Cutts are stocked in Mountain Goat Lake and work their way down to Mountain Sheep Lake. Count on more fish in the upper lake and larger ones in the lower.

Plan on seeing other anglers, although the tough hike around Glacier Lake probably thins out the competition. Fewer hikers go to Moon and Shelf Lakes, as the trail seems steeper and longer than it is. Shelf Lake harbors hefty brookies, while Moon grows above-average cutts.

MILES AND DIRECTIONS

0.0 Start at Glacier Lake Trailhead.

0.5 Bridge over Moon Creek.

4.0 Arrive back at Glacier Lake Trailhead.

THE BEARTOOTH HIGHWAY

Driving the Beartooth Highway (US 212) is an adventure for some people, especially flatlanders who haven't seen many winding mountainous roads. In addition to offering stunning scenery, the high-altitude highway (topping out at 10,965 feet) provides the unique opportunity to start hiking trips well above timberline at 9,500 to 10,000 feet elevation. Gardner Lake has the distinction of being the highest trailhead I've ever used—10,595 feet. Some trailheads, like Island Lake, Beartooth Lake, Clay Butte, and Clarks Fork, get heavy use, but others get minimal use. Experienced hikers can stop at almost any pullout and start hiking almost anywhere, going off-trail over the open, treeless terrain.

Hikers often ignore the undesignated wilderness south of the Beartooth Highway and flock to the heavily used trails in the designated Absaroka-Beartooth Wilderness to the north. Yet the area south of the highway is also wild and scenic—and less crowded. Although not designated as wilderness, the Forest Service manages the area with a priority on backcountry recreation. Unlike trails north of the highway, some trails heading south are open to mountain biking. Also, backcountry horseback riders commonly use the trails south of the highway.

A mile west of the Island Lake Trailhead, check out the aptly named Top of the World Store. Looking in all directions from the store certainly makes it easy to see the reason for its name. It's hard to believe this landscape wasn't included in the designated wilderness, which coincides with the Montana-Wyoming border. Fortunately, though, the Forest Service essentially manages it as though it was included.

Hikers can find dozens of lakes within a short walk of the Beartooth Highway trailheads. Many trails are at least partly in Wyoming, so if you plan to fish, be sure you have the correct fishing license—or in some cases, one from both states.

Many lakes were stocked with brook trout in the first half of the twentieth century. The rationale was that since brookies are hearty and reproduce easily, they could establish reproducing populations, which they certainly did. However, brookies tend to overpopulate these lakes, resulting in smaller, stunted fish. On the positive side, 8- to 9-inch brookies may be the tastiest trout of the Beartooths—and don't feel bad about keeping some for dinner. You're actually doing the environment a favor.

The Forest Service has developed several excellent vehicle campgrounds along the highway, often strategically located near trailheads—and often full, too. Campers who prefer undeveloped camping can also find good sites on short spur roads off the highway, particularly on the west side of Beartooth Pass.

Beartooth Lake lies in the shadow of famous 10,514-foot Beartooth Butte, which dominates the western horizon on the west side of the pass. Beartooth Butte is an enigma, a tiny island of sedimentary rock in a sea of granite making up the Beartooth Mountains. Beartooth Butte and neighboring Clay Butte to the east and Table Mountain to the

Green Lake, a wilderness gem about halfway along the Green Lake loop.

south are the only outcrops on the entire Beartooth Plateau still covered with sedimentary rock. Erosion removed the sedimentary rock from the rest of the area, but for some reason, still somewhat unclear to geologists, these three remnants survived. Geologists do know, however, that Beartooth Butte contains fossils of some the oldest known plants ever found in North America.

Most people are in a big hurry to hit the trail when they get to the trailhead, but at the Clay Butte Trailhead, it's worth taking an extra 15 minutes to drive to the top of Clay Butte for the view. It's only another mile to the lookout, where—at 9,811 feet—you'll find a splendid view of the Beartooth Plateau. From this vista, much of the terrain covered by the trails leaving from this trailhead can be seen.

Anyone who has been to the Clarks Fork Trailhead could mount a strong argument that it's the most beautiful trailhead in the Beartooths. It rests on the south shoreline of the Clarks Fork of the Yellowstone as the river leaves the Beartooths right at a spectacular falls and large, sparkling pool perfect for a chilly dip after a long, hot week in the wilderness. The large grassy area with picnic tables is especially nice for people wanting a leisurely picnic in a gorgeous setting followed by a short day hike. In fact, a worthwhile attraction lies just beyond the trailhead, where a major footbridge spans the Clarks Fork where it squeezes through a narrow gorge.

With the exception of Lake Abundance and Fisher Creek, all Beartooth Highway trailheads are easy to find and located right on the highway. The mileage along US 212 from Red Lodge or Cooke City is as follows:

Lake Abundance—0.5 mile from Cooke City, 61 miles from Red Lodge

Lady of the Lake—2 miles from Cooke City, 59.5 miles from Red Lodge

Clarks Fork of the Yellowstone—3.4 miles from Cooke City, 58.1 miles from Red Lodge

Crazy Creek—11 miles from Cooke City, 50.5 miles from Red Lodge

Clay Butte—21.2 miles from Cooke City, 40.3 miles from Red Lodge

Beartooth Lake—22.7 miles from Cooke City, 38.8 miles from Red Lodge

Island Lake—25.8 miles from Cooke City, 35.7 miles from Red Lodge

Long Lake—27.3 miles from Cooke City, 34.2 miles from Red Lodge

Gardner Lake—34.1 miles from Cooke City, 27.4 miles from Red Lodge

Rock Creek—50.6 miles from Cooke City, 10.9 miles from Red Lodge

Lake Fork of Rock Creek—52.5 miles from Cooke City, 9.3 miles from Red Lodge

West Fork of Rock Creek—61.4 miles from Cooke City, 0.1 mile from Red Lodge

34 GARDNER LAKE

A short but steep day trip to a high-elevation lake within sight of the Beartooth Highway.

Start: Gardner Lake Trailhead
Distance: 1.5 miles out and back
Difficulty: Easy

Maps: USGS Deep Lake; RMS Wyoming Beartooths; and at least 1 wilderness-wide map

FINDING THE TRAILHEAD

Drive 34.1 miles east from Cooke City or 27.4 miles west from Red Lodge and turn into a large pullout on the south side of the Beartooth Highway (US 212). Plenty of parking. No toilet. **GPS:** 44.972032 N, 109.462081 W

THE HIKE

When you start hiking from a trailhead at 10,595 feet (the highest in the Beartooths), there's only one way to go, and the trail to Gardner Lake does exactly that. It's only 0.75 mile to the lake, but it's all steeply downhill to reach it, which, of course, makes the hike back a major calf-stretcher.

Gardner Lake from the trailhead.

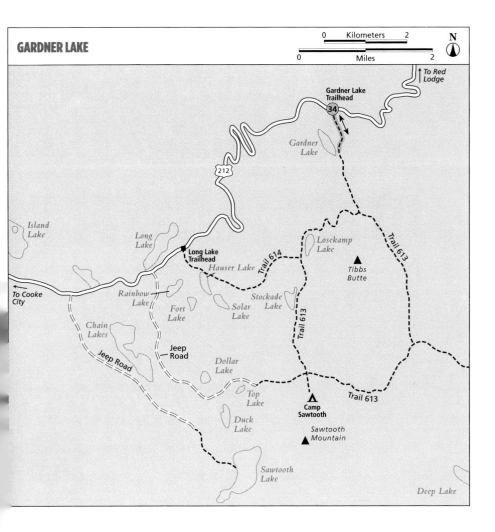

The trail to Gardner Lake is also the beginning of the Beartooth Loop National Recreation Trail, a long backpacking route.

Gardner Lake is a fairly large lake, and the steep climb down drops to 9,950 feet at the lake, making it a Category H climb to get back to the trailhead from the lake. This extra-high elevation stifles tree growth, so the entire route goes through open, alpine terrain. Along the trail you can note many species of delicate alpine wildflowers, usually downsized by the extreme climate they endure.

CAMPING

Although it's possible and legal to camp at Gardner Lake, very few people do.

FISHING

Gardner Lake has a good population of easy-to-catch brookies.

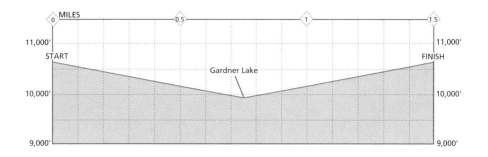

MILES AND DIRECTIONS

0.0 Start at Gardner Lake Trailhead.

0.75 Gardner Lake.

1.5 Arrive back at Gardner Lake Trailhead.

Backpacking along Green Lake, a hidden gem deep in the Beartooths.

35 BEARTOOTH RECREATION LOOP

A fairly short, easy, uncrowded loop with multiple side-trip possibilities, proof that you can have a wonderful backpacking adventure without having designated wilderness.

Start: Gardner Lake Trailhead
Distance: 10.75-mile (not counting side trips) lollipop loop
Difficulty: Easy, unless you go to Deep Lake

Maps: USGS Deep Lake; RMS Wyoming Beartooths; and at least 1 wilderness-wide map

FINDING THE TRAILHEAD

Drive 34.1 miles east from Cooke City or 27.4 miles west from Red Lodge and turn into a large pullout on the south side of the Beartooth Highway (US 212). Plenty of parking. No toilet. **GPS:** 44.972032 N, 109.462081 W

RECOMMENDED ITINERARY

Like most hikes this route could be lengthened, but unlike most routes this could also be a short, easy backpacking trip. You're here—why not spend some time hiking around, fishing, and enjoying the wildness before heading back to the highway?

- First night: Camp Sawtooth
- Second night: Same campsite

THE HIKE

This could be a moderate day hike, but because there is so much to see along the way, it's better suited for an easy—or perhaps a first—backpacking trip. The route is mostly flat and scenic, mostly above timberline, with no steep climbs except a short calf-stretcher at the end of the hike—and no hazards, unless you go to Deep Lake. The trail is well defined all the way with good signage, a plethora of good campsites, and lots of lakes and streams filled with little brookies that love to get caught by kids. In general this is not an austere place. Instead, it's a gentle, elegant, peaceful place, just as wild and beautiful as the Tetons you can see on the western horizon, but not so rugged or crowded.

At 10,595 feet, Gardner Lake Trailhead is the highest in the Northern Rockies, but that changes quickly as the trail plunges down to Gardner Lake. It's a good trail with no switchbacks, which you might wish for when climbing back up to your vehicle. At Gardner Lake, the trail levels out and stays that way most of the trip. It's amazing how fast the wilderness takes over from civilization. Even at Gardner Lake, less than a mile away from the highway, you get the feeling you're in the middle of a great wild area. You can look up and see motor homes cruising the highway in the distance, but try to avoid this.

From Gardner Lake the trail goes south for 0.75 mile to the junction with the Littlerock Creek Trail (Trail 613) that you use to complete the loop, which essentially circles 10,676-foot Tibbs Butte. Turn right (west) here and gain about a hundred feet of elevation to 10,060-foot Tibbs Butte Pass. It's not much of a pass—and not a place to get caught in a lightning storm, as we almost did. Start enjoying the carpet of wildflowers that lines most of the route—lupine, bottle cleaners, elephant head, lady slippers, and many more.

After Tibbs Butte Pass you drop down a few hundred feet, almost to timberline, where you find Losekamp Lake. The trail goes around the lake to the right, and on the other side you see the Hauser Lake Trail coming in from the west. Turn left (south) here. In another 0.75 mile, slightly downhill, you hit Stockade Lake with its small "stockade" at the north end of the lake. At both lakes you can plan on being greeted by clouds of mosquitoes unless you waited until late summer to take this trip. From Stockade Lake you get a great view of Tibbs Butte to the northeast and 10,262-foot Sawtooth Mountain to the south.

After Stockade Lake the trail goes through scattered stands of conifers interspersed with a series of beautiful meadows complete with a small, unnamed meandering stream. Watch for moose and elk. You also drop slightly below timberline and stay there until after you leave Camp Sawtooth.

The trail from Chain Lakes joins the loop 0.5 mile below the south end of Stockade Lake. Turn left (east) here and continue hiking through an open, forested landscape for another mile to the spur trail leading to Camp Sawtooth, a good choice for your camp.

Camp Sawtooth is on the north edge of a huge meadow about a half mile south of the main trail. Unless spring runoff has already washed it away, you can cross Littlerock Creek on a rapidly deteriorating old bridge. At Camp Sawtooth you can find many good campsites and the remains of several old structures. If you don't camp here, spend an hour or so exploring.

Back on the main trail, turn right (east) and hike about another quarter mile to another sign for another spur trail leading to Camp Sawtooth. Either spur trail will take you to Camp Sawtooth, but the first one seemed more heavily used—and when we were there, it had a classic old trail sign that had been chewed on by a bear.

After leaving Camp Sawtooth, you go through a big, wet meadow and then up a small, 200-foot hill and into the lower end of the delightful Littlerock Creek Valley, a truly wonderful high-altitude mountain basin. When you reach the junction with the Lower Highline Trail, turn left (north). You actually gain some elevation hiking through the Littlerock Creek Valley, but it's so pleasant and seemingly flat that you don't notice. You cross Littlerock Creek twice—no bridges, but late in the year, you can usually cross on rocks without getting wet feet.

At the upper end of the valley, you come back to the junction south of Gardner Lake. Turn right (north) here and retrace your steps past Gardner Lake to your vehicle. Allow a little extra time to get up the short Category H hill from the lake to the highway.

OPTIONS

You can do this loop in reverse with no added difficulty. If you do it in reverse, you can make a shuttle out of it by going out to Chain Lakes or Hauser Lake.

SIDE TRIPS

The logical side trip is to Deep Lake, but this transforms the trip from a pleasant walk in the park into a difficult, strenuous adventure. Deep Lake is austere and ruggedly

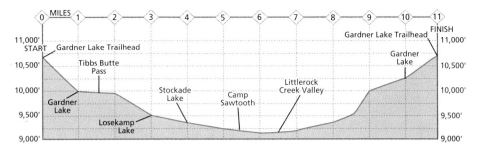

beautiful. Three inlet streams come in at the same place at the north end of the lake, which is a good place to visit but not to camp. The terrain more or less forces all visitors to go to the same place right at the inlet, creating the potential for conflict and overuse. In late summer you can cross the inlet stream and hike a short way along the east side of Deep Lake.

In general the trip to Deep Lake is not for families with small kids or the faint-hearted. To get there, fight through the brush and several small streams in the monstrous meadow south of Camp Sawtooth. At the other end of the meadow, just west of where an unnamed stream comes in from two small tarns, you start up a hill, a gradual, 400-foot, 1.5-mile climb on a good but unofficial trail. Then it's a 1,150-foot plunge down to the lake in less than a mile with no trail and lots of rocks—very tough going and borderline hazardous in a few spots. A few cairns mark the way, but it's basically route-finding. Don't try it unless you are experienced and fit and have lots of time. And keep in mind that after your visit to Deep Lake, you face this Category H climb to get back to your base camp, but it's so steep that it might be easier going uphill than downhill.

Other side-trip opportunities are fairly easy treks to Hauser, Dollar, and Christmas Lakes.

CAMPING

The entire route is lined with great campsites, so you'd have to work hard to find a bad one. Stockade Lake has a big outfitter camp on the east side of the lake, but you can still find a good campsite on the lake's west side. Camp Sawtooth is a conveniently located camping area with a great view and plenty of room for several parties without sacrificing privacy. You usually can find enough downed wood for a campfire, but try to resist. If you have a campfire, keep it small and as close to low-impact as possible.

FISHING

Most lakes and streams along this route have small brookies. Deep Lake has larger brookies and cutthroats.

MILES AND DIRECTIONS

0.0 Start at Gardner Lake Trailhead.

0.75 Gardner Lake.

1.5 Junction with Littlerock Creek Trail; turn right.

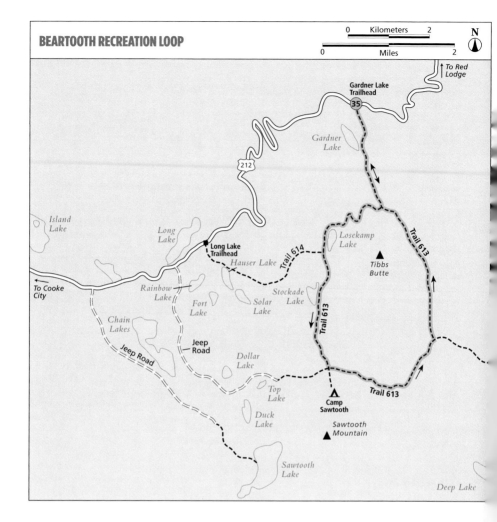

0   Kilometers   2

0   Miles   2

N

1.75 Tibbs Butte Pass.

3.0 Losekamp Lake.

3.25 Junction with Hauser Lake Trail; turn left.

4.0 Stockade Lake.

4.5 Junction with trail from Chain Lakes; turn left.

5.5 Junctions with spur trails to Camp Sawtooth; turn left.

6.5 Littlerock Creek Valley.

6.75 Junction with Lower Highline Trail; turn left.

9.25 Junction with Losekamp Lake Trail; turn right.

10.0 Gardner Lake.

10.75 Arrive at Gardner Lake Trailhead.

36 HAUSER LAKE

A seemingly remote day trip or overnighter to a spectacular area accessible with a very short hike.

Start: Long Lake Trailhead
Distance: 1.5 miles out and back or an easy base camp
Difficulty: Easy

Maps: USGS Deep Lake; RMS Wyoming Beartooths; and at least 1 wilderness-wide map

FINDING THE TRAILHEAD

Drive 27.3 miles east from Cooke City or 34.2 miles west from Red Lodge and turn into a large pullout on the north side of the Beartooth Highway (US 212) just east of Long Lake. Room for 5 to 10 vehicles at the pullout. No toilet. In addition, the Forest Service has recently developed a small parking area for the Morrison Jeep Trail with toilet just south of Long Lake. Take a short gravel road to the parking area. You can start the hike from here or the pullout along the highway. **GPS:** 44.946113 N, 109.495807 W

THE HIKE

This trail is similar to the Gardner Lake hike (Hike 34) minus the big hill, and is ideal for beginning backpackers who like to fish or families with young children out for their first night in the wilderness.

Hauser Lake.

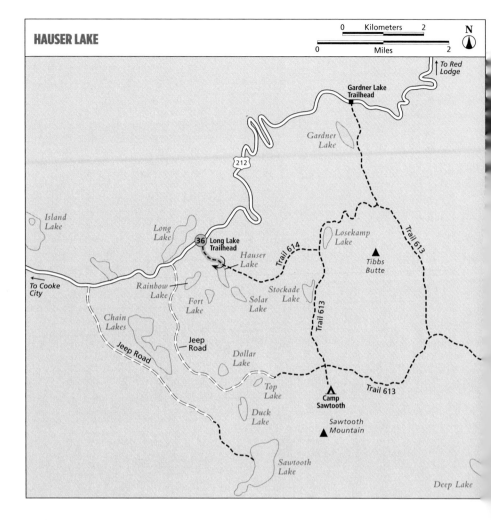

0   Kilometers   2   N

0   Miles   2

To Red Lodge

Gardner Lake Trailhead

Gardner Lake

212

Island Lake

Long Lake

36 Long Lake Trailhead

Hauser Lake

Losekamp Lake

Trail 614

Trail 613

Tibbs Butte

To Cooke City

Rainbow Lake

Fort Lake

Solar Lake

Stockade Lake

Chain Lakes

Jeep Road

Jeep Road

Dollar Lake

Trail 613

Top Lake

Camp Sawtooth

Trail 613

Duck Lake

Sawtooth Mountain

Sawtooth Lake

Deep Lake

There's a trailhead information sign on the south side of the road for the Beartooth Recreation Loop (Hike 35), which can be hiked from this trailhead as easily as from the Gardner Lake Trailhead (Hike 34). The trail is not well defined in the meadow along the road, so keep your eyes peeled for a few big cairns that mark its location.

Once you get near the trees, the trail becomes easy to follow and stays so all the way to Hauser Lake. The elevation on this hike is much lower than the trail to Gardner Lake—starting at 9,841 feet and dropping to Hauser Lake at 9,650 feet. The area is mostly open and very scenic.

SIDE TRIPS

If you have some extra time and energy (and don't mind off-trail hiking), you can visit three more lakes that are very short walks from Hauser Lake—Solar, Fort, and Rainbow Lakes.

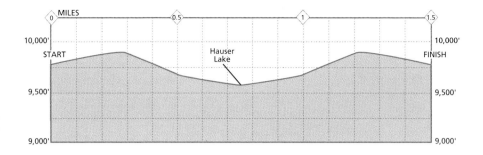

CAMPING

You can set up a camp at Hauser Lake or any of the other three lakes, all of which have excellent campsites on scenic benches above the shorelines.

FISHING

All four lakes in the vicinity offer fair fishing. Hauser, Solar, and Rainbow Lakes have cutthroats, and Fort has brookies. Make sure you have a Wyoming fishing license.

MILES AND DIRECTIONS

0.0 Start at Long Lake Trailhead.

0.75 Hauser Lake.

1.5 Arrive back at Long Lake Trailhead.

37 BECKER LAKE

An easy day hike, overnighter, or base camp with a remarkable number of lakes to enjoy on such a short hike.

Start: Island Lake Trailhead
Distance: 7 miles out and back
Difficulty: Easy

Maps: USGS Beartooth Butte; RMS Wyoming Beartooths; and at least 1 wilderness-wide map

FINDING THE TRAILHEAD

Drive 25.8 miles east from Cooke City or 35.7 miles west from Red Lodge on US 212 and turn north onto a short access road to the Island Lake Campground. Just before entering the campground, turn right to find the trailhead parking lot. Large parking area with toilet. Drinking water available near the boat ramp. **GPS:** 44.943190 N, 109.538964 W

THE HIKE

This is not only a great day hike, but also a perfect choice for that first backpacking experience with family or children. Expect to get your feet wet, though, because three safe stream crossings have no bridges. The trail gains only 175 feet in elevation over 3.5

Becker Lake, a popular base-camp destination. CASEY SCHNEIDER

miles, but just because it's flat doesn't mean it's lacking in scenery. To the contrary, this is one of the most scenic routes in the Beartooths.

From the trailhead the trail crosses an inlet stream before reaching the boat ramp parking area, then crosses another stream. From here, the trail closely follows the west shore of Island Lake for most of the first mile, then leads less than a quarter mile to Night Lake, once again following the west shore. Small children love this section of trail, but they tend to go slowly because there are so many discoveries for them to make.

Continue past Flake Lake, also to the east, until you leave Trail 620 and head straight north (to the right) toward Becker Lake. Be alert not to miss the trail heading to Becker Lake—this is not an official Forest Service trail, nor does it show up on the Forest Service or USGS maps. This "unofficial" trail is, however, as well defined and more heavily used than most official trails.

The trail turns north in a wet meadow just after you leave Flake Lake behind and Trail 620 turns to the west. The first 50 feet or so is overgrown and hard to see. Then it becomes an excellent trail, and almost as crowded as Trail 620. If you miss the trail, simply head cross-country along the continuous lake between Flake Lake and Jeff Lake. Stay on the west side of the lakes, and you'll soon see the trail.

Go between Mutt Lake and Jeff Lake, crossing over a small stream between the lakes. The two lakes are essentially one lake, since the elevation drop between them is about 5 inches. Just past Mutt and Jeff, navigate through a small boulder field. The trail disappears here, so look ahead to where it's clearly defined.

After climbing a small hill (the only one on this trip), hikers are treated to their first view of Becker Lake, with incredibly sheer cliffs on its west bank and 11,409-foot Lonesome Mountain dominating the northern horizon.

SIDE TRIPS

A Becker Lake base camp offers plenty of choices for day trips, all of them off-trail or on well-established social trails. Anglers like the trip to Albino, Golden, and Jasper Lakes (all off-trail routes), and peak baggers opt for the climb up Lonesome Mountain.

CAMPING

You can camp at Jeff Lake, off to the right just as you first see the lake. However, most people prefer to go on to Becker Lake. When you reach the bench where you can first see the lake, leave the trail and head off along the south shore of the lake. It's fairly easy to find a good campsite for one or two tents, but campsites suitable for large parties are scarce.

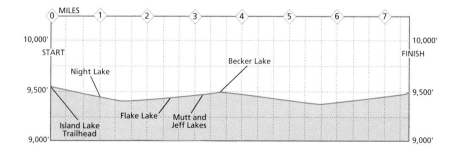

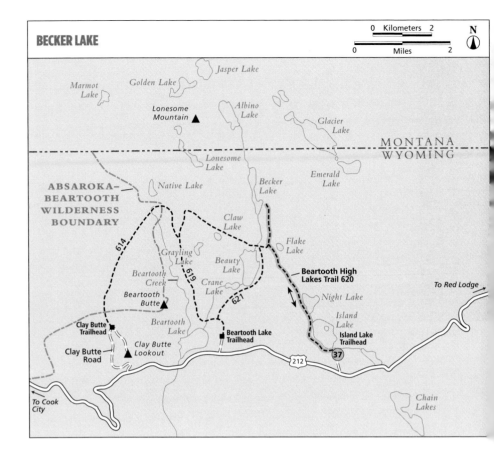

0   Kilometers   2

0   Miles   2

N

Jasper Lake

Marmot
Lake

Golden Lake

Lonesome
Mountain ▲

Albino
Lake

Glacier
Lake

MONTANA
WYOMING

Lonesome
Lake

Emerald
Lake

Becker
Lake

Native Lake

ABSAROKA–
BEARTOOTH
WILDERNESS
BOUNDARY

Claw
Lake

614

Grayling
Lake

Beauty
Lake

Flake
Lake

Beartooth High
Lakes Trail 620

To Red Lodge

Beartooth
Creek

619

Crane
Lake

Beartooth
Butte ▲

621

Night Lake

Island
Lake

Clay Butte
Trailhead

Beartooth
Lake

Beartooth Lake
Trailhead

Island Lake
Trailhead

Clay Butte
Road

Clay Butte
Lookout ▲

212

37

To Cook
City

Chain
Lakes

FISHING

This hike has become popular with anglers, in part because there is very little elevation gain. The fishing along this route leans toward brook trout, a good fish for youngsters learning to fish as well as oldsters looking for lots of action. Keep in mind that brook trout are often easier to catch on hardware (lures) than hackle (flies). Island and Night Lakes have been stocked with rainbows, but now these two lakes are primarily brook trout fisheries. Becker Lake may hold some cutthroats that have migrated down from Albino Lake.

For some variety and a chance to hook cutthroat trout, head up over the saddle at the end of Becker Lake into Montana and to Albino Lake, which is stocked on a four-year cycle and also has some natural reproduction to provide some variation in size.

Golden and Jasper Lakes, just over the hill from Albino, harbor slightly larger cutts. Heading west cross-country, anglers can try the Cloverleaf Lakes, which sport some of the best cutthroat fishing in the Beartooths.

Albino Lake, a popular day hike destination from a Becker Lake base camp. CASEY SCHNEIDER

MILES AND DIRECTIONS

0.0   Start at Island Lake Trailhead.

1.0   Night Lake.

2.5   Flake Lake.

2.7   Turn off Beartooth High Lakes Trail 620.

3.2   Mutt and Jeff Lakes.

3.5   Becker Lake.

7.0   Arrive back at Island Lake Trailhead.

38 BEARTOOTH HIGH LAKES

A truly spectacular route best suited for long day trips, and perhaps the best way to see the essence of the unique Beartooth high lakes country.

Start: Island Lake Trailhead
Distance: 8.5-mile shuttle
Difficulty: Moderate

Maps: USGS Beartooth Butte; RMS Wyoming Beartooths; and at least 1 wilderness-wide map

FINDING THE TRAILHEADS

Drive 25.8 miles east from Cooke City or 35.7 miles west from Red Lodge on US 212 and turn north onto a short access road to the Island Lake Campground. Just before entering the campground, turn right to find the trailhead parking lot. Large parking area with toilet. Drinking water available near the boat ramp. **GPS:** 44.943190 N, 109.538964 W

To reach the Beartooth Lake Trailhead, drive 22.7 miles east from Cooke City or 38.8 miles west from Red Lodge on US 212 and turn north onto a well-marked turnoff for Beartooth Lake Campground. The trailhead is at the north end of the campground, and the last 100 yards are on a narrow dirt road. Limited parking, so be sure to take only one space. Toilets in the campground. **GPS:** 44.94648 N, 109.58554 W

Hiking the open terrain along the Beartooth High Lakes route.

T Lake, one of many along the Beartooth High Lakes route.

THE HIKE

This is one of those pesky shuttle trails that requires arranging transportation in advance. Leave a vehicle at the Beartooth Lake Trailhead, or arrange with another party to start at Beartooth Lake and meet at Claw Lake or Beauty Lake for lunch so you can trade keys. You can also leave a bicycle at Beartooth Lake and elect somebody to ride it back to your vehicle at the Island Lake Trailhead (only about 4 miles).

Although relatively long and sometimes used for an easy overnighter, this route is also well suited for a delightful moderate day hike, but plan on taking the entire day to cover the distance, leaving plenty of time to enjoy the scenery. Carry a water filter to save weight rather than packing several full water bottles; the route follows streams and lakes virtually every step of the way.

The first section of this trail goes along Island, Night, and Flake Lakes. It's flat and scenic, and it stays that way for the rest of the trip.

The trail turns left (west) just after Flake Lake and soon drops down into Beauty Lake, where the scenery matches the name. Just before the lake, look for Trail 621 heading off to the south along the east shore of Beauty Lake. This route offers a shorter hike for those so inclined, but you'd miss some great vistas by cutting the trip short.

After a short, easy upgrade out of the Beauty Lake basin, continue through an open, alpine plateau to Claw Lake. For an overnight stay, Claw Lake or Grayling Lake (just to the south) probably offer the best choices for campsites. Wood is scarce, so please go without campfires.

After passing Claw Lake and laboring up another small hill, follow a string of lakes (Shallow, Marmot, Horseshoe, and others). This stretch of trail embodies the essence of the Beartooth high lakes country—water is everywhere, with Lonesome Mountain dominating the northern horizon and Beartooth Butte on the western horizon. It really doesn't get much better than this, especially on such an accessible trail.

Lakes everywhere along the Beartooth High Lakes Trail.

After Horseshoe Lake the trail turns south toward Beartooth Lake. For about a quarter mile, the trail fades away, but it's marked by clearly visible cairns. At the well-marked junction with Trail 619, turn left (south) and continue 2.7 miles in the shadow of Beartooth Butte to the Beartooth Lake Trailhead on US 212.

OPTIONS

This shuttle trip can be done in reverse with no added difficulty.

If this route isn't a long enough hike, consider the option of leaving a vehicle at the Clay Butte Trailhead and adding about 3 miles to the trip. For this option turn right at the junction with Trail 619 and head north around the north side of Beartooth Butte. This option includes another (and longer) section where the trail fades away to a series of cairns, but once you hit Trail 614 to Clay Butte, the trail is well defined. On the way to Clay Butte, the trail passes through a huge meadow that is one of the best places in the Beartooths for wildflower enthusiasts. The downside of taking the Clay Butte option is a 2-mile climb up to the trailhead from the meadow.

You can also make the trip shorter by turning south at Beauty Lake but still ending up at the Beartooth Lake Trailhead.

SIDE TRIPS

If you have the time, this trip offers a nearly endless selection of side trips, including the chance to simply wander through the open, trailless terrain with no particular destination in mind.

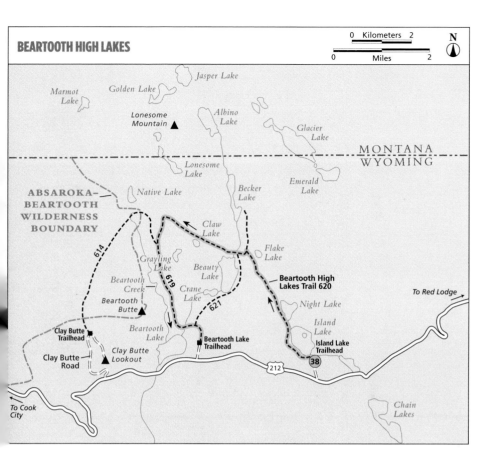

BEARTOOTH HIGH LAKES

CAMPING

Although most hikers day hike this route, it has plenty of good campsites, such as the north end of Beauty Lake, the south end of Claw Lake near Grayling Lake, or somewhere in the vicinity of Horseshoe, Finger, or T Lakes.

FISHING

Fishing along this trail leans toward brook trout, although several other species have been planted over the brook trout populations. Fishing is usually excellent in lakes with brookies, but some days even these fish are hard to catch—and sometimes hardware users can outfish the fly casters. Beauty Lake has had cutts stocked over the brookies. Claw, Horseshoe, and Beartooth Lakes have all had lake trout planted to feed on the brookies to control their population. Beartooth Lake has had several other species introduced, including rainbows, cutts, goldens, and grayling.

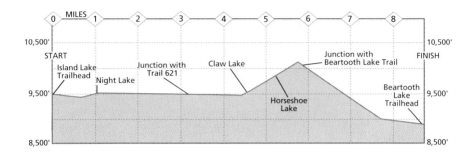

MILES AND DIRECTIONS

0.0 Start at Island Lake Trailhead.

1.0 Night Lake.

2.5 Flake Lake.

3.2 Junction with Trail 621 to Beartooth Lake Trailhead; stay to the right.

3.3 Beauty Lake.

4.5 Claw Lake.

4.9 Shallow Lake.

5.1 Marmot Lake.

5.3 Horseshoe Lake.

5.8 Junction with Trail 619 to Beartooth Lake Trailhead; turn left.

8.5 Arrive at Beartooth Lake Trailhead.

39 BEAUTY LAKE

A nice day hike suitable for children and families.

Start: Beartooth Lake Trailhead
Distance: 4.8 miles out and back
Difficulty: Easy

Maps: USGS Beartooth Butte; RMS Wyoming Beartooths; and at least 1 wilderness-wide map

FINDING THE TRAILHEAD

Drive 22.7 miles east from Cooke City or 38.8 miles west from Red Lodge on US 212 and turn north onto a well-marked turnoff for Beartooth Lake Campground. Once in the campground it might take a few minutes to find the trailhead. A likely-looking spot on the left just past the entrance is actually a picnic area and boat launch. The trailhead is at the north end of the campground, and the last 100 yards is on a narrow dirt road. Limited parking, so be sure to take only one space. Toilets in campground. **GPS:** 44.94648 N, 109.58554 W

THE HIKE

This trail leaves from a major vehicle campground and is one of the most accessible trails in the Beartooths. Consequently, the trail to Beauty Lake receives heavy use compared to

At the trailhead, Beartooth Lake and Beartooth Butte, a prominent feature along the Beartooth Highway.

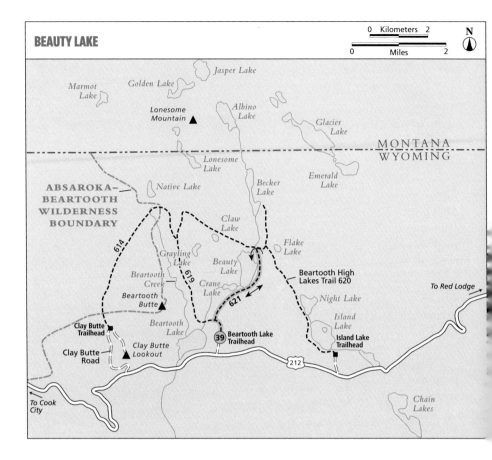

most other trails in the Beartooths, but not heavy compared to short day hikes in most national parks.

Right at the trailhead the trail is faint. After crossing a stream on a footbridge by the trailhead, however, the trail becomes well defined and easy to follow all the way to Beauty Lake. In less than a quarter mile from the trailhead, the trail splits. Trail 619 veers off to the left toward Beartooth Butte. Go right (north) on Trail 621 to Beauty Lake.

From this junction the trail gradually climbs about 500 feet through lush forest with lots of wildflowers and mushrooms. The trail is rocky in a few places but is still nicely suited for families with small children. It's rare for such great scenery to grace such a short hike. And it's all downhill on the way back from the lake to the trailhead.

After 1.4 miles look for Crane Lake off to the left (west) and a trail splitting off in that direction. Take the right fork in the trail and continue north for less than a quarter mile to Beauty Lake.

Undoubtedly, visitors here will all agree that this lake lives up to its name. This large, clear, alpine lake boasts several sandy beaches just right for wading on a warm day.

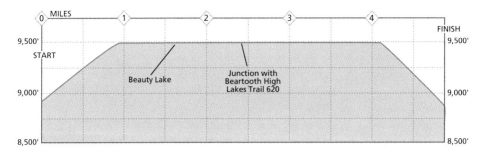

CAMPING

Most people consider Beauty Lake a leisurely day trip. Others hurry by on their way to some more remote spot. But it's also a nice spot to camp. If you do, however, please resist the temptation to build a campfire. Overnighters might actually find better campsites along the south shore of Crane Lake than at Beauty Lake.

FISHING

Even though other species have been planted in Beauty Lake, the fishing is still dominated by brook trout. Crane Lake has had cutts stocked over the brookies. Fishing in both lakes is excellent.

Beartooth Lake has been stocked with lake trout, which have thinned the brook trout population. The remaining brookies are larger than average size. Beartooth Lake has had several introductions of other species including rainbows, cutts, goldens, and grayling.

MILES AND DIRECTIONS

0.0   Start at Beartooth Lake Trailhead.

0.2   Junction with trail to Beauty Lake; turn right.

1.4   Junction with trail to Crane Lake; turn right.

1.6   South edge of Beauty Lake.

2.4   Junction with Beartooth High Lakes Trail 620.

4.8   Arrive back at Beartooth Lake Trailhead.

40 CLAW LAKE

A moderate day hike or easy overnighter—a rare loop route and a good choice for that first backpacking trip.

Start: Beartooth Lake Trailhead
Distance: 8.3-mile loop
Difficulty: Moderate

Maps: USGS Beartooth Butte; RMS Wyoming Beartooths; and at least 1 wilderness-wide map

FINDING THE TRAILHEAD

Drive 22.7 miles east from Cooke City or 38.8 miles west from Red Lodge on US 212 and turn north onto a well-marked turnoff for Beartooth Lake Campground. Once in the campground it might take a few minutes to find the trailhead. A likely-looking spot on the left just past the entrance is actually a picnic area and boat launch. The trailhead is at the north end of the campground, and the last 100 yards is on a narrow dirt road. Limited parking, so be sure to take only one space. Toilets in the campground. **GPS:** 44.94648 N, 109.58554 W

THE HIKE

Most trips of this length are shuttle or out-and-back trails, but this is a rare loop route.

Perhaps the most troublesome spot on the entire trip is the stream crossing right at the trailhead. Earlier in the season, in June and July, this stream carries lots of water, so be careful. Even though children might have some difficulty crossing this stream, the rest of the trip is quite safe. There are five more stream crossings, but none hazardous, and it's usually possible to cross on rocks to keep your feet dry.

Less than a quarter mile from the trailhead, watch for the junction with Trail 621 to Beauty Lake. To do this trip clockwise, turn left to stay on Trail 619 and head for Beartooth Butte. The return route of this loop comes down Trail 621 to this junction on the final leg to the trailhead.

The first part of the trail hugs the north shoreline of beautiful and expansive Beartooth Lake. Some parts of the trail can get quite marshy, especially in June and July. Then, after crossing Beartooth Creek, the trail turns north through the shadow of spectacular Beartooth Butte for another 2 miles to the junction with Beartooth High Lakes Trail 620.

Turn right onto the Beartooth High Lakes Trail, and don't be surprised when the trail fades away for about a quarter mile. A series of cairns clearly marks the way. At the top of a small ridge (the highest point on this trail, about 9,900 feet), the trail becomes well defined again. From this point on to Claw Lake, the trail skirts the south edge of a chain of lakes. Beyond the lakes to the north looms awesome, 11,409-foot Lonesome Mountain, standing out like the Lonely Mountain in the *Hobbit* movies.

Continue 1 mile down the trail to Claw Lake. From Claw Lake it's slightly more than a mile to the junction with Trail 621, which heads south along the east shore of Beauty Lake and past Crane Lake back to the Beartooth Lake Trailhead. When you're at the junction of Trails 620 and 621, drop your pack and walk over to the rocky ledge on the north end of Beauty Lake for a fantastic view of the well-named lake. This is a great place to eat lunch for day hikers on this loop. There are several more views to equal this one farther along the lake's edge.

Taking in the views near Claw Lake.

OPTIONS

This trip works either clockwise or counterclockwise, but clockwise seems slightly easier.

SIDE TRIPS

The route offers a wide variety of side trips, such as a trek around the sprawling Grayling Lake, south of Claw Lake. Pick a spot on the map and go for it.

CAMPING

The Claw Lake–Grayling Lake area may be the most logical place for an overnight camp on this loop. There are several excellent campsites on the southwestern shore of Claw Lake, some suitable for large parties. Downed wood is scarce here, so please refrain from building a campfire. For more privacy, move your camp out of sight of the trail by going a few hundred more yards south to Grayling Lake. You can also camp along Horseshoe and Finger Lakes as well as at several other places along this route.

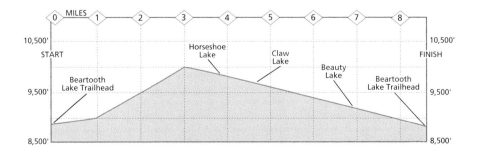

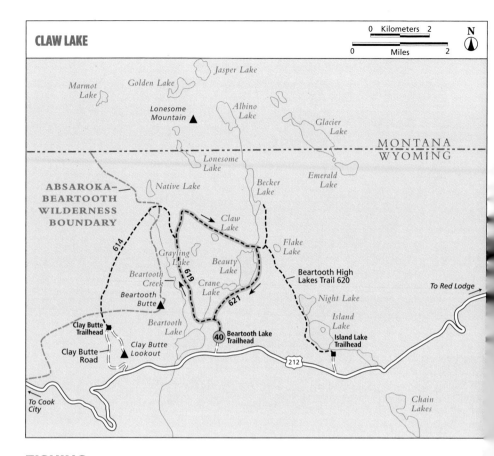

CLAW LAKE

0 Kilometers 2
0 Miles 2

N

Jasper Lake
Marmot Lake
Golden Lake
Lonesome Mountain ▲
Albino Lake
Glacier Lake

MONTANA
WYOMING

Lonesome Lake
Becker Lake
Emerald Lake

ABSAROKA-
BEARTOOTH
WILDERNESS
BOUNDARY

Native Lake
Claw Lake
Flake Lake

614
Grayling Lake
Beauty Lake
Beartooth Creek
619
621
Crane Lake
Beartooth High Lakes Trail 620

To Red Lodge

Beartooth Butte ▲
Night Lake
Island Lake

Clay Butte Trailhead
Beartooth Lake
40 Beartooth Lake Trailhead
Island Lake Trailhead

Clay Butte Road
Clay Butte Lookout ▲
212

To Cook City

Chain Lakes

FISHING

Claw, Horseshoe, and Beartooth Lakes have all been planted with lake trout to act as predators to the brook trout populations. For the most part the fishing along this route is the standard brook trout fare. Sorry, there aren't any grayling left in Grayling Lake.

MILES AND DIRECTIONS

0.0 Start at Beartooth Lake Trailhead.

0.2 Junction with Trail 621 to Beauty Lake; turn left onto Trail 619.

2.9 Junction with Beartooth High Lakes Trail 620; turn right.

3.9 Horseshoe Lake.

4.1 Marmot Lake.

4.3 Shallow Lake.

4.7 Claw Lake.

5.9 Junction with Trail 621; turn right.

6.7 South end of Beauty Lake.

6.9 Crane Lake.

8.3 Arrive back at Beartooth Lake Trailhead.

41 NATIVE LAKE

An easily accessible base-camp hike with an incredible number of alpine lakes nearby.

Start: Beartooth Lake Trailhead
Distance: 8 miles (not counting side trips) out and back with shuttle option
Difficulty: Easy

Maps: USGS Beartooth Butte, Muddy Creek, Castle Mountain, and Silver Run Peak; RMS Wyoming Beartooths and Alpine–Mount Maurice; and at least 1 wilderness-wide map

FINDING THE TRAILHEAD

Drive 22.7 miles east from Cooke City or 38.8 miles west from Red Lodge on US 212 and turn north onto a well-marked turnoff for Beartooth Lake Campground. Once in the campground it might take a few minutes to find the trailhead. A likely-looking spot on the left just past the entrance is actually a picnic area and boat launch. The trailhead is at the north end of the campground, and the last 100 yards is on a narrow dirt road. Limited parking, so be sure to take only one space. Toilets In campground. **GPS:** 44.94648 N, 109.58554 W

Native Lake base camp with easy access to dozens of scenic day trips.

Waiting for a trout, Native Lake sunrise.

THE HIKE

Native Lake is an ideal place for a base camp for those who don't want to carry their big packs long distances but still want some serious remoteness. Unlike some base-camp locations, many remote destinations can easily be reached from Native Lake both on-trail and off-trail.

How to get to Native Lake, however, can be a tough decision. Going in at the Beartooth Lake Trailhead is the shortest way. But the Clay Butte and Island Lake Trailheads also offer access to this area. Regardless of which trailhead you use, the hike into Native Lake can seem nearly effortless compared to many trails in the Beartooths. All three trails go through gorgeous, open, alpine country, dotted with lakes and carpeted with wildflowers.

From Beartooth Lake Trailhead, head north on Trail 619. In less than a quarter mile from the trailhead, the trail splits. Trail 619 veers off to the left toward Beartooth Butte; be careful not to get on Trail 621 to Beauty Lake. If you do, the punishment will be 2 extra miles of famous Beartooth high lakes country before reaching Native Lake.

Start out hiking around the north edge of Beartooth Lake on the edge of some moist meadows. Beartooth Butte provides a magnificent backdrop on the western horizon most of the way to Native Lake. The trail crosses Beartooth Creek twice, but it's usually easy to find a way across on rocks without getting your feet wet.

At the junction with Beartooth High Lakes Trail 620, bear left and keep going north on Trail 619. About a half mile after the junction, watch for a trail and a string of cairns heading west through the pass on the north side of Beartooth Butte. These cairns lead down to Trail 614 to Clay Butte.

Continue northwest on the main trail for about another half mile to Native Lake. The trail is well defined the entire way.

Five minutes later.

From Native Lake there are plenty of options for adventurous side trips. Set up camp and start exploring the area. This is a great place to practice using a compass and topo map and your GPS.

OPTIONS

You can reach Native Lake from three major trailheads: Beartooth Lake, Clay Butte, and Island Lake. Consider arranging a shuttle at a different trailhead to avoid retracing your steps on the way out. With two vehicles, it's best to leave one at Beartooth Lake and then go in at the Clay Butte Trailhead. Then the entire trip is downhill, with the exception of a minor bump just before Native Lake. The start at Clay Butte is at 9,600 feet, and the end at Beartooth Lake is at 8,900 feet.

SIDE TRIPS

Please refer to "Where to Go from Native Lake" (page 217).

CAMPING

Camp on the bench above the trail on the west side of the lake. There are several excellent campsites here, and they're spacious enough for large parties. This campsite is at 9,500 feet, just above timberline; even though there is a limited supply of firewood in this area, please don't give in to the temptation of starting a campfire.

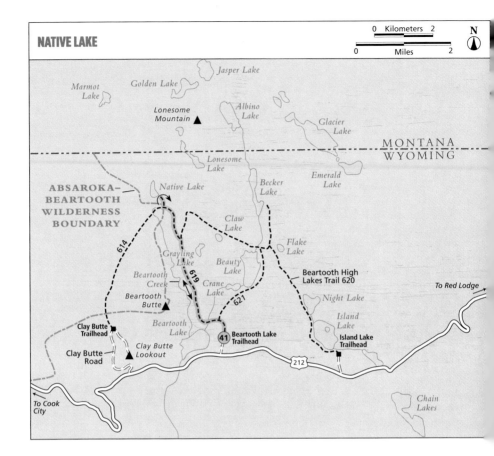

FISHING

Native Lake is a cutthroat exception to the brook trout theme found throughout this area. If the cutts are being stubborn, many of the lakes in the area sport voracious populations of brookies. The nearby Beartooth High Lakes Trail provides access to many of these lakes, and lake trout have been added to both T and Lamb Lakes.

The Montana state line is about 1 mile north of Native Lake, so anglers must make sure they have the proper state license(s). North of Lonesome Lake, heading cross-country, are Golden and Jasper Lakes, both offering cutthroat trout fishing. Just to the west is the Cloverleaf chain of lakes, a famous cutthroat fishery.

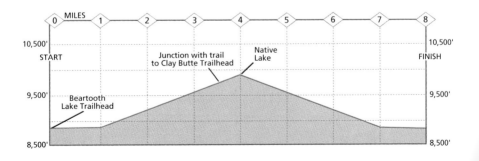

WHERE TO GO FROM NATIVE LAKE

The Beartooth high lakes area provides abundant opportunities for moderately easy, off-trail side trips. Day trips in this area are less advanced than in other areas of the Beartooths, and they provide a good chance to familiarize yourself with off-trail travel without getting in over your head. Here's a list of suggestions rated for difficulty as follows: Human (easy for almost everyone, including children), Semi-human (moderately difficult), or Animal (don't try it unless you're very fit and wilderness-wise). Also refer to more detailed rating information in "How to Use This Guide" (page 4).

Destination	Difficulty
Box Lakes	Human
Surprise Lake	Human
Mule Lake	Human
Thiel Lake	Human
Martin Lake Basin	Human
Hidden Lake	Semi-human
Swede Lake	Semi-human
Lonesome Mountain	Animal
Cloverleaf Lakes	Animal
Jasper and Golden Lakes	Animal
T Lake	Semi-human
Lonesome Lake	Semi-human
Beartooth Butte	Animal
Claw and Grayling Lakes	Human

MILES AND DIRECTIONS

0.0 Start at Beartooth Lake Trailhead.

0.2 Junction with Trail 621 to Beauty Lake; turn left.

2.9 Junction with Beartooth High Lakes Trail 620; turn left.

3.6 Turnoff to Trail 614 and Clay Butte Trailhead; turn right.

4.0 Native Lake.

8.0 Arrive back at Beartooth Lake Trailhead.

42 UPPER GRANITE LAKE

An out-and-back trip on a well-used trail suitable for a long day trip or an overnighter to one of the largest, deepest, most majestic mountain lakes in the Absaorka-Beartooth Wilderness.

Start: Clay Butte Trailhead
Distance: 10.4 miles out and back
Difficulty: Moderate

Maps: USGS Muddy Creek and Castle Mountain; RMS Wyoming Beartooths and Alpine–Mount Maurice; and at least 1 wilderness-wide map

FINDING THE TRAILHEAD

Drive 21.2 miles east from Cooke City or 40.3 miles west from Red Lodge on US 212 and turn north onto the well-marked Clay Butte Road 142. Any passenger car can make it up the moderately steep, well-maintained gravel road to Clay Butte Lookout, but it isn't recommended for vehicles pulling trailers. The turnoff to the trailhead is on your left 2 miles from the Beartooth Highway. Small parking area (way too small for its popularity). Some overflow parking in pullouts farther up the road. No toilet. **GPS:** 44.95176 N, 109.63294 W

The author's grandkids fishing Granite Lake.

An evening campfire always makes the wilderness spirit grow.

THE HIKE

This is the typical hike in the mountains, only in reverse. It's downhill all the way to the lake and uphill all the way out. Because the trail to Upper Granite Lake stays moist until late in the season, it isn't suited for use by backcountry horseback riders. Regrettably, they frequently use it anyway, so don't be surprised if you have to negotiate around a few horse bogs.

The route is popular with backpackers and fit day hikers, and when you get to Granite Lake the reason for this becomes clear. It's hard to believe (thankfully!) such a large, beautiful lake so close to a paved highway doesn't have a road to it, vehicle campgrounds, cabins lining the shoreline, and motorboats pulling water-skiers. Instead, visitors find a pristine, forested lake straddling the Montana-Wyoming border, protected on all sides by the Absaroka-Beartooth Wilderness.

The first 2 miles of the trail go through open meadows that are very rich in wildflowers, especially early in the season. For wildflower buffs this is one of the best trails in the Beartooths. And if you ever grow weary of wildflowers, look up. In every direction, on every horizon, the rich greens of the high mountain meadows rise to a panorama of snowcapped peaks. To name a few of many, Lonesome Mountain looms to the northeast and Pilot and Index Peaks mark the western view.

Early in the season the mosquito crop can come close to blotting out the sun on a clear day, so be prepared with bug dope. To avoid the bloodsuckers, wait until mid- to late-August.

A sign of a wild environment.

CAMPING

Upper Granite Lake has several good campsites along the branches of the inlet stream (Lake Creek), but because it's in a location that becomes a logical overnight stay, it gets heavy use. Stock parties frequently use this camping area and magnify the impact. You might be able to find enough downed wood for a campfire.

FISHING

Granite Lake straddles the Wyoming-Montana border, but there is no official agreement between the states on this joint jurisdiction. Technically, anglers should be careful to fish only in the state for which they carry a license. Perhaps the safest approach is to carry licenses from both states.

Granite Lake supports brook trout, rainbows, and cutthroats. There is also talk of planting lake trout. Brook trout dominate the fishery, but there are plenty of other fish. Montana FWP also stocks grayling, when available, in nearby Spaghetti and Skeeter Lakes.

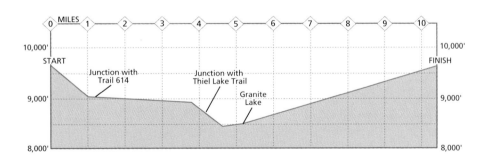

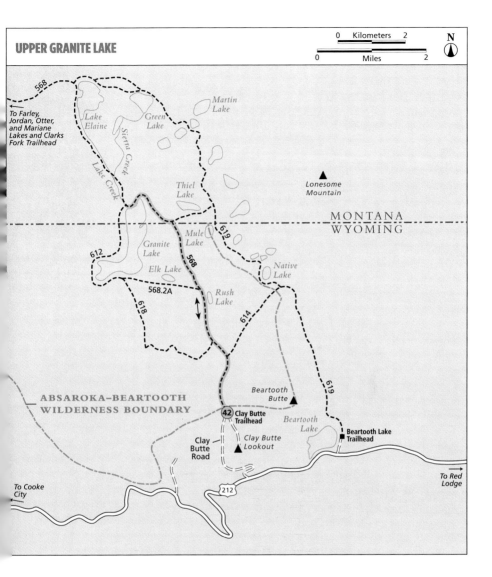

MILES AND DIRECTIONS

0.0 Start at Clay Butte Trailhead.

1.2 Junction with Trail 614 to Native Lake; turn left.

1.7 Junction with connecting trail to Muddy Creek Trailhead; turn right.

4.1 Junction with trail to Thiel Lake; turn left.

5.2 Upper Granite Lake.

10.4 Arrive back at Clay Butte Trailhead.

43 MARTIN LAKE

An ideal base-camp trip into one of the most scenic sections of the Beartooths, with many opportunities for side trips and a multitude of scenic, trout-filled lakes—even a high-altitude waterfall.

Start: Clay Butte Trailhead
Distance: 13 miles out and back
Difficulty: Moderate
Maps: USGS Muddy Creek, Beartooth Butte, Silver Run Peak, and Castle

Mountain; RMS Wyoming Beartooths and Alpine–Mount Maurice; and at least 1 wilderness-wide map

FINDING THE TRAILHEAD

Drive 21.2 miles east from Cooke City or 40.3 miles west from Red Lodge on US 212 and turn north onto the well-marked Clay Butte Road 142. Any passenger car can make it up the moderately steep, well-maintained gravel road to Clay Butte Lookout, but it isn't recommended for vehicles pulling trailers. The turnoff to the trailhead is on your left 2 miles from the Beartooth Highway. Small parking area (way too small for its popularity). Some overflow parking in pullouts farther up the road. No toilet. **GPS:** 44.95176 N, 109.63294 W

Last pitch down into the fabulous Martin Lake Basin.

Spogen Falls at almost 10,000 feet of elevation.

THE HIKE

For those who like to spend one moderately hard day getting into a really beautiful base camp and then spend several days doing scenic day trips, this is an ideal choice.

Trail 614 starts out downhill but turns uphill after about 1 mile at the junction of Trail 568 to Upper Granite Lake. Turn right here and stay on Trail 614. For the first 2.5 miles, the trail travels through an enormous, high-altitude meadow carpeted with wildflowers. At one point the trail fades away into a string of cairns, so watch carefully for the next trail marker.

About a quarter mile before Native Lake, the trail meets Trail 619 coming from Beartooth Lake. Turn left (west) onto Trail 619. Native Lake is the beginning of a long string of lakes. It's tempting to look for campsites along the way, but the best is yet to come at Martin Lake. Be prepared for short, steep climbs just before and after Mule Lake and a long, strenuous climb into the Martin Lake Basin that starts at Thiel Lake. Be careful not to miss Thiel Lake. It's off to the left (south) at the bottom of the hill after Mule Lake, just after the trail breaks out into a small, lush meadow.

Martin Lake Basin is one of the most fascinating places in the Beartooths. A gorgeous mountain stream packed with brook trout flows through the basin and connects four major lakes (Martin, Wright, Spogen, and Whitcomb), also loaded with hungry brookies. There is also a spectacular high-altitude waterfall between Wright and Spogen Lakes, which seems mysteriously larger and more majestic here at 9,600 feet.

As is obvious on the map, this is major-league lake country. Dozens of lakes lie within a day's trek from this basin. Even avid explorers could spend a week here and not see the same lake twice. Don't forget to spend one of those days simply hiking around the four lakes in the basin to fully appreciate a place that puts most national parks to shame.

OPTIONS

You can make a long loop out of this by following the route described under the Green Lake trip (Hike 44).

Another reason Martin Lake is a better base camp than most is that hikers don't have to retrace the exact same route on the way out. On the return trip, from the bottom of the steep hill down to Thiel Lake, leave Trail 619 and follow a well-used trail that traverses the east side of Thiel Lake. This isn't an official Forest Service trail and is not shown on the topo or national forest maps, but it's well maintained and well signed at the south end. In less than a mile, it intersects with Trail 568, which goes to Upper Granite Lake. Turn left (south) at this junction and follow this well-used trail back to the Clay Butte Trailhead. This still means retracing your steps the last uphill mile to the trailhead from the junction of Trails 568 and 614, but most of the return trip will be new country.

SIDE TRIPS

From Martin Lake, hikers have an almost countless number of choices for day trips. Refer to "Where to Go from Martin Lake," above.

CAMPING

You can camp almost anywhere in the basin, but the most convenient sites are around Wright and Martin Lakes, both surrounded with excellent campsites. This is, in fact, a five-star hotel: Every room has a knockout view, and the air-conditioning is always on.

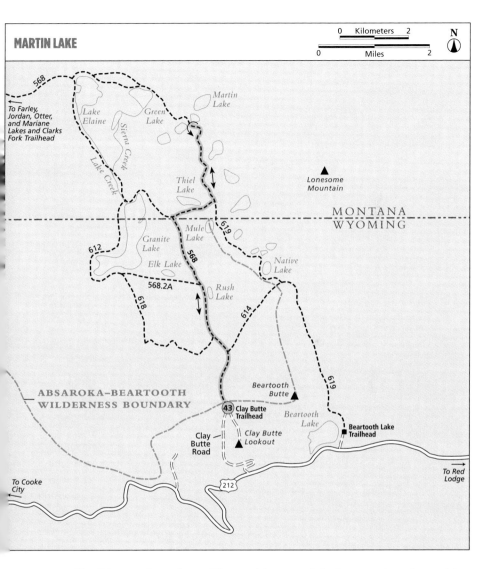

You could call it nature's penthouse. Firewood, however, is in short supply and essential to the extraordinary charm of this basin, so resist the temptation to have a campfire.

FISHING

Most of the lakes in this area were stocked with brook trout, and, in fact, the chain of lakes in Martin Lake Basin is named after the men who hauled in the brook trout. The brookies here are average for the Beartooths, with Whitcomb Lake having slightly larger fish.

For variation, Trail Lake (appropriately named) has cutthroats that are stocked but also reproduce. Also, head upstream from Martin Lake to reach the cutthroat hotbed found in the Cloverleaf Lakes.

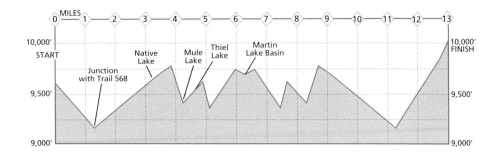

Earlier along the route in, a side trip to Swede or Hidden Lakes is worthwhile for the cutthroats found there. Goldens were once found in Hidden Lake, and a few may remain there.

MILES AND DIRECTIONS

0.0 Start at Clay Butte Trailhead.

1.2 Junction with Trail 568 to Upper Granite Lake; turn right.

2.9 Junction with Trail 619 from Beartooth Lake Trailhead; turn left.

3.1 Native Lake.

4.2 Mule Lake.

4.7 Thiel Lake.

6.5 Martin Lake Basin.

13.0 Arrive back at Clay Butte Trailhead.

44 GREEN LAKE

A long loop on the southwest edge of the Beartooth Plateau, best suited for at least two nights out, with one short off-trail section; a short section is impassable for horses, and plenty of opportunities to get your feet wet.

Start: Clay Butte Trailhead
Distance: 19.4-mile loop
Difficulty: Difficult
Maps: USGS Muddy Creek, Beartooth Butte, Silver Run Peak, and Castle

Mountain; RMS Wyoming Beartooths and Alpine–Mount Maurice; and at least 1 wilderness-wide map

FINDING THE TRAILHEAD

Drive 21.2 miles east from Cooke City or 40.3 miles west from Red Lodge on US 212 and turn north onto the well-marked Clay Butte Road 142. Any passenger car can make it up the moderately steep, well-maintained gravel road to Clay Butte Lookout, but it isn't recommended for vehicles pulling trailers. The turnoff to the trailhead is on your left 2 miles from the Beartooth Highway. Small parking area (way too small for its popularity). Some overflow parking in pullouts farther up the road. No toilet. **GPS:** 44.95176 N, 109.63294 W

Crossing Sierra Creek on the Green Lake loop.

RECOMMENDED ITINERARY

This is one of those hikes that you don't have to meticulously plan in advance. There are so many places to see and camp that you can sort of "play it by ear," and when you get ready to camp, you can quickly find a good spot. You should take at least three days to do this loop, but you can spend much longer by setting up base camps at several points such as around Native Lake, Martin Lake, Green Lake, or Lake Elaine.

HIKE

Clay Butte is one of those rare trailheads that allow backpackers to go downhill instead of up at the beginning of a trip. In fact, the trailhead, at 9,600 feet, is almost the highest point on any trail leaving from it. The trail edges a few feet over 10,000 on the top of the ridge overlooking Martin Lake, but most of the trip is at a lower elevation than the trailhead.

Clay Butte and neighboring Beartooth Butte to the east and Table Mountain to the south are the only outcrops on the entire Beartooth Plateau still covered with sedimentary rock. Erosion removed the sedimentary rock from the rest of the area, but for some reason, still somewhat unclear to geologists, these three remnants survived.

Most people are in a big hurry to hit the trail when they get to the trailhead, but here it's worth taking an extra 15 minutes to drive to the top of Clay Butte for the view. It's only another mile to the lookout, where (at 9,811 feet) you can enjoy a truly splendid view of the Beartooth Plateau. From this vista much of the terrain covered on this hike can be seen.

Trail 614 starts out downhill but turns uphill after about 1 mile at the junction of Trail 568 to Upper Granite Lake. Turn right and stay on Trail 614. For the first 2.5 miles, the trail travels through an enormous, high-altitude meadow carpeted with wildflowers. At one point the trail fades away into a string of cairns, so watch carefully for the next trail marker.

About a quarter mile before Native Lake, the trail meets Trail 619 coming from Beartooth Lake. Turn left (west) onto Trail 619. Native Lake is the beginning of a long string of lakes. Native, Box, Mule, and Thiel Lakes all boast excellent campsites. Thiel Lake is a frequent overnight stay for backcountry horseback riders and probably not a great choice for backpackers. Be careful not to miss Thiel Lake. It's off to your left (south) at the bottom of the hill after Mule Lake, just after the trail breaks out into a small, lush meadow and heads uphill again.

Regardless of where you spend your first night, continue along Trail 619 the next morning. Just after Thiel Lake, start a long, strenuous climb into the Martin Lake Basin. It's a fairly tough, Category 3 grind, but with a big reward at the end of it.

Martin Lake Basin is one of the most alluring spots in the Beartooths. A gorgeous mountain stream packed with brook trout flows through the basin and connects four major lakes (Martin, Wright, Spogen, and Whitcomb), also loaded with hungry brookies. There is also a spectacular, high-altitude waterfall between Wright and Spogen Lakes, which seems mysteriously larger and more majestic here at 9,600 feet.

You can camp almost anywhere in the basin, but most conveniently around Wright and Martin Lakes where you'll find many superb campsites. This is a five-star hotel where every room has a view sort of like nature's penthouse. Firewood, however, is in short supply and essential to the extraordinary charm of this basin, so resist the temptation to have a campfire.

Enjoying the last peaceful minutes of the day.

As is obvious with a quick look at the map, this is major-league lake country. Dozens of lakes lie within a day's trek from this basin. Even avid explorers could spend a week here and not see the same lake twice. Don't forget to spend one of those days simply hiking around the four lakes in the basin to fully appreciate a place that puts most national parks to shame.

Because this is one of the most spectacular spots in the Beartooths, plan to spend at least one night in the basin. For those who hiked all the way in on their first day, this area is worth a two-night stay, or more, and has plenty of enticing day trip options.

You have to ford the creek between Wright and Spogen Lakes, so when selecting a campsite consider whether you want wet feet that night or first thing the next morning. You'll find excellent campsites on both sides of the creek.

After spending a night or two or three in the Martin Lake Basin, you might have to force yourself to hit the trail the next morning. After climbing a small hill to get out of the basin, the route skirts Trail Lake before heading down a very steep hill into the gorgeous Green Lake valley. Going down this grade is all the argument needed against doing this trip in reverse. This hill makes the climb from Thiel Lake to Martin Lake Basin seem like a knoll.

At Green Lake don't continue around the lake to the south, even though the trail appears to head in that direction. Instead, turn north, ford the braided inlet stream, and head around the north side of Green Lake on a less-defined social trail. This isn't an official Forest

Lake Elaine.

Service trail, nor is it shown on the national forest map or topo map, but it's an easily followed pathway around the lake to Sierra Creek. If you decide not to camp in the Martin Lake Basin, camp instead at the head of Green Lake or after crossing Sierra Creek.

The Sierra Creek ford is also braided, and it can be fairly difficult early in the season, so be careful. After the ford the trail leaves the Green Lake shoreline and heads straight west to Lake Elaine. Again, this isn't an official trail, and it isn't maintained or marked, but it's still fairly easy to navigate. The trail through this section fades away in several wet meadows. Stay on the south edge of these meadows and you'll find the trail again.

At Lake Elaine traverse the north shoreline—including a short boulder field—until you hit well-used Trail 568. Be careful in the boulder field; it can be dangerous, especially if you're carrying a big pack or if the rocks are wet. After the boulder field and another stream crossing, turn left (south) onto Trail 568, which hugs the west shore of Lake Elaine for about a mile.

Campsites at Lake Elaine are sparse and marginal, but you can find one if this fits your schedule. We did this route many times, and we preferred to forge on to Upper Granite Lake to camp.

Shortly after leaving Lake Elaine, the trail drops down a steep hill, another good reason not to do this trip in reverse. This downhill grade receives heavy horse traffic, which has ground up the rock into a fine dust that can make footing precarious, so watch your step. From the bottom of this climb, it's a pleasant 2 miles to upper Granite Lake.

Granite Lake is a huge mountain lake fed by massive Lake Creek, which splinters into six channels just before tumbling into Granite Lake. Some folks moan and groan about having to cross six streams, but imagine how difficult the crossing would be if Lake Creek stayed in one channel. Fording Lake Creek as it leaves Granite Lake (not part of this route) is probably the most difficult and dangerous ford in the Beartooths.

The first view of Granite Lake is all the enticement most people need to stay, so why not? Choose from any of the numerous campsites at the upper end of the lake, some of which have been pounded by stock parties.

From Granite Lake the trail gradually climbs all the way to the Clay Butte Trailhead. This final stretch can become fairly muddy and have horse bogs. The hardest part of the trip, it seems, is the last uphill mile, which seemed so pleasant three or four days ago.

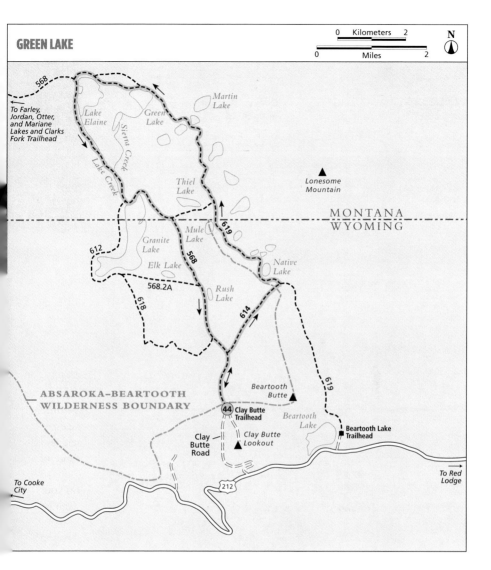

OPTIONS

Any loop can be done in reverse, but on this hike that option would require a steep climb with poor footing just south of Lake Elaine and another after Green Lake. This trip is also a good choice for backpackers who like to set up base camps and explore some of the surrounding terrain without a big pack.

SIDE TRIPS

Refer to "Where to Go from Martin Lake" (page 224). Another great side trip would be spending a day hiking up Sierra Creek to several lakes and perhaps as far as Castle Rock Glacier. From Lake Elaine you can go west on Trail 568 to see numerous lakes—Jordan, Hatcher, Farley, Lennon, and more.

CAMPING

There are delightful places to camp everywhere along this route, with the possible exception of Lake Elaine, where campsites are marginal. Be sure to set up a zero-impact camp.

FISHING

Most of the lakes in this area were stocked with brook trout, and, in fact, the chain of lakes in Martin Lake Basin is named after the men who hauled in the brook trout. The brookies here are average for the Beartooths, with Whitcomb Lake having slightly larger fish.

For variation, Trail Lake (appropriately named) has cutthroats that are stocked but also reproduce. Head upstream from Martin Lake to reach the cutthroat hotbed found in the Cloverleaf Lakes.

Earlier along the route in, a side trip to Swede and Hidden Lakes is worthwhile for the cutthroats found there. Goldens were once found in Hidden Lake, and a few may still remain.

MILES AND DIRECTIONS

0.0 Start at Clay Butte Trailhead.

1.2 Junction with Trail 568 to Granite Lake; turn right.

2.9 Junction with Trail 619 from Beartooth Lake Trailhead; turn left.

3.1 Native Lake.

4.2 Mule Lake.

4.7 Thiel Lake.

6.5 Martin Lake Basin.

7.8 Green Lake.

8.8 Sierra Creek.

10.1 Upper Lake Elaine and junction with Trail 568 to Farley Lake; turn left.

10.9 Lower Lake Elaine.

13.7 Upper Granite Lake and junction with Trail 618; turn left.

14.9 Junction with trail to Thiel Lake; turn right.

18.2 Junction with Trail 614; turn right.

19.4 Arrive back at Clay Butte Trailhead.

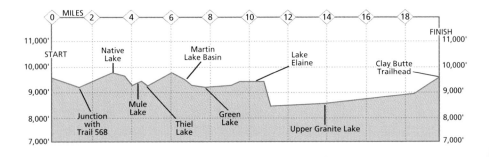

45 JORDAN LAKE

A long shuttle along a series of large, trout-filled lakes on the south-west edge of the Beartooth Plateau, best suited for at least three nights out.

Start: Clay Butte Trailhead
Distance: 23.9-mile shuttle
Difficulty: Moderate
Maps: USGS Muddy Creek, Fossil Lake, and Castle Mountain; RMS Wyoming Beartooths and Alpine-Mount Maurice; and at least 1 wilderness-wide map

FINDING THE TRAILHEADS

Drive 21.2 miles east from Cooke City or 40.3 miles west from Red Lodge on US 212 and turn north onto the well-marked Clay Butte Road 142. Any passenger car can make it up the moderately steep, well-maintained gravel road to Clay Butte Lookout, but it isn't recommended for vehicles pulling trailers. The turnoff to the trailhead is on your left 2 miles from the Beartooth Highway. Small parking area (way too small for its popularity). Some overflow parking in pullouts farther up the road. No toilet. **GPS:** 44.95176 N, 109.63294 W

To leave a vehicle at the Clarks Fork Trailhead, drive 3.4 miles east from Cooke City or 58.1 miles west from Red Lodge and turn north on the well-marked road to the hiking trailhead. Don't turn onto FR 306, which is about a quarter mile west of the hiking trailhead, and goes only to the stock trailhead. Huge trailhead with plenty of parking, toilet, picnic area, and interpretive displays. **GPS:** 45.01762 N, 109.86935 W

RECOMMENDED ITINERARY

If you want to extend this trip, set up a base camp at Jordan Lake and spend a day or two exploring the area.

- First night: Upper Granite Lake
- Second night: Jordan Lake
- Third night: Fox Lake or Rock Island Lake

THE HIKE

The first 5.2-mile stretch is fairly easy, all downhill to Upper Granite Lake. Because the trail to Upper Granite Lake stays moist until late in the season, it isn't suited for use by backcountry horseback riders. Regrettably, they frequently use it anyway, so don't be surprised if you have to negotiate around a few horse bogs.

The route is also popular with backpackers, and when you get to Granite Lake the reason for this becomes clear. It's hard to believe such a large, beautiful lake so close to a paved highway doesn't have a road to it, vehicle campgrounds, cabins lining the shoreline, and motorboats pulling water-skiers. Instead, visitors find a pristine, forested lake straddling the Montana-Wyoming border, protected on all sides by the Absaroka-Beartooth Wilderness.

Camping at Jordan Lake.

The first 2 miles of the trail go through open meadows rich in wildflowers, especially early in the season. And if you ever grow weary of wildflowers, look up. In every direction, on every horizon, the rich greens of the high mountain meadows rise to a panorama of snowcapped peaks. To name a few of many, Lonesome Mountain looms to the northeast and Pilot and Index Peaks highlight the western horizon.

Early in the season the mosquito crop can come close to blotting out the sun on a clear day, so be prepared. Lots of wildflowers seem to go hand-in-hand with lots of mosquitoes. To avoid the bloodsuckers, wait until mid- to late-August.

Upper Granite Lake is a good place to camp the first night out, particularly for those who started late in the day. Lake Elaine offers only limited camping, especially marginal for large parties, and it would be a long day with a backpack to get to Farley or Jordan Lake for the first night out. So, Upper Granite is your best choice.

From Granite Lake the trail climbs gradually along Lake Creek until just before Lake Elaine. Here it goes madly uphill with poor footing. Heavy horse traffic has pounded this section into dust, making it slippery even when not wet.

At the top of the hill, the forest opens up to beautiful Lake Elaine. Follow the trail along the west shore of the lake for about a mile until the trail veers off to the left (northwest) at the upper end of the lake. There are two small but marginal campsites along the west shore.

Shortly after leaving Lake Elaine, you climb just enough to break out above timberline. It's about a mile to Farley Lake, and a little over 2 miles to Jordan Lake. Both lakes have plenty of quality campsites and are similar in appearance, with Jordan Lake the larger of the two—and are a popular destination for backcountry horseback riders. Jordan Lake and Farley Lake are both good choices for setting up a base camp and extending your trip for a day or two.

From Jordan Lake you start a delightful trek along a string of beautiful lakes in both forested and subalpine environments all the way to Trail 567 coming down from Fossil Lake, which you hit about 3 miles northwest of Otter Lake. The trail from Otter Lake to Russell Lake isn't on the national forest or topo map, but it's there—and well defined most of the way. In a few places around Otter and Mariane Lakes, the trail might fade away, but the route is still easy to follow. After dropping down a steep grade from Mariane Lake to Russell Lake, the route dips below timberline into a fairly moist forested landscape. It then meets The Beaten Path (i.e., the main thoroughfare through the Beartooths, Trail 567) about a quarter mile from Russell Lake. Turn left (south) onto Trail 567.

You can camp at Russell Lake for your last night out, but the campsites and the upper and lower end of the lake are heavily used. If you have energy left in the tank, you might want to continue on to Fox or Rock Island Lake for better camping and fishing.

Approaching Kersey Lake, the aftermath of the dramatic fires of 1988 becomes apparent, but the rest of the trip travels through unburned forest. Also, be sure to watch for the point where the trail splits into horse and footpaths just after Kersey Lake. Parties with stock go right to a separate trailhead, and parties on foot stay left.

OPTIONS
At Farley Lake you can turn left on Trail 568 and exit at either the Crazy Creek Trailhead or make a loop out of this by going back to Clay Butte.

SIDE TRIPS
If you have extra time at Farley Lake, check out Hipshot or Wade Lake. If you set up a base camp at Jordan Lake, spend a day visiting the Desolation Lake area, but make sure you have good weather. On the way out you might save some time to visit Fox, Rock Island, or Vernon Lakes.

CAMPING
Upper Granite Lake has a few good campsites, but because it's a logical overnight camp, it gets heavy use. Stock parties frequently use this camping area and magnify the impact.

Jordan Lake has a large selection of good campsites, so it shouldn't be difficult finding a good one for a base camp.

Russell Lake offers a conveniently located campsite for the last night out. Like Upper Granite Lake, again because of its convenient location, Russell Lake is very heavily used. As a result the Forest Service discourages camping at Russell Lake, especially by

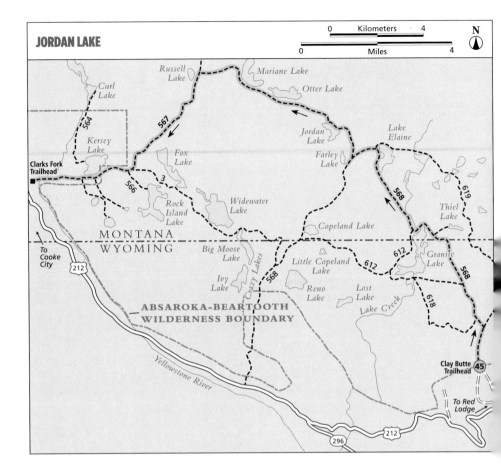

backcountry horseback riders because of the heavy impact stock has had on this area. You can camp at either the upper end or lower end of the lake but may have to cross the stream to reach the best campsites. You can also push on to Fox or Rock Island Lake to camp. Both lakes have a limited number of campsites not well-suited for horses. However, there's a good chance that these campsites will be occupied. Both Fox and Rock Island are popular overnight camping destinations from the Clarks Fork Trailhead.

FISHING

Jordan Lake holds a reproducing population of cutthroat trout that adequately complements the scenery. There are two creeks that enter the north side of Jordan Lake, both of which originate at Widowed Lake. Starting with Desolation Lake and ending with Widowed Lake, Montana FWP is trying to establish a reproducing population of golden trout. Many of the lakes along this route contain brook trout, but anglers willing to get off the trail can find other species. Keep in mind, however, that not all lakes contain fish. Fox Lake sports larger-than-average brookies, nice rainbows, and an occasional grayling that works its way down from Cliff Lake.

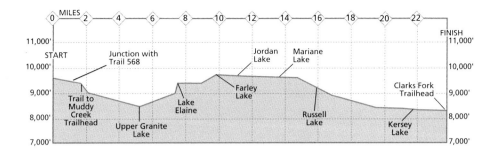

MILES AND DIRECTIONS

0.0   Start at Clay Butte Trailhead.

1.2   Junction with Trail 568 to Upper Granite Lake; turn left.

1.7   Junction with connecting trail to Muddy Creek Trailhead; turn right.

4.1   Junction with trail to Thiel Lake; turn left.

5.2   Upper Granite Lake and junction with Trail 612; turn right.

7.5   Lower Lake Elaine.

9.8   Farley Lake and junction with trail to Jordan Lake; turn right.

11.1   Jordan Lake.

12.6   Otter Lake.

13.7   Mariane Lake.

15.7   Junction with Trail 567; turn left.

15.9   Russell Lake.

18.7   Junction with trail 575 to Fox Lake; turn right.

19.9   Junction with Crazy Lakes Trail 3; turn right.

20.1   Junction with Rock Island Lake Trail 566; turn right.

21.7   Kersey Lake.

22.1   Junction with Vernon Lake Trail 565; turn right.

22.8   Junction with Curl Lake Trail 564; turn left.

22.1   Junction with stock trail/jeep road 305; turn left

23.9   Arrive at Clarks Fork Trailhead.

46 LOWER GRANITE LAKE

A fairly long, but not strenuous, day hike or an easy overnighter to a sprawling subalpine lake with good fishing.

Start: Clay Butte Trailhead
Distance: 7.4 miles out and back
Difficulty: Moderate

Maps: USGS Muddy Creek; RMS Wyoming Beartooths; and at least 1 wilderness-wide map

FINDING THE TRAILHEAD

Drive 21.2 miles east from Cooke City or 40.3 miles west from Red Lodge on US 212 and turn north onto the well-marked Clay Butte Road 142. Any passenger car can make it up the moderately steep, well-maintained gravel road to Clay Butte Lookout, but it isn't recommended for vehicles pulling trailers. The turnoff to the trailhead is on your left 2 miles from the Beartooth Highway. Small parking area (way too small for its popularity) with some overflow parking in pullouts farther up the road. No toilet. **GPS:** 44.95176 N, 109.63294 W

THE HIKE

Until recently this hike started at the Muddy Creek Trailhead, but the Forest Service has abandoned that trailhead, mainly because the trail went through an expansive wet meadow. You can still go to Lower Granite Lake from that trailhead, but be prepared to

Hiking the massive meadows near Clay Butte and Beartooth Butte.

Early morning wading in Granite Lake.

have very wet feet when you reach the lake—unless you like hiking in hip boots. The abandoned trailhead isn't signed, but with a little research (or an old map), you can find it.

I've rewritten this hike to start from the Clay Butte Trailhead, which is actually shorter, but does involve some steep climbs on the way back to the trailhead.

The first mile or so of the trail to the first junction (turn left here) drops steeply, and then keeps dropping, but not quite as steeply. A short 0.5 mile later you come to the Muddy Creek Cutoff Trail, which very precipitously drops into Muddy Creek. You can reach Lower Granite Lake that way, but for this route, turn right here and continue on to Rush Lake.

When you reach well-named Rush Lake on your right, watch for a junction with Trail 568.2A (a new trail built when the Muddy Creek Trailhead was abandoned) to Lower Granite Lake. You'll see Elk Lake on your right just before reaching massive and gorgeous Granite Lake.

The trail arrives at the south end of Granite Lake and continues west, fording the outlet stream, Lake Creek. Beware: Fording Lake Creek at this point can be dangerous. A tremendous amount of water leaves Granite Lake, and the flow can be powerful and chest-deep on a short person. This is probably the most hazardous ford in the Beartooths.

Instead of risking the ford, you can camp or relax for an hour or two along the lake, staying on the east side of Lake Creek, before heading back to the trailhead.

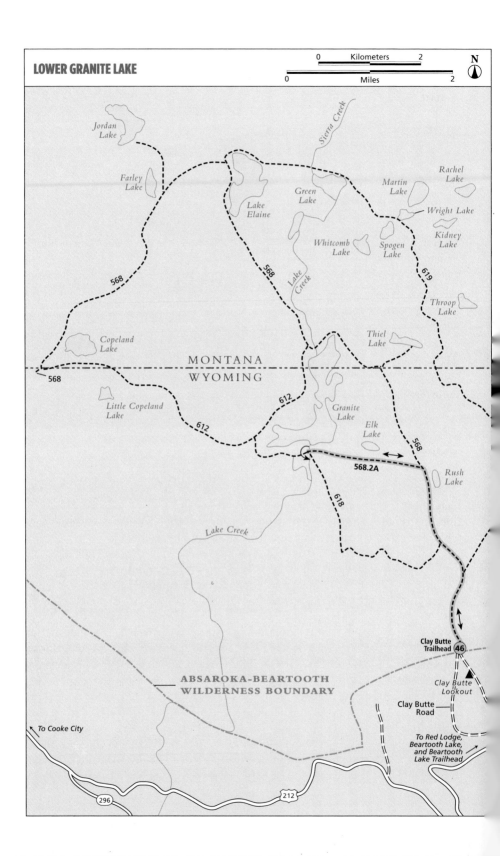

0   Kilometers   2

0   Miles   2

N

Jordan
Lake

Sierra Creek

Farley
Lake

Martin
Lake

Rachel
Lake

Green
Lake

Lake
Elaine

Wright Lake

Kidney
Lake

Whitcomb
Lake

Spogen
Lake

619

568

568

Lake Creek

Throop
Lake

Copeland
Lake

Thiel
Lake

MONTANA
WYOMING

568

Little Copeland
Lake

612

612

Granite
Lake

Elk
Lake

568

568.2A

Rush
Lake

618

Lake Creek

Clay Butte
Trailhead 46

ABSAROKA-BEARTOOTH
WILDERNESS BOUNDARY

Clay Butte
Lookout

Clay Butte
Road

To Cooke City

To Red Lodge,
Beartooth Lake,
and Beartooth
Lake Trailhead

296

212

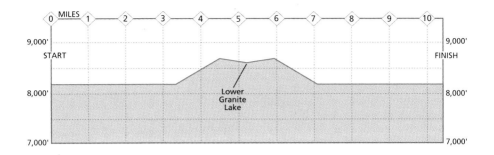

OPTIONS

You can make a lollipop loop out of this hike by going down the Muddy Creek Cutoff Trail to Granite Lake and then back via Rush Lake. You'd want to do this loop clockwise to avoid the steep hill climb on the cutoff trail.

If you go late in the year, the abandoned Muddy Creek Trail might be dry, so you could leave a vehicle or bicycle at the old Muddy Creek Trailhead and make this a shuttle hike.

SIDE TRIPS

If you have extra time and the courage and skill to ford Lake Creek, try the pleasant hike along the west shore of the Granite Lake.

CAMPING

There are excellent campsites on both sides of Lake Creek where it leaves the lake.

FISHING

Granite Lake supports rainbows and cutthroats, but brook trout dominate the fishery. All three species grow larger than normal. Elk Lake has a nice cutthroat population.

MILES AND DIRECTIONS

0.0   Start at Clay Butte Trailhead.

1.2   Junction with Trail 568 to Upper Granite Lake; turn left.

1.7   Junction with Muddy Creek Cutoff Trail; turn right to stay on Trail 618.

2.4   Rush Lake and junction with Trail 568.2A; turn left.

3.5   Elk Lake.

3.7   Lower Granite Lake.

7.4   Arrive back at Clay Butte Trailhead.

47 COPELAND LAKE

A long loop to several large wilderness lakes best suited for a three- or four-night backpack.

Start: Clay Butte Trailhead
Distance: 23.7-mile lollipop loop
Difficulty: Moderately difficult, with 2 difficult stream crossings and 1 steep hill

Maps: USGS Muddy Creek and Castle Mountain; RMS Wyoming Beartooths; and at least 1 wilderness-wide map

FINDING THE TRAILHEAD

Drive 21.2 miles east from Cooke City or 40.3 miles west from Red Lodge on US 212 and turn north onto the well-marked Clay Butte Road 142. Any passenger car can make it up the moderately steep, well-maintained gravel road to Clay Butte Lookout, but it isn't recommended for vehicles pulling trailers. The turnoff to the trailhead is on your left 2 miles from the Beartooth Highway. Small parking area (way too small for its popularity) with some overflow parking in pullouts farther up the road. No toilet. **GPS:** 44.95176 N, 109.63294 W

RECOMMENDED ITINERARY

You can easily spend more than four days exploring along this route, but for a three-night trip:

- First night: Lower Granite Lake
- Second night: Farley, Hipshot, or Wade Lake
- Third night: Copeland Lake

THE HIKE

This hike used to start at the recently abandoned Muddy Creek Trailhead. You can still go to Lower Granite Lake from the old Muddy Creek Trailhead and make this route a bit easier (although not shorter), but be prepared to have very wet feet when you reach Granite Lake. The abandoned trailhead isn't signed, but with a little research (or an old map), you can find it.

I've rewritten this hike to start from the Clay Butte Trailhead, which actually makes the total distance slightly shorter, but probably not easier because it involves some steep climbs on the way back to the trailhead.

The first mile or so of the trail to the first junction (turn left here) drops steeply, and then keeps dropping, but not quite as steeply. Only 0.5 mile later you come to the Muddy Creek Cutoff Trail, which very precipitously drops into Muddy Creek. You can reach your destination that way, but for this route, turn right here and continue on to Rush Lake.

When you reach well-named Rush Lake on your right, watch for a junction with Trail 568.2A (a new trail built when the Muddy Creek Trailhead was abandoned) to Lower Granite Lake. You'll see Elk Lake on your right just before reaching massive and gorgeous Granite Lake.

The trail arrives at the south end of Granite Lake and continues west, fording Lake Creek, the outlet stream. Beware: Fording Lake Creek at this point can be dangerous. A tremendous amount of water leaves Granite Lake, and the flow can be powerful and possibly chest-deep. This is probably the most hazardous ford in the Beartooths.

Lake Creek leaves the huge lake amid several excellent campsites. Shortly after the ford, look for the trail coming in from Copeland Lake on the left. That will be the return leg of this loop. Turn right (north) and follow Trail 612 along the west shore of Granite Lake, one of the largest lakes in the Beartooths and shared by Montana and Wyoming. At the lake's upper end, Lake Creek splits into six channels before melting into Granite Lake, but you don't have to cross them on this route.

From here the trip to Lake Elaine starts out easy and mostly flat. But just before Lake Elaine, you face a short but tough climb up to the lake. This half-mile climb is not only steep but also dusty and slick. Heavy horse traffic has ground the rock down to fine sand, creating precarious footing, especially when wet. Believe it or not, it's easier going up than down this slope.

At Lake Elaine the forest starts to open up, giving great views of another of the largest lakes in the Beartooths. Despite its size, Lake Elaine really doesn't offer much in the way of quality camping or fishing, so after soaking in the scenery over lunch, head west on the trail to Farley Lake for the second night's campsite.

Just before Farley Lake the trail meets the trail going right (north) to Jordan Lake. Turn left to Farley Lake, which has several campsites but not enough wood for a campfire. Those with energy to spare and who don't mind getting off the trail can go another mile or so to a more secluded camp at Hipshot Lake or Wade Lake. It's a short cross-country trip to these lakes, but check the topo map carefully before heading off-trail. Both lakes are about a half mile south of Farley Lake—Wade Lake to the east of the trail and Hipshot Lake to the west.

From Farley Lake the trail goes south, and just before Copeland Lake it meets a trail coming in from the Crazy Creek Trailhead. Turn left (east) and continue about a half mile to Copeland Lake, which is nestled in a forested pocket with lots of wood for campfires—and a few more mosquitoes than any lake deserves. If you camp at Copeland for the third night, you have an 8.4-mile trek out to the Clay Butte Trailhead, mostly uphill, for the final day. The grade is easy down to Lower Granite Lake and the Lake Creek ford. From here retrace your steps back to the Clay Butte Trailhead.

OPTIONS
If you prefer to hike down the Lake Elaine hill, you can hike this route in reverse.

SIDE TRIPS
Attractive side trips include Jordan, Hipshot, and Wade Lakes. If you're especially ambitious, stay an extra night at Farley Lake and spend the down day exploring the Desolation Lake area.

CAMPING
You'll probably want to spend the first night at one of several scenic campsites at the lower end of Granite Lake. It might be tempting to march on for another 2.5 miles to the upper end of Granite Lake, but there are fewer nice campsites there, and they're often occupied. Rich forests surround aesthetic Granite Lake, and there is ample fuel for building a low-impact campfire.

For the second night out, you can choose from a large selection of campsites at Farley, Hipshot, or Wade Lake.

On the third night, Copeland Lake is the best choice, even though good campsites are limited and hard to see through the clouds of mosquitoes.

FISHING

Most lakes along this route, including Lake Elaine, contain brook trout. However, Hipshot Lake contains stocked cutthroats, and Jordan Lake has natural cutts. Farley Lake provides the best brook trout eatery with the fish being an inch or so larger than nearby lakes.

MILES AND DIRECTIONS

0.0 Start at Clay Butte Trailhead.

1.2 Junction with Trail 568 to Upper Granite Lake; turn left.

1.7 Junction with Muddy Creek Cutoff Trail; turn right to stay on Trail 618.

2.4 Rush Lake and junction with Trail 568.2A; turn left.

3.5 Elk Lake.

3.7 Lower Granite Lake and junction with Trail 568.2A; turn right.

3.9 Lake Creek ford.

4.6 Junction with Trail 612; turn right.

6.2 Upper Granite Lake.

6.3 Junction with Trail 568; turn left.

8.9 Lower end of Lake Elaine.

9.8 Upper end of Lake Elaine.

11.0 Farley Lake and junction with trail to Jordan Lake; turn left.

15.1 Junction with Trail 624; turn left.

15.3 Copeland Lake.

16.3 Little Copeland Lake.

18.9 Junction with Trail 568.2A; turn right.

19.8 Lower end of Granite Lake and Lake Creek ford.

20.0 Junction with Trail 568.2A; turn left.

20.2 Elk Lake.

21.3 Rush Lake and junction with Trail 618; turn right.

22.0 Junction with Muddy Creek Cutoff Trail; turn left.

22.5 Junction with Trail 614.1; turn right.

23.7 Arrive back at Clay Butte Trailhead.

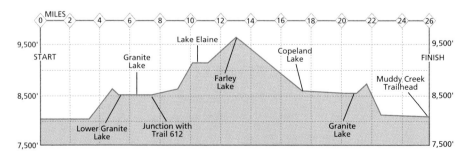

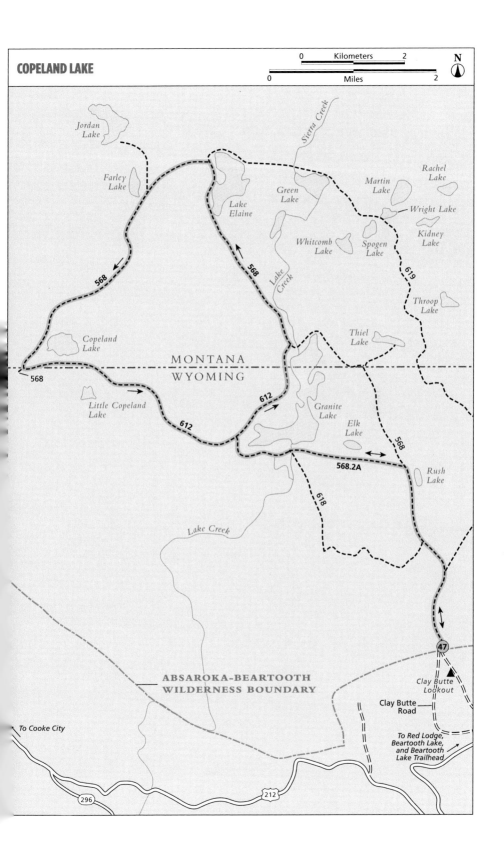

48 IVY LAKE

A moderately long day hike or easy overnighter where you can see Crazy Falls and have a better chance of seeing wildlife than most places in the Beartooths.

Start: Crazy Creek Trailhead
Distance: 7.6 miles out and back
Difficulty: Moderate

Maps: USGS Jim Smith Peak; RMS Wyoming Beartooths; and at least 1 wilderness-wide map

FINDING THE TRAILHEAD

Drive 11 miles east from Cooke City or 50.5 miles west from Red Lodge on US 212 and turn north into a turnout across the highway from the Crazy Creek Campground. Limited parking. No toilet at trailhead, but toilets are at the vehicle campground across the highway. **GPS:** 44.94292 N, 109.77359 W

THE HIKE

The Ivy Lake trail starts off with a bang. The first quarter mile or so parallels cascading Crazy Creek Falls. You'll want to stop and marvel at it a few times along the way.

Much of this trail goes through a drier, sagebrush-type environment with Pilot and Index Peaks highlighting the western horizon. Plan to hike this route in the early

Hiking to Ivy Lake through sagebrush flats. Pilot and Index Peaks on the horizon.

Ivy Lake.

morning or evening to avoid the heat—and for a better chance of seeing elk and moose that sleep during the hot midday.

About halfway to Ivy Lake the trail goes around a big, wet meadow. At the 3-mile mark, look to the left, down the hill to Little Moose Lake. For a short side trip, drop down and note the unusual "floating shoreline" here.

About a quarter mile after Little Moose Lake, the trail meets a jeep road coming from the Lily Lake area to the east. Continue north along the jeep road for another quarter mile or so to where the Crazy Lakes Trail veers off to the right. You continue to follow the old jeep road, which turns into a singletrack, then left down to Ivy Lake. Some maps might not show the trail going down to Ivy Lake, but it's there.

SIDE TRIPS
Try the short spur trail to Little Moose Lake.

CAMPING
There are campsites on the left and right just before the lake. This area was partly burned during the 1988 fires, so there's plenty of wood for a campfire.

FISHING
Ivy Lake is the lowest of a chain of lakes on Crazy Creek. This chain of lakes harbors both brook trout and rainbow trout, and the variety provides for some nice (though not exceptional) fishing. The rainbows are much harder to catch than brookies. Little Moose

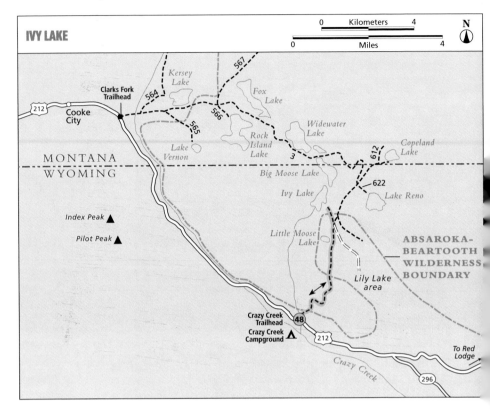

Lake is stocked occasionally with cutthroat trout. The weedy nature of the lake makes it a good home for food organisms, so fish grow larger here.

MILES AND DIRECTIONS

0.0   Start at Crazy Creek Trailhead.

3.0   Little Moose Lake.

3.1   Junction with jeep road coming in from Lily Lake area.

3.3   Turn off jeep road onto trail to Ivy Lake.

3.8   Ivy Lake.

7.6   Arrive back at Crazy Creek Trailhead.

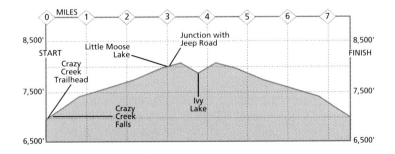

49 **CRAZY LAKES**

A two- or three-night late-summer shuttle trip to a string of large, forested lakes.

Start: Crazy Creek Trailhead
Distance: 12.6-mile shuttle
Difficulty: Moderate
Maps: USGS Jim Smith Peak and Fossil Lake; RMS Wyoming

Beartooths and Cooke City–Cutoff Mountain; and at least 1 wilderness-wide map

FINDING THE TRAILHEADS

Drive 11 miles east from Cooke City or 50.5 miles west from Red Lodge on US 212 and turn north into a turnout across the highway from the Crazy Creek Campground. Limited parking. No toilet at trailhead, but toilets in the vehicle campground across the highway. **GPS:** 44.94292 N, 109.77359 W

To leave a vehicle or bicycle at the Clarks Fork Trailhead, drive 3.4 miles east from Cooke City or 58.1 miles west from Red Lodge on US 212 and turn north onto FR 306. Drive about a half mile to the trailhead. Be careful not to go to the special trailhead for backcountry horseback riders, which is just west of the hiker trailhead. Huge trailhead with plenty of parking, toilet, picnic area, and interpretive displays. **GPS:** 45.01762 N, 109.86935 W

THE HIKE

The first order of business is leaving a vehicle or a bicycle at the Clarks Fork Trailhead. If you are trading keys with another party, plan on joining up at approximately the halfway point on the west shore of Big Moose Lake.

Trail 568.1 starts off with a bang. The first quarter mile or so parallels cascading Crazy Creek Falls. You'll want to stop and marvel at it two or three times along the way.

Much of the first few miles of this trail wander through a drier, sagebrush–type environment with Pilot and Index Peaks highlighting the western horizon. Plan to hike this route in the early morning or evening to avoid the heat—and for a better chance of seeing elk and moose that sleep during the hot midday.

About halfway to Ivy Lake the trail goes around a big, wet meadow. At the 3-mile mark, look to the left, down the hill to Little Moose Lake. For a short side trip, drop down to see the little lake's unusual "floating shoreline." About a quarter mile after Little Moose Lake, the trail meets a jeep road coming from the Lily Lake area to the east. Continue north along the jeep road for another quarter mile or so to the Ivy Lake/Crazy Lakes junction. Go right here, staying on Trail 568.1.

Actually, if you're out for two nights, make a note of this junction and continue on up the road to Ivy Lake, a good spot for the first night out. Come back to this junction the next morning. Rock Island or Fox Lakes would be good choices for the second night.

Note of caution: From the Ivy Lake junction, the next few miles of trail can be confusing. When I was last there, several junctions were missing signs. Plus, outfitter use in the area had created several well-worn social trails. So stay alert.

Crazy Creek Falls, a short stroll from the trailhead.

After following the Crazy Lakes Trail for about a quarter mile, you reach the junction with Trail 617 to Lost Lake, where you turn right and stay on Trail 568.1.

About a mile later the trail enters a huge mountain meadow and splits. You can go either way here. If you want a side trip to Lake Reno, go right. Otherwise go left on Trail 567. Trail 568 goes straight, on to Copeland Lake. The left fork is a shortcut social trail to an outfitter camp. Both forks eventually go right through the outfitter camp and on to Big Moose Lake.

At Big Moose Lake it becomes clear why this trip isn't recommended for early in the hiking season, even though the snow burns off this lower-elevation area earlier than most of the Absaroka-Beartooth Wilderness. Big Moose Lake is, more or less, a big, wide, shallow section of Crazy Creek. To continue the trek, hikers must, in essence, ford Big Moose Lake. In June this could turn into an exhilarating experience, to say the least. In August, though, it isn't difficult as long as you don't ford it right where the trail meets the shoreline. It's better to go slightly north where the water has some current and isn't so deep.

From Big Moose Lake it's about 4 miles to the junction with Trail 3, a heavily used trail called The Beaten Path. Turn left (west) here and go less than a quarter mile to the junction with Trail 566 to Rock Island Lake. Turn right (west) and head for Kersey Lake. Just past this lake, turn right (west) at the junction with the trail to Lake Vernon. From Big Moose Lake the trail is in excellent shape and easy to follow. From Rock Island Lake it's a leisurely 2.4 miles out to the Clarks Fork Trailhead, with one minor climb at Kersey Lake.

OPTIONS
This shuttle trip can be started at the Clarks Fork Trailhead with no extra difficulty.

SIDE TRIPS
If there's time for a side trip, it's only 0.5 mile over to Lake Reno. If you camp at Rock Island Lake, you might want to set aside several hours of free time to walk around this lake or go over to see Fox Lake.

CAMPING
There are several places to camp at Ivy Lake; the best site is on the left just before the lake. Camping at Lake Reno is limited, and the area tends to be marshy. At Big Moose Lake, the best campsite is on the west side of the lake, just north of the trail. There's room for a large party or several parties without anybody losing much privacy. Another good choice for the second night out is Rock Island Lake. Camping is somewhat limited at Rock Island, but once you find a spot big enough for a tent, you'll relish your stay at this gorgeous, forested lake that seems to sprawl everywhere. Fox Lake is another good choice, but it only has one large campsite at the inlet to the lake.

FISHING
The Crazy Lakes are a chain of lakes starting with Fox and Widewater Lakes in Montana, Moose Lake straddling the border, and Ivy Lake in Wyoming. The chain of lakes has both brook and rainbow trout and a few grayling. The streams between the lakes sport the same type of fish, and they're easier to locate.

Fox Lake has some above-average brookies and some nice rainbows. Rock Island has a nice mix of cutts and brookies, but many people know this, and anglers can count on some competition, as it is an easy day hike from the Clarks Fork Trailhead to Rock Island Lake.

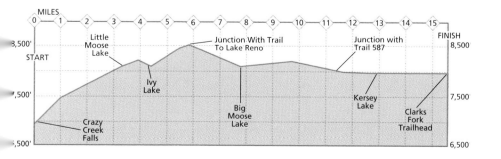

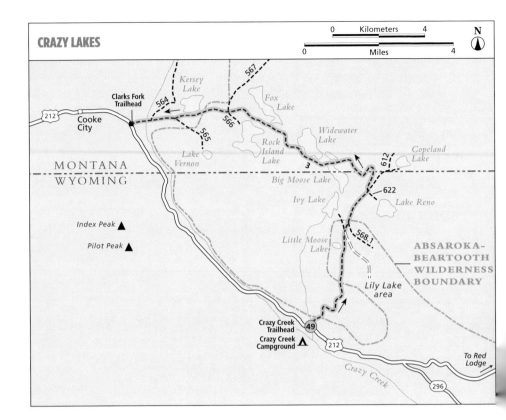

0   Kilometers   4

0   Miles   4

N

MILES AND DIRECTIONS

0.0   Start at Crazy Creek Trailhead.

3.0   Little Moose Lake.

3.1   Junction with jeep road coming in from Lily Lake area; turn left.

3.3   Junction with Crazy Lakes Trail 568.1; turn right.

3.7   Junction with Trail 617 to Lost Lake; turn left.

4.7   Three-way junction with Trail 568 to Copeland Lake and Trail 622 to Lake Reno; turn left.

6.5   Big Moose Lake and the ford.

10.1   Junction with Trail 3; turn left.

10.2   Junction with Trail 566 to Rock Island Lake; turn right.

11.0   Kersey Lake.

11.6   Junction with Trail 565 to Lake Vernon; turn right.

12.6   Arrive at Clarks Fork Trailhead.

50 **CURL LAKE**

A seldom-used trail suitable for day trips or an overnight stay.

Start: Clarks Fork Trailhead
Distance: 7 miles out and back
Difficulty: Moderate to difficult

Maps: USGS Fossil Lake; RMS Cooke City–Cutoff Mountain; and at least 1 wilderness-wide map

FINDING THE TRAILHEAD

Drive 3.4 miles east from Cooke City or 58.1 miles west from Red Lodge and turn north on the well-marked road to the hiking trailhead. Don't turn onto FR 306, which is about a quarter mile west of the hiking trailhead and goes only to the stock trailhead. Huge trailhead with plenty of parking, toilet, picnic area, and interpretive displays. **GPS:** 45.01762 N, 109.86935 W

THE HIKE

For a moderately short trip to a rarely visited lake, the Curl Lake hike is a good choice. The lack of use shows on the trail, which is difficult to follow in places, especially just before the lake. Early in the year you'll have to skirt several bogs. With the exception of the first mile or so, the trail goes through forests burned by the 1988 fires, including along the entire shoreline of Curl Lake.

To find Curl Lake, take Trail 3 from the Clarks Fork Trailhead. After 0.5 mile turn left (northeast) at the well-marked junction with the Kersey Lake jeep road. From this point on, it's a moderate uphill grade all the way to Curl Lake. Follow the road for another 0.5 mile and turn left (north) onto Trail 564.

Trail 564 passes through partially burned forest and several wet meadows. Off to the left, watch for the Broadwater River rushing down to meet the Clarks Fork. Follow this beautiful cascading stream the rest of the way to Curl Lake. Along the way lies one of the Broadwater Meadow Lakes, essentially a scenic wide spot in the stream.

Stay alert at the head of this Broadwater Meadow Lake. Just past this point the trail gets more difficult to find, especially just before Curl Lake.

CAMPING

The shoreline of Curl Lake is steep and rocky, but you can find a few small campsites.

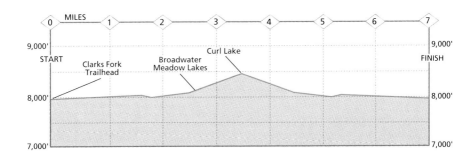

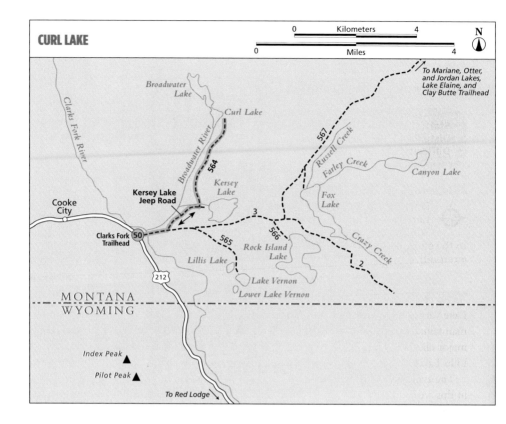

FISHING

The Broadwater River provides a beautiful setting to fish a mountain stream. The Broadwater Meadow Lakes are known for their brook trout, providing a good opportunity to work on fly casting. Curl and Broadwater Lakes are both brook trout fisheries.

MILES AND DIRECTIONS

0.0 Start at Clarks Fork Trailhead.

0.5 Kersey Lake jeep road.

1.1 Junction with Trail 564 to Curl Lake; turn left.

2.7 Broadwater Meadow Lakes.

3.5 Curl Lake.

7.0 Arrive back at Clarks Fork Trailhead.

51 LAKE VERNON

An easy day hike to two forested lakes.

Start: Clarks Fork Trailhead
Distance: 5 miles out and back
Difficulty: Easy

Maps: USGS Fossil Lake; RMS Cooke City–Cutoff Mountain; and at least 1 wilderness-wide map

FINDING THE TRAILHEAD

Drive 3.4 miles east from Cooke City or 58.1 miles west from Red Lodge and turn north on the well-marked road to the hiking trailhead. Don't turn onto FR 306, which is about a quarter mile west of the hiking trailhead and goes only to the stock trailhead. Huge trailhead with plenty of parking, toilet, picnic area, and interpretive displays. **GPS:** 45.01762 N, 109.86935 W

THE HIKE

Lake Vernon is a great choice for a day hike with small children. The entire trail is well maintained and easy to follow. It passes through a rich, unburned forest, and there are no major climbs. Keep a sharp eye out for moose, especially in the big meadow just before Lillis Lake.

The trail doesn't have abundant drinking water, so bring an extra bottle. Like all trails in this area, mosquitoes can be bothersome, especially early in the summer.

To reach Lake Vernon, take Trail 3 from the Clarks Fork Trailhead for about 1.2 miles to a well-signed junction with Trail 565 to Lake Vernon. Turn right (south) and head up a moderate grade. After another half mile or so, look for little, jewellike Lillis Lake in the foreground with majestic Pilot Peak and Index Peak as a backdrop.

The trail continues around the northwest shoreline of Lillis Lake less than a mile more to your destination, Lake Vernon. This forest-lined lake is larger than Lillis but offers a similar view of Pilot and Index. Just south of Lake Vernon is Lower Lake Vernon, more appropriately called Reed Lake on some maps since it's little more than a scenic marsh.

On the way out of Lake Vernon, the trail climbs the biggest hill of the trip, about a half mile long. Once at the top, however, it's downhill all the way back to the trailhead.

CAMPING

Although better suited for day hiking (fairly short for an overnighter), Lake Vernon has a few campsites. Perhaps the best campsite is on the left just before the trail hits the lake.

FISHING

This short day hike offers some surprising fishing. Brook trout have trouble reproducing in Lillis Lake, and the smaller population translates into bigger brookies. Be sure to stop at this small lake on the way to Lake Vernon, which hosts both cutthroat and brook trout. Just over the hill, you could find yourself alone catching stocked cutthroats at Margaret Lake.

Clarks Fork of the Yellowstone at the Clarks Fork Trailhead.

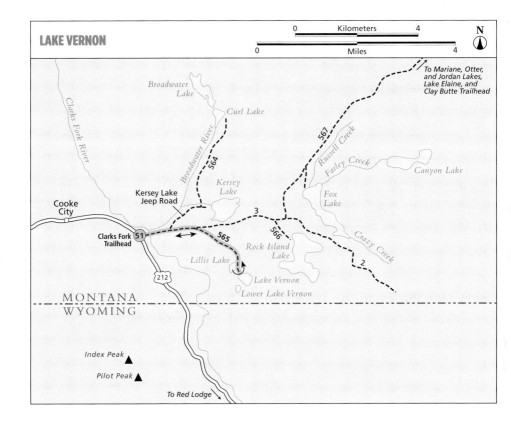

MILES AND DIRECTIONS

0.0 Start at Clarks Fork Trailhead.

0.5 Junction with Kersey Lake jeep road.

1.2 Junction with Lake Vernon Trail 565; turn right.

1.8 Lillis Lake.

2.5 Lake Vernon.

5.0 Arrive back at Clarks Fork Trailhead.

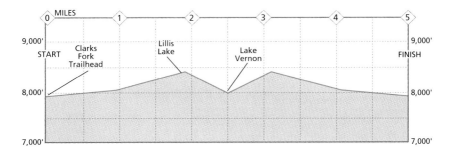

52 ROCK ISLAND LAKE

An easy day hike or overnighter to an unusually large, forest-lined lake.

Start: Clarks Fork Trailhead
Distance: 6 miles out and back
Difficulty: Easy

Maps: USGS Fossil Lake; RMS Cooke City–Cutoff Mountain; and at least 1 wilderness-wide map

FINDING THE TRAILHEAD

Drive 3.4 miles east from Cooke City or 58.1 miles west from Red Lodge and turn north on the well-marked road to the hiking trailhead. Don't turn onto FR 306, which is about a quarter mile west of the hiking trailhead and goes only to the stock trailhead. Huge trailhead with plenty of parking, toilet, picnic area, and interpretive displays. **GPS:** 45.01762 N, 109.86935 W

THE HIKE

Rock Island Lake differs from many high-elevation lakes. Instead of forming a small, concise oval in a cirque, it sprawls through flat and forested terrain, seemingly branching off in every direction. Visitors can spend an entire day just walking around it, which is about the only way to realize how big it really is.

To get to Rock Island Lake, take Trail 3 from the Clarks Fork Trailhead to the junction with Trail 566 to Rock Island Lake. Turn right (east) here for about another half

Trying to catch dinner in Rock Island Lake.

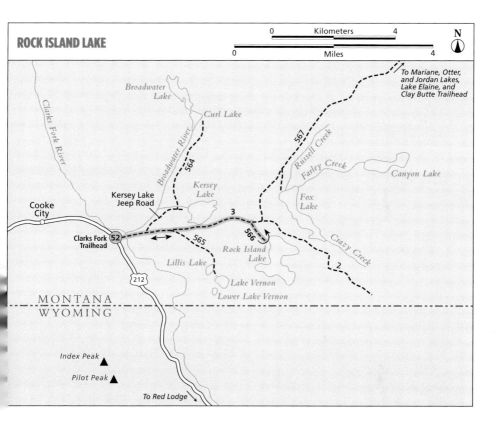

mile to the lake. The trail is well used and well maintained the entire way, with only one noteworthy hill (near Kersey Lake). The 1988 fires scorched the area around Kersey Lake but missed Rock Island Lake.

Because Rock Island Lake is so easy to reach (3 miles on a near-level trail), it's a perfect choice for a family's first trip into the Absaroka-Beartooth Wilderness. Drinking water is readily available on the trail and at the lake (boiled or filtered, of course), but the mosquitoes can be thick in early summer.

CAMPING

Those planning an overnight stay can camp at one of several places along the west side of the lake. However, camping spots are more limited than at many other lakes in the Beartooths, and you might have to search for a while to find an unoccupied spot. Although there might be enough wood for a campfire at the lake, consider using a stove for cooking. The area receives heavy use, and if everyone had a fire, the area would soon show signs of overuse.

FISHING

This popular lake has a combination of homegrown brookies and cutthroats stocked on a three-year rotation, both of which grow well in this lake. The fishing should generally be good enough to count on for dinner.

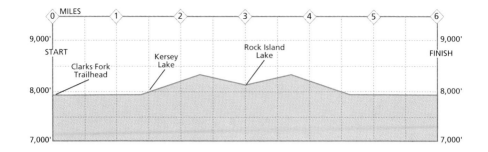

MILES AND DIRECTIONS

0.0 Start at Clarks Fork Trailhead.

0.5 Junction with Kersey Lake jeep road; turn right.

1.2 Junction with Trail 565 to Lake Vernon; turn left.

1.5 Kersey Lake.

2.4 Junction with Trail 566 to Rock Island Lake; turn right.

3.0 Rock Island Lake.

6.0 Arrive back at Clarks Fork Trailhead.

Viewing Pilot Peak and Index Peak, frequently seen landmarks from trails in the Cooke City area.

53 FOX LAKE

A moderate day hike or overnighter to a large lake.

Start: Clarks Fork Trailhead
Distance: 8 miles out and back
Difficulty: Moderate

Maps: USGS Fossil Lake; RMS Cooke City–Cutoff Mountain; and at least 1 wilderness-wide map

FINDING THE TRAILHEAD

Drive 3.4 miles east from Cooke City or 58.1 miles west from Red Lodge and turn north on the well-marked road to the hiking trailhead. Don't turn onto FR 306, which is about a quarter mile west of the hiking trailhead, and goes only to the stock trailhead. Huge trailhead with plenty of parking, toilet, picnic area, and interpretive displays. **GPS:** 45.01762 N, 109.86935 W

THE HIKE

Fox Lake is the first of a long chain of lakes called Crazy Lakes, and it's a good choice for a moderate overnight trip.

To get to Fox Lake, take Trail 3 from the Clarks Fork Trailhead. The trail passes through mostly unburned forest (except for a section by Kersey Lake) for 2.6 miles, climbing gradually as it heads toward the high plateau. Be careful not to take the right-hand turns to Rock Island Lake or Crazy Lakes. Then turn left onto Trail 567 to Russell

Big meadow at the head of Fox Lake.

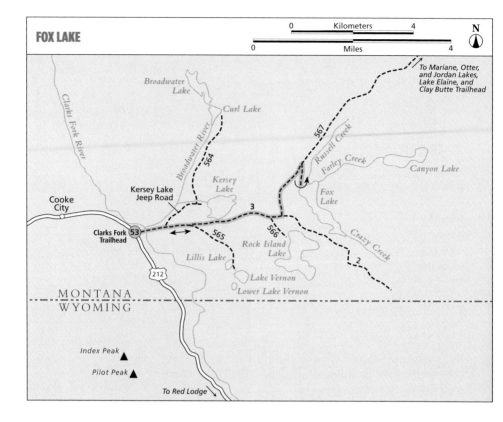

0   Kilometers   4

0   Miles   4

N

Broadwater Lake

Curl Lake

Clarks Fork River

Broadwater River

564

567

Russell Creek

Farley Creek

Canyon Lake

To Mariane, Otter, and Jordan Lakes, Lake Elaine, and Clay Butte Trailhead

Kersey Lake Jeep Road

Kersey Lake

Fox Lake

Cooke City

3

Clarks Fork Trailhead

53

565

566

Rock Island Lake

Crazy Creek

2

Lillis Lake

Lake Vernon

Lower Lake Vernon

212

MONTANA

WYOMING

Index Peak ▲

Pilot Peak ▲

To Red Lodge

Creek, and in 1 mile look for a trail heading right (southeast) to Fox Lake. The turn onto the Fox Lake Trail 575 leads to a steep descent, about a half mile, to the lake.

Fox Lake is large and striking. Explorers can follow the shoreline around to the right (west) but not to the left, where steep cliffs jut up from the lake.

Farley Creek also tumbles into Fox Lake just to the east of Russell Creek. These two streams merge in Fox Lake and leave the lake as Crazy Creek.

On the way out of Fox Lake, be prepared to climb that major hill you came down on the way in. But once on top, it's downhill all the way back to the trailhead except for a short slope along Kersey Lake.

SIDE TRIPS

For a fairly rough side trip, follow a crude anglers' trail up Farley Creek to Canyon Lake. This is a steep, difficult-to-follow unofficial trail for experienced hikers only. Cliff Lake is another option, but again, no trail and for hardy hikers only.

CAMPING

There's a large camping area on the west side of where Russell Creek slips into Fox Lake. This is the only campsite, but it's suitable for a large party or more than one small group. The site is not suited for backcountry horseback riders.

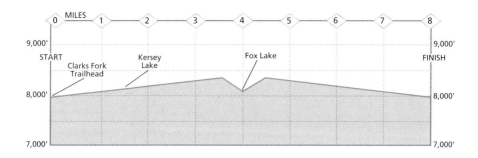

FISHING

Fox Lake is a personal favorite. Most day hikers stop at Kersey Lake or head over to Rock Island Lake. Overnighters generally pass by on The Beaten Path (Trail 567, Hike 20). Fox has oversize brookies, nice rainbows, and an occasional grayling that slipped down from Cliff Lake, which has an abundance of 8- to 12-inch grayling, if you have the energy to make the tough climb up to the remote lake.

MILES AND DIRECTIONS

0.0   Start at Clarks Fork Trailhead.

0.5   Junction with Kersey Lake jeep road.

1.2   Junction with Trail 565 to Lake Vernon; turn left.

1.5   Kersey Lake.

2.4   Junction with Trail 566 to Rock Island Lake; turn left.

2.6   Junction with Trail 567 to Russell Creek; turn left.

3.6   Junction with trail 575 down to Fox Lake; turn right.

4.0   Fox Lake.

8.0   Arrive back at Clarks Fork Trailhead.

54 LADY OF THE LAKE

An easy day hike or overnighter to a gorgeous forested lake.

Start: Lady of the Lake Trailhead
Distance: 3.6 miles out and back
Difficulty: Easy

Maps: USGS Cooke City; RMS Cooke City–Cutoff Mountain; and at least 1 wilderness-wide map

FINDING THE TRAILHEAD

Drive 2 miles east from Cooke City or 59.5 miles west from Red Lodge on US 212 and turn north onto the Lulu Pass Road, less than a quarter mile west of Colter Campground. Drive about 1.5 miles to the Forest Service trailhead on your right (east) of the Lulu Pass Road just before you cross Fisher Creek and before you reach the Goose Lake Jeep Road. You can also access Lady of the Lake from an old unofficial trailhead about a half mile farther up the road. No toilet. Undeveloped camping sites at the trailhead and nearby. **GPS:** 45.04609 N, 109.91201 W

THE HIKE

Lady of the Lake is an ideal choice for an easy day hike or overnighter with small children. Besides being a short hike, watching the weather isn't as critical as it is at the higher elevations.

It's about 0.3 mile from the new official trailhead to the old unofficial trailhead. After crossing Fisher Creek on a bridge, the trail goes by a small inholding with a cabin and then heads down a well-maintained, forest-lined trail to Lady of the Lake. The trail sign says 1 mile to the lake, but it's probably more like 1.5 miles. The trail breaks out of the trees into a large marshy meadow at the foot of the lake. The trail goes up and down, but no big hills.

Giving young ones a fishing break on Lady of the Lake.

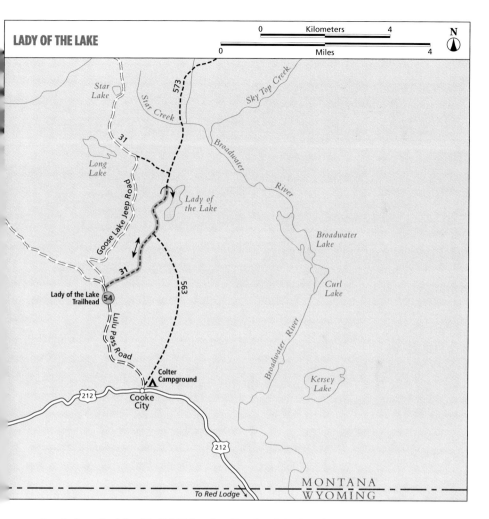

Just before the lake, Trail 563 heads off to the right (south) to Lower Lady of the Lake Trailhead near Colter Campground on US 212. (Trail 563 also offers fairly easy access to Lady of the Lake, but the route described here is much shorter and faster.) Stay to the left on Trail 31 to the lake.

The return trip involves more climbing than the way in, so allow extra time, especially if traveling with small children.

OPTIONS

You can also reach Lady of the Lake by taking Trail 563 from Lower Lady of the Lake Trailhead near Colter Campground, or use this trail to make this a shuttle trip, which means leaving a vehicle at the Lower Lady of the Lake Trailhead or Colter Campground.

CAMPING

The lake has a few good campsites, but they show some major wear and tear along the trail, so please be sure to have a zero-impact camp. Campfires are allowed but discouraged.

Lady of the Lake.

FISHING

Lady of the Lake is a personal favorite of places to take kids for their first wilderness camping experience. The hike is easy, and the brook trout are always willing. For those with some wilderness experience, there are four small lakes nestled in the trees to the southeast. They're a bit tough to find, but they promise solitude. Grayling are stocked in Mosquito Lake when available, while the other lakes are scheduled for stocking with cutthroats. Don't bother to fish Fisher Creek. Acid effluent from mines abandoned before environmental protection laws were in place keeps this stream close to sterile.

MILES AND DIRECTIONS

0.0 Start at Lady of the Lake Trailhead.

0.3 Old access point and trailhead.

1.3 Junction with Trail 563; stay left.

1.8 Lady of the Lake.

3.6 Arrive back at Lady of the Lake Trailhead.

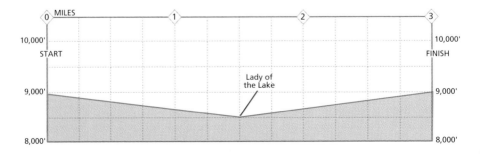

55 AERO LAKES

A base-camp backpacking adventure to the stark beauty of this high plateau area with a wide diversity of potential side trips.

Start: Lady of the Lake Trailhead
Distance: 12 miles out and back
Difficulty: Difficult

Maps: USGS Cooke City, Fossil Lake, and Granite Peak; RMS Cooke City–Cutoff Mountain; and at least 1 wilderness-wide map

FINDING THE TRAILHEAD

Drive 2 miles east from Cooke City or 59.5 miles west from Red Lodge on US 212 and turn north onto the Lulu Pass Road, less than a quarter mile west of Colter Campground. Drive about 1.5 miles to the Forest Service trailhead on your right (east) of the Lulu Pass Road just before you cross Fisher Creek and before you reach the Goose Lake Jeep Road. You can also access Lady of the Lake from an old unofficial trailhead about a half mile farther up the road. No toilet. Undeveloped camping sites at the trailhead and nearby. **GPS:** 45.04609 N, 109.91201 W

RECOMMENDED ITINERARY

You could hike into Aero Lakes and out the same day, but that would be a shame. Instead, plan on a long day hike to get to the lakes and spend the extra time finding an idyllic campsite. Then spend two or three days exploring this incredible high country.

THE HIKE

This trailhead is slightly harder to locate than most others in the Beartooths, but that hasn't lessened its popularity. The area has lots to offer, and it receives heavy use both by locals and by those who travel from afar for a chance to experience this spectacular wild area.

The trailhead lies on the eastern fringe of the section of the Beartooths that has been extensively mined, logged, and roaded. Even in the 2 miles of gravel road to the trailhead, the contrast between this area and the pristine wilderness is clearly evident. To get an early start, camp at the undeveloped campground at the trailhead.

At Aero Lakes you're many miles from the nearest machine. At night neither city lights nor smog blocks the view of the stars. Nearly one million acres of pristine land surrounds you, more than enough for a lifetime of wandering.

At this altitude the summer season is very short. Ice may not free the lakes until mid-July. The moist tundra tends to produce a prodigious number of mosquitoes when the wind isn't blowing, but it usually is.

The first leg of the trip down Trail 31 takes you to Lady of the Lake. After the bridge over Fisher Creek the trail goes by a small private inholding with a cabin and then heads down a well-maintained, forest-lined trail to Lady of the Lake. The trail sign says 1 mile to the lake, but it's probably more like 1.5 miles. The trail breaks out of the trees into a large marshy meadow at the foot of the lake.

Amazing scenery around Aero Lakes. GREG SCHNEIDER

Just before the lake, Trail 563 heads off to the right (south) to Lower Lady of the Lake Trailhead near Colter Campground on US 212. (Trail 563 also offers fairly easy access to Lady of the Lake, but the route described here is shorter and faster.)

Once at Lady of the Lake, follow the trail along the west side of the lake. At the far end of the lake, the trail heads off to the left for about a quarter mile to a meadow on the north side of the lake where two trails depart. The left-hand trail (Trail 31) heads northwest to Long Lake. Take the righthand trail (Trail 573), which leads almost due north for about a mile to the confluence of Star and Zimmer Creeks. Ford the stream here and continue north along Zimmer Creek another mile or so until you see Trail 573 switchbacking up the steep right side of the cirque. If you see a major stream coming in from the left, you have gone too far up the drainage.

There are several social trails in this area, and it can be confusing, and there is a shortage of signage. Some of the unofficial trails are better than the official trail. The key is making sure you don't cross Zimmer Creek until just before you turn right (east) and head up the switchbacks to Aero Lakes. Also, make sure to ford Star Creek west of the junction with Zimmer Creek and head up the west side of Zimmer Creek until you see cairns on the right (east) that indicate the start of the climb up to Aero Lakes.

The scramble up the Trail 573 switchbacks is short but steep and requires good physical conditioning. Locals call it Cardiac Hill and for good reason. It climbs almost 900 feet in about a mile, close to a Category H on our hill-rating chart.

At the top of Cardiac Hill, the trail suddenly emerges from the timber and pauses above Lower Aero Lake. Be sure to notice the dramatic contrast between the treeless plateau here and the timbered country below.

The shoreline around Lower Aero is rocky and punctuated with snowbanks. There are a number of places to camp. They all have great scenery, and the air-conditioning is always on. Those planning to stay here for two or three nights should spend some extra time searching for that five-star campsite. Drop the packs and look around for an hour or so. Don't expect to have a campfire on this treeless plateau.

To proceed to Upper Aero Lake, follow the north shore of Lower Aero Lake until you reach the stream connecting the two lakes and then follow the stream to the upper lake. Another good camping spot is just below the outlet of the upper lake. It provides a good view of the lake and prominent Mount Villard with its spiny ridges. It also makes a good base camp for fishing both lakes and for exploring east to Rough Lake and then north up the Sky Top Lakes chain.

Although most people visit Rough Lake or Lone Elk Lake on side trips, there's also good camping there. Both are large, deep lakes similar to Aero Lakes. Sky Top Lakes might look inviting on the map, but camping is very limited in this rocky basin.

After a day or two of exploring the high country, retrace your steps down Cardiac Hill to Zimmer Creek—and then, regrettably, back to civilization.

OPTIONS

This trip could turn into a long (four- or five-day) shuttle for experts only by continuing east from Aero Lakes through the "top of the world" and exiting the Beartooths at the East Rosebud or Clarks Fork Trailheads.

You can also make a loop out of your trip by exiting on an off-trail route down Sky Top Creek, but be careful on the steep upper section of the stream where it tumbles off the plateau from Lone Elk Lake. Be forewarned: This route is only for the fit, agile, and adventuresome. It requires carrying your pack cross-country over to Rough Lake

---

WHERE TO GO FROM AERO LAKES

While in the Aero Lakes area, set aside a day or two for exploring the top of the world. Day trips in this area are generally more advanced than in other parts of the Beartooths. Here's a list of suggestions rated for difficulty as follows: Human (easy for almost everyone, including children), Semi-human (moderately difficult), or Animal (don't try it unless you're very fit and wilderness-wise). Also refer to more detailed rating information in "How to Use This Guide" (page 4).

Destination	Difficulty
Aero Lakes perimeter	Semi-human
Upper Aero Lake	Human
Leaky Raft Lake	Human
Rough Lake	Semi-human
Lone Elk Lake	Semi-human
Sky Top Lakes	Animal
Zimmer Lake	Animal
Iceberg Peak	Animal
Grasshopper Glacier	Animal
Mount Villard	Animal
Glacier Peak	Animal

Looking down into Upper Aero Lake. GREG SCHNEIDER

(probably named for how hard it is to reach) and then down to Lone Elk Lake. From Lone Elk Lake it's a scramble down a steep route with no trail to a meadow where the stream from Splinter Lake slips into Sky Top Creek. This is a long, slow mile, and it can be hazardous, so be careful and patient. But it's also very beautiful, especially the falls where Sky Top Creek leaves Lone Elk Lake. At the meadow there is an unofficial trail along Sky Top Creek all the way to the main trail. Follow cascading Sky Top Creek until near its end, when it veers off to the left to join up with Star Creek to form the Broadwater River. The track comes out into the same meadow (where Star and Zimmer Creeks join) you passed through on the way up Zimmer Creek on Trail 573. From here retrace your steps back to Lady of the Lake and the trailhead.

SIDE TRIPS

Refer to "Where to Go from Aero Lakes" (page 269).

CAMPING

No problem finding a quality campsite, but they're all high elevation and treeless, so please use zero-impact camping principles to preserve this fragile landscape.

FISHING

Lady of the Lake is a favorite place to take kids for their first wilderness camping experience. The hike is easy, and the brook trout are always willing. For those with some

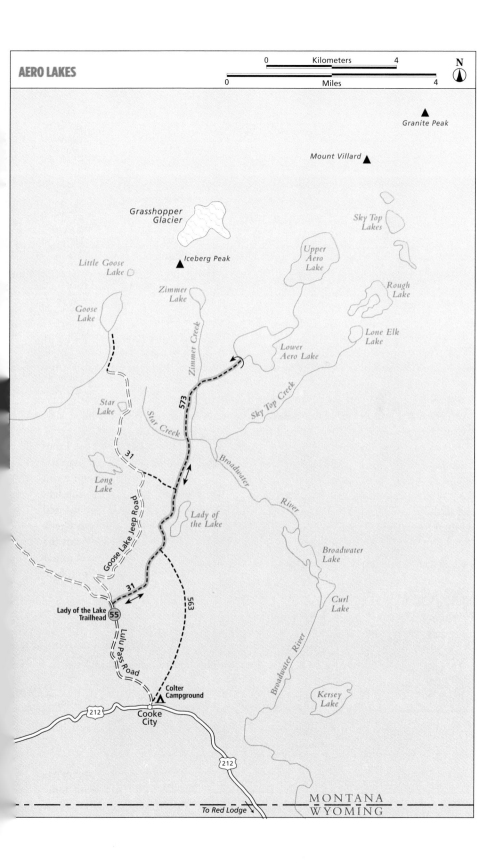

AERO LAKES

0   Kilometers   4

0   Miles   4

N

Granite Peak ▲

Mount Villard ▲

Sky Top
Lakes

Grasshopper
Glacier

Upper
Aero
Lake

Little Goose
Lake

Iceberg Peak ▲

Rough
Lake

Zimmer
Lake

Goose
Lake

Lone Elk
Lake

Zimmer Creek

Lower
Aero
Lake

Sky Top Creek

573

Star Creek

Star
Lake

31

Broadwater

Long
Lake

Goose Lake Jeep Road

River

Lady of
the Lake

Broadwater
Lake

31

Curl
Lake

563

Lady of the Lake
Trailhead   55

Lulu Pass Road

Broadwater River

Kersey
Lake

Colter
Campground

212

Cooke
City

212

MONTANA
WYOMING

To Red Lodge

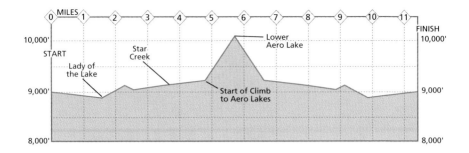

wilderness experience, there are four small lakes nestled in the trees to the southeast. They're a bit tough to find, but they promise solitude. Grayling are stocked in Mosquito Lake when available, while the other lakes are scheduled for stocking with cutthroats.

Don't bother to fish Fisher Creek. Acid effluent from mines abandoned before environmental protection laws were in place keeps this stream pretty sterile.

Fishing is generally slow in both Upper and Lower Aero Lakes, but the rewards can be worth it. Lower Aero has large brookies, occasionally a pound or more. They're supplemented with cutthroats that migrate down from Upper Aero and seem to be reproducing. Cutts can be seen trying to spawn between the lakes through most of July. Upper Aero is stocked with cutts. Fishing is tough here as the cutthroats tend to school, and they can be hard to find in a lake this size.

Sky Top Lakes were once stocked with grayling, and these worked down into Rough and Lone Elk Lakes, but all seem to have disappeared, leaving just brook trout in Lone Elk and Rough. The Sky Tops will probably be stocked once again to maintain a fishery in this chain originating on the slopes of Granite Peak.

To the east of Sky Top Creek are a number of lakes supporting mostly brook trout, although Weasel, Stash, and Surprise Lakes are stocked with cutts. For hearty souls Recruitment Lake holds a few extremely large brookies, but the chances of getting skunked are good. Nevertheless, just one hefty fish from this lake would be the high point of a summer vacation.

MILES AND DIRECTIONS

0.0 Start at Lady of the Lake Trailhead.

0.3 Old access point and trailhead.

1.8 Lady of the Lake and junction with Trail 563; turn left.

2.8 Junction with Trail 31 to Long Lake; turn right.

3.1 Stream coming in from Long Lake.

3.9 Star Creek.

5.1 Start of climb to Aero Lakes on Trail 573.

6.0 Base of Lower Aero Lake.

12.0 Arrive back at Lady of the Lake Trailhead.

56 GOOSE LAKE

An unusual hike partially on a jeep road to a large, fish-filled mountain lake in a treeless, high-altitude basin.

Start: Lady of the Lake Trailhead
Distance: 10.6 miles out and back
Difficulty: Moderate

Maps: USGS Cooke City, Fossil Lake, and Granite Peak; RMS Cooke City–Cutoff Mountain; and at least 1 wilderness-wide map

FINDING THE TRAILHEAD

Drive 2 miles east from Cooke City or 59.5 miles west from Red Lodge on US 212 and turn north onto the Lulu Pass Road, less than a quarter mile west of Colter Campground. Drive about 1.5 miles to the Forest Service trailhead on your right (east) of the Lulu Pass Road just before you cross Fisher Creek and before you reach the Goose Lake Jeep Road. You can also access Lady of the Lake from an old unofficial trailhead about a half mile farther up the road. No toilet. Undeveloped camping sites at the trailhead and nearby. **GPS:** 45.04609 N, 109.91201 W

THE HIKE

I purposely left this route out of the first edition of this book because, at the time, a Canadian mining company had proposed a massive open-pit mine near Goose Lake. When environmental and economic concerns finally defeated the mining plans, I added this route. That doesn't mean the area is pristine, though, because the landscape around Goose Lake is still pockmarked with mining scars from the 1900s or earlier. Thankfully now, nature has made great strides in reclaiming many of the mine sites, and many millions of Superfund money has hurried nature along. The end result is a reasonably attractive landscape dotted with trout-filled lakes.

Unfortunately, most of this area is not in the Absaroka-Beartooth Wilderness, withheld from the original legislation because of mining activity. This allows several old jeep roads to remain open to motorized travel, including the Goose Lake Jeep Road along the route described here, another reason I didn't include it in the first edition.

Later, I hiked into Goose Lake again and with some reservation decided to include it in the third edition, even though about half the route involves hiking on the Goose Lake Jeep Road. I found that hiking in the morning on a weekday meant I had the road all to myself. I enjoyed the hike and didn't encounter any ATVs. However, on the way out of Goose Lake that afternoon, I did meet a few, but even that didn't ruin the trip, mainly because this is such a scenic area that it's hard not to enjoy it.

The first part of the Goose Lake hike follows the route to Lady of the Lake.

After the bridge over Fisher Creek the trail goes by a small inholding with a cabin, then heads down a well-maintained, forest-lined trail to Lady of the Lake. The Forest Service sign says 1 mile to the lake, but it's probably more like 1.5 miles. The trail breaks out of the trees into a large marshy meadow at the foot of the lake.

Just before the lake, Trail 563 heads off to the right (south) to Colter Campground on US 212. (Trail 563 also offers fairly easy access to Lady of the Lake, but the route described here is much shorter and faster.)

Taking a fishing break, common on many trails in the Beartooths.

Walk along the west shoreline of the lake and then about a half mile past the lake to a junction with Trail 31 heading up to the jeep road. There's a sign saying Goose Lake Jeep Road, but it's set back away from the trail and is easy to miss. If you get to Star Creek, you've missed it, so backtrack to the junction.

This section of trail has one confusing spot. Shortly after the junction, you reach a large meadow, and the trail fades away. Don't take the logical route angling off to the right, which leads back to the Aero Lakes trail. Instead, your trail takes off up the hill at about two o'clock from the point where you enter the meadow. It's a steady climb with a few switchbacks for almost a mile until you reach the jeep road at Long Lake.

From here to Goose Creek, about a half mile from the lake, you walk on the jeep road, passing Long Lake and Star Lake along the way. The jeep road is actually an easy trail—and a very rugged drive made for people who like to punish their vehicles. At Goose Creek you enter the wilderness; motorized travelers must park here and walk the last half mile to the lake.

Goose Lake has a few mining scars, but the stunning scenery makes it easy to overlook them. The lake is ringed with some of the most precipitous mountains in the wilderness—Wolf Mountain, Sawtooth Mountain, and Iceberg Peak to the north; Mount Fox to the west; and Mount Zimmer to the east. Scenery doesn't get much better than this.

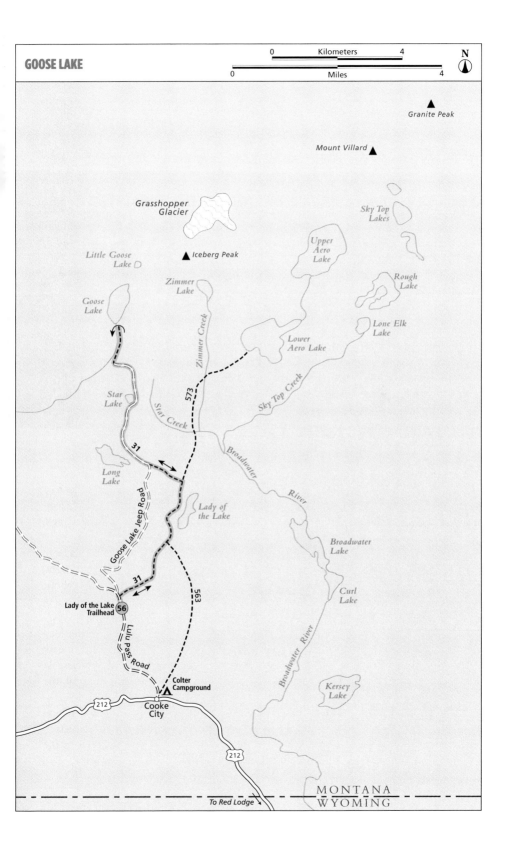

Kilometers

0 4

0 Miles 4

N

Granite Peak

Mount Villard

Grasshopper
Glacier

Sky Top
Lakes

Little Goose
Lake

Iceberg Peak

Upper
Aero
Lake

Rough
Lake

Goose
Lake

Zimmer
Lake

Zimmer Creek

Lower
Aero Lake

Lone Elk
Lake

Star
Lake

573

Star Creek

Sky Top Creek

31

Broadwater

Long
Lake

Goose Lake Jeep Road

Lady of
the Lake

River

Broadwater
Lake

31

Curl
Lake

563

Lady of the Lake
Trailhead

56

Lulu Pass Road

Broadwater River

Colter
Campground

Kersey
Lake

Cooke
City

212

212

MONTANA
WYOMING

To Red Lodge

OPTIONS

You can make a loop out of this trip, sort of, by continuing down the jeep road at Long Lake instead of taking the trail back to Lady of the Lake. This bypasses the hill up from Lady of the Lake and takes you past Round Lake, but it also provides more risk of encountering jeeps and ATVs.

SIDE TRIPS

At Goose Lake cross the outlet stream and walk along an old mining road above the east side of the lake to Little Goose Lake. If you have some extra time on the way back to Lady of the Lake Trailhead, check out nearby Huckleberry and Ovis Lakes, both a short walk west of the jeep road.

CAMPING

You'll find limited camping at the lower end of Goose Lake and a slightly better selection of campsites at the upper end between the big lake and Little Goose Lake.

FISHING

Goose Lake and Little Goose Lake have good, self-sustaining cutthroat fishing, but because of the easy assess, they see lots of flies and lures and can be difficult to catch. You can depend on the other lakes in the area (Long, Huckleberry, Round, and Chris) to provide a catch of tasty brook trout for dinner. Ovis and Star Lakes have cutthroats.

MILES AND DIRECTIONS

0.0 Start at Lady of the Lake Trailhead.

0.3 Old access point and trailhead.

1.8 Lady of the Lake.

2.3 Junction with trail to Long Lake; turn left.

3.1 Long Lake.

3.8 Star Lake.

4.8 Wilderness boundary.

5.3 Goose Lake.

10.6 Arrive back at Lady of the Lake Trailhead.

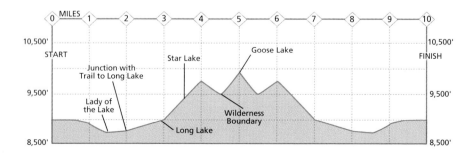

57 HORSESHOE LAKE

A long and strenuous loop through some of the most remote and untamed country covered in this book.

Start: Lake Abundance Trailhead
Distance: 28.7-mile loop
Difficulty: Very difficult and demanding; strictly for the fit and experienced hiker

Maps: USGS Cooke City, Cutoff Mountain, Little Park Mountain, Granite Peak, and Pinnacle Mountain; RMS Cooke City–Cutoff Mountain; and at least 1 wilderness-wide map

FINDING THE TRAILHEAD

Most trailheads in the Beartooths are quite accessible. This one is the other extreme. Just getting here can be quite the experience. From Cooke City drive 0.5 mile east on US 212 and turn north onto Daisy Pass Road. It's then about 8 miles to the trailhead. The first 4 miles are on a well-maintained gravel road that can be traversed by any two-wheel-drive vehicle. About a half mile after the top of Daisy Pass, turn left (west) onto the Lake Abundance Jeep Road, which is not maintained. From this point on, don't proceed without a high-clearance, four-wheel-drive vehicle and the experience to use it. Plenty of parking. No toilet. An undeveloped campground at the trailhead. **GPS:** 45.08390 N, 110.00376 W

RECOMMENDED ITINERARY

This route is about the right length for four nights out, but when considering good camping options, it works better for three nights out. If you decide on this recommended option, plan on a long last day to get back to your vehicle. If you decide on four nights, it's an easy decision to stay at Horseshoe Lake on the third night. If you decide on three nights out but don't want to hike 11-plus miles on the last day, bypass Horseshoe Lake and find a campsite somewhere along Rock Creek or Lake Abundance Creek. Regrettably, neither area has good camping areas.

- First night: Along the Stillwater River near Glacier, Octopus, or Horseshoe Creek
- Second night: Lake of the Woods or Peace Lake
- Third night: Horseshoe Lake

THE HIKE

This trip is not for the beginner or the fainthearted. It goes through the wildest, most isolated country in the Beartooths, and most of the trail is poorly maintained and, in places, hard to find. Be sure to allow extra travel time for covering rough ground and for route-finding. In fact, I consider this the most difficult trip in this book.

On the plus side, travelers here will think they have the entire universe to themselves because the area receives so little use. In this realm of solitude and untamed grandeur, you become immersed in the true spirit of the wilderness, sort of like having the feeling you're the last person on the planet.

From the trailhead head down Stillwater River Trail 24, which takes off just across the little stream meandering through a large, high-altitude meadow east of the trailhead. Goose Creek is the headwaters of the Stillwater River, though it doesn't look like much of a river at this point. That changes about 2 miles downstream when Goose Creek joins the upper Stillwater.

After a pleasant half-mile walk through the flat meadow, the trail drops over the end of the plateau and starts a steep downhill grade along the still small Stillwater River. When Goose Creek cascades in from the east, the gradient flattens out a bit and grows steadily more gradual all the way to the junction with Trail 34 up Horseshoe Creek. Cross the Stillwater where Goose Creek comes in—no bridge, but safe to cross (plan on wet feet).

The first 4 miles of this trail traverse a somewhat stark landscape, carpeted with flat, glaciated rock and punctuated like a pincushion with whitish snags. It was semi-stark before the fires of 1988, but one of the burns scorched its way down the Stillwater to finish the job. It's a lonely, seemingly haunted, slice of wilderness.

The landscape soon becomes more diverse and moist, supporting abundant wildlife populations, especially elk and deer. You should start looking for the first night's campsite somewhere along this reach of the upper Stillwater. There's no shortage of campsites, so where to camp depends mostly on how many miles you want to put in on your first day out.

About 9 miles into the trek, start watching for the turnoff to Horseshoe Creek. This junction is easy to miss, and it'd be a long detour if you do. Refer to a topo map frequently to be sure you've crossed Horseshoe Creek. Shortly after the stream crossing, Trail 34 heads west out of a small meadow. There probably won't be a sign, but look for the post that once held the sign. The grassy meadow also tends to swallow up the trail as it departs, but attentive hikers won't miss it. After the first 50 yards, the trail becomes easy to follow, although from here onward the trail has received little trail maintenance.

Trail 34 climbs moderately to Lake of the Woods, following the creek all the way. About a mile before Lake of the Woods, the trail breaks out into a scenic subalpine landscape that burned only in spots. Lake of the Woods is a shallow, pristine lake surrounded by marshy meadows. Those who camp here for the second night should set aside some time for the short side trip over to Peace Lake and, if there's time and energy to spare, the bushwhack up a short, 600-foot climb to Heather Lake, which is about 2 miles northwest of Lake of the Woods.

About 100 feet before hitting the shoreline at Lake of the Woods, Trail 109 takes off to the south. This junction can be difficult to find; backtrack from the lake if necessary and look carefully for the trail as it starts to switchback up a steep grade to the south. Again, the trail is easy to follow after the first 100 yards.

After the tough but short climb (gaining about 900 feet), the trail breaks out above timberline at 9,500 feet and follows a narrow ridge for a while. Set an easy pace and soak in the great scenery. Look west to 10,111-foot Horseshoe Mountain, north to 10,272-foot Timberline Mountain, and 8 miles south to 10,500-foot Wolverine Peak on the northwest boundary of Yellowstone National Park. As the trail drops off the ridge, keep the topo map and compass or GPS out—the trail fades away in several places.

Soon you'll see a trail veering off to the right to Horseshoe Lake. This is a nice side trip if you have the time, and you can camp there. The lake still bears a few signs of early twentieth-century mining activity around its shores, but you'll still be overwhelmed by the extreme remoteness of the place.

From Horseshoe Basin descend gradually toward Lake Abundance Creek, following Rock Creek most of the way. This area escaped the 1988 fires and is loaded with wildlife, including a healthy bear population, so stay alert.

About 3 miles from Horseshoe Basin, turn left (east) onto Trail 84 at the only easy-to-find junction on this trip. Then follow Lake Abundance Creek all the way back to the trailhead, about 7.5 miles. This drainage is moist and lush, excellent wildlife habitat. When I hiked this route, the trail needed a trail crew badly, and I spent the day climbing over downed trees. The trail skirts the north shore of Lake Abundance for about half of the final mile to the trailhead.

OPTIONS
The route can be hiked in reverse, but it wouldn't be any easier.

SIDE TRIPS
Peace Lake and Horseshoe Lake are easy side trips on trails, and if you're fit and adventurous (which you probably are or you wouldn't be on this trip), try Heather Lake.

CAMPING
It's always comforting to know that you can find a place that looks like you might be the first person to ever camp there. This is such a place, so when you set up your camp, please make sure you do your part to keep it that way.

FISHING
For anglers the highlight of this trip is the possibility of catching aboriginal Yellowstone cutthroat trout. Peace and Heather Lakes have never been stocked and contain original cutthroats. It seems that someone took a few of these over the pass and placed them in Lake of the Woods, as the same stock is found there. While none of these fish are large, just catching them may be satisfying.

The entire Slough Creek drainage supports only cutthroats. Stocking of Yellowstone cutthroats has occurred in many places, including the creek itself. Currently only Lake Abundance (on a three-year cycle) and Horseshoe Lake (on an eight-year cycle) are stocked. Fish grow exceptionally well in Lake Abundance, and it's certainly worth the stop.

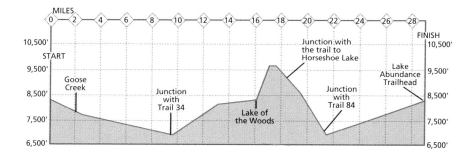

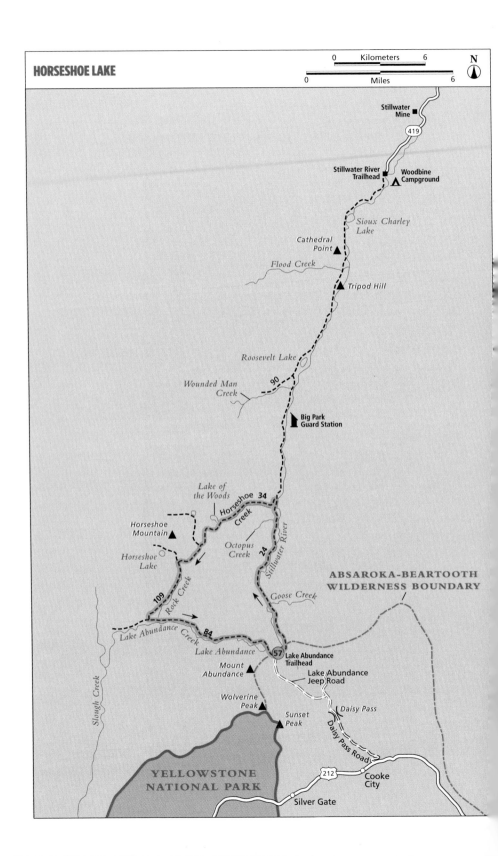

0   Kilometers   6

0   Miles   6

N

Stillwater
Mine

419

Stillwater River
Trailhead

Woodbine
Campground

Sioux Charley
Lake

Cathedral
Point

Flood Creek

Tripod Hill

Roosevelt Lake

Wounded Man
Creek

90

Big Park
Guard Station

Lake of
the Woods

Horseshoe   34

Horseshoe Creek

Horseshoe
Mountain

Octopus
Creek

24

Stillwater River

Horseshoe
Lake

109

Rock Creek

Goose Creek

ABSAROKA-BEARTOOTH
WILDERNESS BOUNDARY

Lake Abundance Creek

84

Lake Abundance

57

Lake Abundance
Trailhead

Mount
Abundance

Lake Abundance
Jeep Road

Slough Creek

Wolverine
Peak

Sunset
Peak

Daisy Pass

Daisy Pass Road

YELLOWSTONE
NATIONAL PARK

212

Cooke
City

Silver Gate

MILES AND DIRECTIONS

0.0   Start at Lake Abundance Trailhead.

2.1   Goose Creek.

9.6   Junction with Horseshoe Creek Trail 34; turn left.

16.0   Lake of the Woods and junction with Trail 109; turn left.

16.5   Junction with trail to Peace Lake; stay left on Trail 109.

18.5   Trail to Horseshoe Lake.

21.2   Junction with Lake Abundance Trail 84; turn left.

27.7   Lake Abundance.

28.7   Arrive back at Lake Abundance Trailhead.

58 THE COMPLETE STILLWATER

A trans-Beartooth route following the Stillwater River all the way, all downhill.

Start: Lake Abundance Trailhead	Granite Peak, Cathedral Point, and
Distance: 27.8-mile shuttle	Pinnacle Mountain; RMS Cooke
Difficulty: Moderate but long	City–Cutoff Mountain and Mount
Maps: USGS Cooke City, Cutoff	Douglas–Mount Wood; and at least 1
Mountain, Little Park Mountain,	wilderness-wide map

FINDING THE TRAILHEADS

Most trailheads in the Beartooths are quite accessible. This one is the other extreme. Just getting here can be quite the experience. From Cooke City drive 0.5 mile east on US 212 and turn north onto Daisy Pass Road. It's then about 8 miles to the trailhead. The first 4 miles are on a well-maintained gravel road that can be traversed by any two-wheel-drive vehicle. About a half mile after the top of Daisy Pass, turn left (west) onto the Lake Abundance Jeep Road, which is not maintained. From this point on, don't proceed without a high-clearance, four-wheel-drive vehicle and the experience to use it. Plenty of parking. No toilet. An undeveloped campground at the trailhead. **GPS:** 45.08390 N, 110.00376 W

To reach the Stillwater River Trailhead: From I-90 at Columbus, drive 15 miles south on MT 78 to Absarokee. Continue south 2 miles, turn west onto the paved Nye Road (CR 419), and go through Fishtail and Nye. Stay on this road, which eventually ends at the trailhead, about 2 miles past the Stillwater Mine. It's about 42 miles southwest of Columbus. Plenty of parking. Toilet. Woodbine Campground near the trailhead. **GPS:** 45.35082 N, 109.90331 W

RECOMMENDED ITINERARY

This route is best suited to two nights out.

- First night: Along the Stillwater River near Octopus or Horseshoe Creek
- Second night: Along the Stillwater River near Wounded Man Creek

THE HIKE

This trip can be traveled from either end, of course, but most people will prefer starting at Lake Abundance because, quite frankly, it's lot easier. In fact, it's downhill all the way. There aren't many trails where hikers can go 28 miles without a single uphill pitch.

Try to arrange for somebody to drop you off at Lake Abundance and then leave a vehicle or arrange for a pickup at the Stillwater River Trailhead. The "trading keys" option doesn't work well on this trail because one party has to agree to walk 28 miles uphill so the other group gets 28 miles downhill. It's also too far to ride to leave a bicycle at the trailhead.

Arranging the shuttle may be a hassle, but it allows the rare chance to travel all the way through the Beartooths along the Stillwater River. There are only two other ways to traverse the entire area and stay on established trails. These are The Beaten Path up the East

The 1988 fires burned through the Stillwater, and fireweed is among the first species to start reclaiming the forest.

Rosebud (Hike 20) and the Slough Creek Divide trail following the East Fork Boulder River and Slough Creek from Boulder River Road into Yellowstone Park (Hike 9).

From the marvelous, high-mountain park at the trailhead, this trail travels through 28 miles of forested river valley. The 1988 fires burned through the Stillwater, but now the forest is springing back, and the entire area is lush and full of wildlife.

To some the prospect of traveling 28 miles through one continuous valley forest might sound monotonous. And granted, this route offers none of the thrills of "bagging" a major peak or watching sunsets burnish the surface of some icy alpine tarn. But it more than makes up for this by immersing the traveler in remote wilderness.

The trail is in good shape all the way, and is well traveled north of the junction with Wounded Man Creek and Trail 90.

For descriptions of the route, refer to the Stillwater to Stillwater trip (Hike 12) and the Horseshoe Lake trip (Hike 57). Be sure to take the time for the short side trip over to Tripod Hill at mile 21.6. There's an obvious trail going east just before the Flood Creek bridge. The point provides a spectacular view of the Stillwater River drainage, including well-named Cathedral Point to the south just past Flood Creek.

At Flood Creek a glance at the map shows that it isn't far to Flood Creek Falls. But this is an extremely difficult bushwhack, which is really too bad because Flood Creek Falls is one of the most spectacular sights in the Beartooths and one that very few people will ever see.

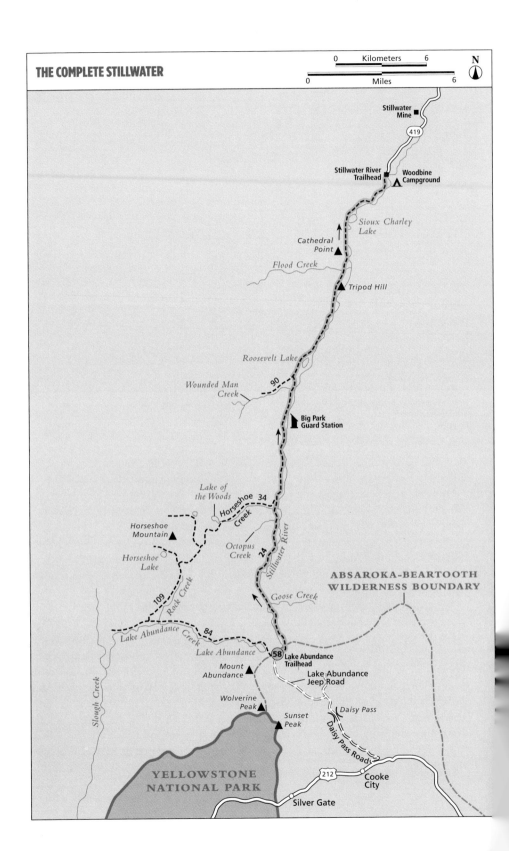

0   Kilometers   6

0   Miles   6

N

Stillwater Mine

419

Stillwater River Trailhead
Woodbine Campground

Sioux Charley Lake

Cathedral Point

Flood Creek

Tripod Hill

Roosevelt Lake

Wounded Man Creek

90

Big Park Guard Station

Lake of the Woods

Horseshoe Creek   34

Horseshoe Mountain

Octopus Creek

24

Stillwater River

Horseshoe Lake

ABSAROKA-BEARTOOTH
WILDERNESS BOUNDARY

109

Rock Creek

Goose Creek

Lake Abundance Creek   84

Lake Abundance

58   Lake Abundance Trailhead

Mount Abundance

Lake Abundance Jeep Road

Slough Creek

Wolverine Peak

Sunset Peak

Daisy Pass

Daisy Pass Road

YELLOWSTONE
NATIONAL PARK

212   Cooke City

Silver Gate

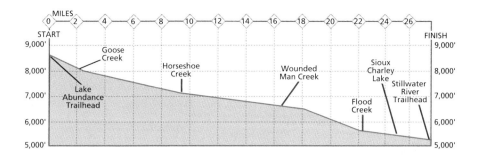

SIDE TRIPS

Take a short side trip over to Tripod Hill for a nice view. Try for Flood Creek Falls if you're up for a short but tough bushwhack.

CAMPING

Potential campsites are abundant along the entire route, and there is plenty of wood for thought-provoking campfires.

FISHING

The Stillwater above, or south of, Goose Creek doesn't support a fishery and probably never has. The steep cascades block upstream migration. Fish begin to appear in the river at Goose Creek; below here there are brook trout as well as rainbows and cutthroats. The farther downstream you go, the better the fishing.

Keep in mind as you fish that the steeper the terrain, the less hospitable it is for trout. Look for fish in the slower water. Rainbows and cutthroats are slightly more suited to faster, colder water, and they do better than brookies in the swifter water.

Most anglers agree that brook trout are the best eating of the three types of trout found here, and eating them will only help the remaining fish to grow bigger. Plan on taking a meal with you when you leave; there will be plenty left for those who follow.

Sioux Charley Lake is really just a wide, slow spot in the river where many people choose to stop and catch a few brookies for dinner.

MILES AND DIRECTIONS

0.0 Start at Lake Abundance Trailhead.

2.1 Goose Creek.

9.6 Junction with Horseshoe Creek Trail 34; turn right.

14.9 Big Park Guard Station.

16.6 Wounded Man Creek.

16.8 Junction with West Stillwater Trail 90; turn right.

21.6 Tripod Hill.

22.3 Flood Creek.

23.8 Sioux Charley Lake.

27.8 Arrive at Stillwater River Trailhead.

ABSAROKA RANGE

The Absaroka Range is circled with trailheads. Trailheads on the east side along the Boulder River Road are covered in that chapter. This chapter includes the rest of the trailheads on the west and south sides of the range. One trailhead, Hellroaring Trailhead, is actually in Yellowstone National Park but accesses a nice loop in the southern Absaroka Mountains.

Wildflowers are abundant everywhere in the Absaroka Range.

59 THE HELLROARING

A trip starting inside Yellowstone National Park, hiking through the open terrain of northern Yellowstone and into the lush upper Hellroaring country in the Absaroka-Beartooth Wilderness.

Start: Hellroaring Trailhead, Yellowstone National Park
Distance: 20-mile loop
Difficulty: Moderate

Maps: USGS Specimen Creek; RMS Gardiner–Mount Wallace; Trails Illustrated Mammoth and Tower Junction; and at least 1 wilderness-wide map

FINDING THE TRAILHEAD

Drive 14.3 miles east from Mammoth, Wyoming, on the Yellowstone Park Grand Loop Road, or 3.3 miles west from Tower, Wyoming, and turn north into the Hellroaring Trailhead. The actual trailhead is 0.3 mile down an unpaved service road. Ample parking. No toilet. **GPS:** 44.94878 N, 110.45121 W

RECOMMENDED ITINERARY

Try a three-day trip, staying two nights somewhere near the Hellroaring Guard Station and spending the second day fishing or day hiking. This might be the most efficient way to do this trip, but it means long days with the overnight pack coming in and going out. You could opt for a longer trip, spending the first night at a designated site in the park along Coyote Creek (2C1 or 2C2), the second (or third, if you have the time) night near the Hellroaring Guard Station, and the last night in one of the many designated campsites along Hellroaring Creek in the park. Make sure you have a permit if you plan to camp in the park.

THE HIKE

This is not the most spectacular hike in this book, but it offers some special features not found on most other backpacking vacations.

The hike penetrates the uncrowded remoteness of the southern Absaroka Mountains. Such privacy is rare in today's popular hiking areas—even though about half the trip lies within Yellowstone Park. It's one of the many park trails, with the exception of the first 2 miles, that receives very little use.

Also, expect to see large wildlife—elk, moose, bison, antelope, wolves, and bears, including the mighty grizzly. Hit the trail early to see wildlife that often retreats to shady daybeds as the landscape heats up in late morning.

This trip makes a nice loop thanks to two trails (Hellroaring and Coyote Creek) that head north out of the park, looping around a grassy butte called Bull Mountain, which is easily viewed from the Coyote Creek Trail.

In Yellowstone the trails go through dry, open terrain where you can hike in May or June of most years with no snowbanks. Don't take this entire trip, though, until at least mid-June because snow will linger in sections outside the park.

In September, hundreds of big-game hunters crowd into the area just north of the park boundary, most using horses and staying in large outfitter camps. In summer months, however, the area is amazingly devoid of people.

The Yellowstone River Trail starts out with a steep drop through mostly open hillside to the suspension bridge over the Black Canyon of the Yellowstone River. From here, go another 0.6 mile to the junction with the Coyote Creek and Buffalo Plateau Trails. Some maps may not have been updated. The outdated maps show the Coyote Creek Trail coming up from Hellroaring Creek instead of branching out from the Buffalo Plateau Trail 0.5 mile after taking a right (north) at this junction.

You can do this loop in either direction with little extra effort, but we took the counterclockwise route, so go right (north) at the Coyote Creek/Buffalo Plateau junction.

About a half mile after leaving the Yellowstone River Trail, the Buffalo Plateau Trail goes off to the right. You go left (north) on the Coyote Creek Trail. In another half mile or so, you might see the abandoned trail coming up from Hellroaring Creek (abandoned but still visible on the ground and shown on many maps).

Before and after the park boundary, the trail goes into a partially burned forest for about a mile. In places the trail seemed to serve as a fire line, with the trees on the west side of the trail green and unburned and those on the east side victims of the 1988 fires.

About a half mile north of the park boundary, turn left (north) at the junction with the Poacher Trail, staying on Trail 97. Shortly after this junction, the trail breaks out into a huge, marshy meadow. This is an easy place to get on the wrong trail. Note on the map that Trail 97 crosses the meadow and goes up the west side. An excellent trail (not on some maps) goes up the east side of the meadow, tempting you to follow it. If you do, you won't be completely lost, but you'll add about a mile to your trip. Both trails intersect with the Trail 36, about a half mile apart. Whichever trail you follow, turn left (west) when you reach Trail 36.

This section of the route goes through a more lush forest than the lower stretches of Coyote and Hellroaring Creeks. Just before crossing Hellroaring Creek, the trail drops steeply for about a half mile, making you happy you didn't do the trip in reverse.

Hellroaring is a huge stream even this far from its eventual merger with the Yellowstone River, and the Forest Service has constructed a massive bridge to handle the heavy horse traffic this area gets during the hunting season.

After the bridge you pass through a large meadow and by the Hellroaring Guard Station. If you're staying overnight outside of the park, pick from the many nice campsites in this area. Four Forest Service trails take off to the north and west from here, but you keep turning left at all the junctions and follow Hellroaring Creek south back into the park. After the guard station the trail stays out of sight of the creek up on the west hillside and passes through mature lodgepole.

After crossing the park boundary until just south of campsite 8H9, the trail stays away from the creek in timber. However, when we hiked this trail, we came through a live forest fire burning on both sides of the trail, including campsite 8H9. Later this fire burned north up to Hellroaring Guard Station. Since this lightning-caused fire was a natural part of the Yellowstone ecosystem (just like rain and wind), the National Park Service rightfully let it burn.

After breaking out into a series of large meadows, you reach the junction with the bridge over Hellroaring Creek. Unless you want to ford Hellroaring Creek, take a left (east) here. On the other side of the bridge, a spur trail to campsite 8H8 goes off to the left and you go right (south), following the stream for 1.5 miles back to the Yellowstone River Trail where you go left (east) and retrace your steps back to the trailhead.

Camping at the large meadow surrounding the Hellroaring Guard Station.

The trail is in excellent shape the entire way, but the many trail junctions (some not on maps) can be confusing, especially when you're outside of the park.

OPTIONS

You can do this loop in reverse, but it might be slightly more difficult because of the hill east of the Hellroaring Guard Station. You can also skip the loop option and go out and back along either Coyote or Hellroaring Creek. And if you're long on fitness and short on time, you can do it all in a long, hard, dry day hike.

SIDE TRIPS

Several trails juncture at the Hellroaring Guard Station, so you have plenty of options for side trips. We only had one extra day, so we took the Carpenter Lake loop. It's about 13 miles around the loop, including some confusing spots on the little-used Carpenter Lake Trail. The 1988 fires burned the Carpenter Lake area, including the lakeshore.

CAMPING

This route has designated campsites within Yellowstone Park along Hellroaring and Coyote Creeks and undesignated camping areas outside the park. All campsites in the park allow campfires unless otherwise indicated, and you usually can have a fire outside the park, too. Likewise, all campsites in the park have bear poles, but outside the park, you'll have to hang your food in trees. You'll need a backcountry camping permit from the National Park Service to camp within the park.

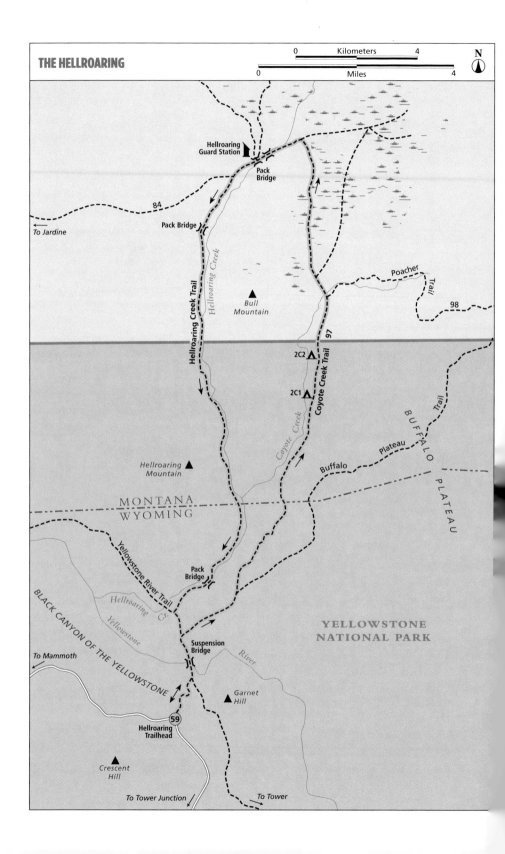

0   Kilometers   4

0   Miles   4

N

Hellroaring
Guard Station

Pack
Bridge

84

Pack Bridge

← To Jardine

Hellroaring Creek

Hellroaring Creek Trail

▲
*Bull
Mountain*

Poacher

Trail

98

97

2C2 ◬

Coyote Creek Trail

2C1 ◬

Coyote Creek

Hellroaring ▲
Mountain

B U F F A L O

Trail

Plateau

Buffalo

P L A T E A U

MONTANA
WYOMING

Yellowstone River Trail

Pack
Bridge

Hellroaring Cr.

Yellowstone

YELLOWSTONE
NATIONAL PARK

BLACK CANYON OF THE YELLOWSTONE

Suspension
Bridge

River

← To Mammoth

▲ *Garnet
Hill*

59

Hellroaring
Trailhead

▲
*Crescent
Hill*

To Tower Junction

To Tower →

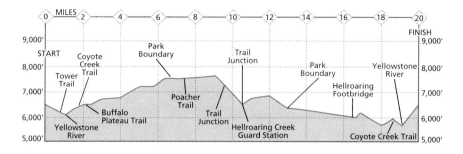

FISHING

Cutthroats abound throughout Hellroaring Creek and in lower Coyote Creek. If you have time, hike a mile or two down to the Yellowstone River for even better cutthroat fishing. Carpenter Lake is loaded with cutthroats, but the treelined shoreline makes fly casting difficult. Fortunately, a roll cast will net you plenty of fish because the cutts hang out near the shoreline.

MILES AND DIRECTIONS

0.0 Start at Hellroaring Trailhead.

0.8 Junction with trail to Tower; turn left.

1.0 Suspension bridge over Yellowstone River.

1.6 Junction with Coyote Creek/Buffalo Plateau Trail; turn right.

2.1 Junction with trail to Buffalo Plateau Trail; turn left.

6.0 Backcountry campsite 2C1.

6.4 Backcountry campsite 2C2.

6.7 Park boundary.

7.2 Poacher Trail 98; turn left.

9.5 Coyote Creek Trail 97; turn left.

9.8 Hellroaring Bridge.

10.2 Hellroaring Guard Station and Horse Creek Bridge.

10.4 Junction with trail to Jardine; turn left.

13.0 Park boundary.

15.8 Backcountry campsite 8H9.

16.3 Junction with trail to campsite 8H8; trail down west side to creek and to campsites 8H5, 8H3, and 8H1; a footbridge; and trail along Hellroaring Creek; turn left and cross creek on bridge.

17.8 Backcountry campsite 8H6.

18.1 Junction with Yellowstone River Trail and spur trail to campsites 8H4 and 8H2; turn left.

18.4 Junction with trail to Coyote Creek and Buffalo Plateau; turn right.

19.0 Suspension bridge over Yellowstone River.

19.2 Junction with trail to Tower; turn right.

20.0 Arrive back at Hellroaring Trailhead.

60 ELBOW LAKE

A long, hard day hike or overnighter with a stunning view of Mount Cowen, an incredible mass of rock and the highest point in the Absaroka Range.

Start: East Fork Mill Creek Trailhead
Distance: 16 miles out and back
Difficulty: Difficult

Maps: USGS Knowles Peak, The Pyramid, and Mount Cowen; RMS Mount Cowen Area; and at least 1 wilderness-wide map

FINDING THE TRAILHEAD

Drive south from Livingston on US 89 for 16 miles and turn left (east) at a well-marked turn onto Mill Creek Road. You cross the Yellowstone River after 0.5 mile. Continue driving southeast on Mill Creek Road (FR 486), which turns to gravel (passable by any vehicle) after 5.6 miles. (You can cut about 2 miles off the route by taking the East River Road south from Livingston and turning left onto the well-signed Mill Creek Road.) Go 8.8 miles from US 89 and turn left (northeast) onto East Fork Mill Creek Road (FR 3280), also well signed, and follow it 1.5 miles to the trailhead, located about a quarter mile before the Snowy Range Ranch. Snowbank Campground, a Forest Service vehicle campground, is on the main Mill Creek Road 1.3 miles past the West Fork Road. Limited parking, so be careful not to block the road. No toilet. **GPS:** 45.31683 N, 110.53658 W

THE HIKE

The rugged north Absaroka Range forms the eastern horizon of the Paradise Valley south of Livingston along the Yellowstone River. Of all these formidable peaks, 11,206-foot Mount Cowen is the highest.

Snow often clings to this trail until mid-July, so if you plan a late June or early July trip, check with the Forest Service about snow conditions before trying it.

As you leave the trailhead on Trail 51, it stays high and skirts around the south side of the Snowy Range Ranch for a little more than a mile before crossing the East Fork Mill Creek on a bridge to the junction with Upper Sage Creek Trail 48. Turn left to head north along Sage Creek. As you cross the bridge, a major social trail comes in from the Snowy River Ranch. Don't go left here. Instead, go down the trail about 200 yards and take a left at a well-defined junction (no trail sign when I hiked this route).

The trail climbs steeply with no switchbacks and then crosses Sage Creek. After the creek it continues an unrelenting, Category 1 climb with good switchbacks (i.e., not too flat or long) across a dry hillside. Carry extra water for this stretch, but the rest of the trail has plenty of water even in late August.

Elbow Lake is 8 miles from the trailhead. You gain almost 3,500 feet of elevation, making this a tough hike even for the extra-fit. The trail is in good shape most of the way. The last 2 miles to the lake get rough, muddy, and difficult for horses. If you hike to Elbow Lake in July, expect to see lots of wildflowers, including an ocean of balsamroot.

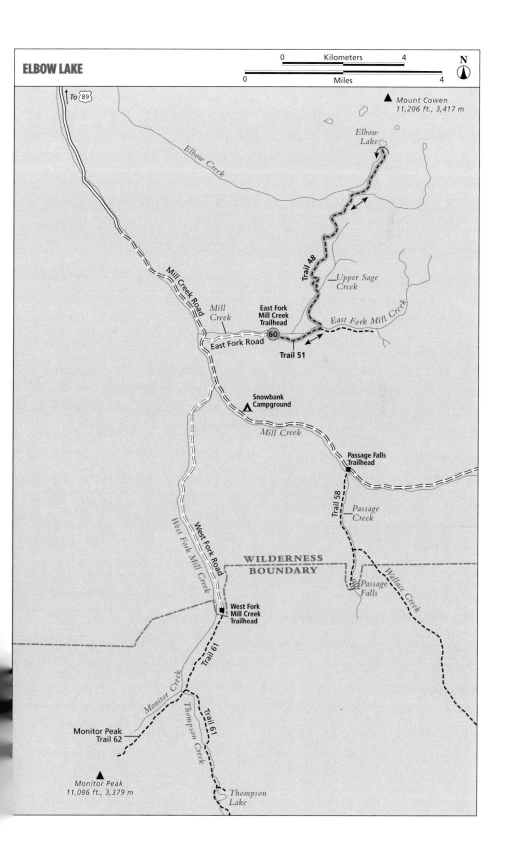

ELBOW LAKE

0 Kilometers 4

0 Miles 4

N

▲ Mount Cowen
11,206 ft., 3,417 m

Elbow
Lake

To 89

Elbow Creek

Trail 48

Mill Creek Road

Mill
Creek

Upper Sage
Creek

East Fork
Mill Creek
Trailhead

60

East Fork Road

Trail 51

East Fork Mill Creek

Snowbank
Campground

Mill Creek

Passage Falls
Trailhead

Trail 58

Passage
Creek

West Fork Road

West Fork Mill Creek

WILDERNESS
BOUNDARY

Wallace Creek

Passage
Falls

West Fork
Mill Creek
Trailhead

Trail 61

Monitor Creek

Trail 62

Monitor Peak
Trail 62

Thompson Creek

Trail 61

▲ Monitor Peak
11,086 ft., 3,379 m

Thompson
Lake

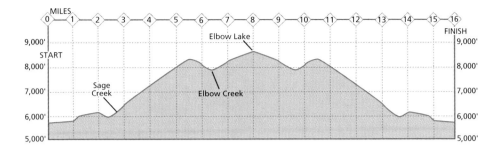

Start early and plan to make the entire hike to the lake in one day, as good campsites are almost nonexistent along the way. Starting early also helps you get through the major climbing before the afternoon sun starts beating you down.

Elbow Lake is very scenic, with a gorgeous waterfall crashing down into the lake. Mount Cowen does lure a fair number of climbers, but do not attempt it unless you know what you're doing. Unlike most of the other peaks in the Absaroka Range, Mount Cowen is a technical climb.

SIDE TRIPS

Explore the nearby unnamed lake (no fish) to the northeast by following the stream that enters Elbow Lake's eastern side. For spectacular views of Mount Cowen, hike up the little valley on the eastern side of Mount Cowen to the top of the ridge. You may spot some mountain goats.

CAMPING

There are no great campsites along the way to the lake, but you can find four or five nice sites at the lake. This lake receives surprisingly heavy use, so the campsites are overused; be sure to set up a zero-impact camp.

FISHING

You can catch some pan-size cutthroats in Elbow Lake and in Elbow Creek, but these fish see lots of artificial flies, so plan on beans and rice for dinner.

MILES AND DIRECTIONS

- **0.0** Start at East Fork Mill Creek Trailhead.
- **1.2** Junction with Upper Sage Creek Trail 48; turn left.
- **2.7** Sage Creek.
- **4.0** Junction with major social trail; turn right.
- **6.5** Elbow Creek.
- **8.0** Elbow Lake.
- **16.0** Arrive back at East Fork Mill Creek Trailhead.

61 THOMPSON LAKE

A moderate day hike or overnighter to a beautiful mountain lake, a rare occurrence in the southern Absaroka Range.

Start: West Fork Mill Creek Trailhead
Distance: 10 miles out and back
Difficulty: Moderate

Maps: USGS Mineral Mountain, The Pyramid, and Mount Cowen; RMS Gardiner–Mount Wallace; and at least 1 wilderness-wide map

FINDING THE TRAILHEAD

Drive south from Livingston on US 89 for 16 miles and turn left (east) at a well-marked turn onto Mill Creek Road. Crossing the Yellowstone River after 0.5 mile, continue driving southeast on Mill Creek Road (FR 486), which turns to gravel after 5.6 miles.

For the West Fork Mill Creek Trailhead, go 0.8 mile past the East Fork Road (9.6 miles from US 89) and turn right (south) onto the West Fork Road. Go 5.9 miles to the end of the road and the trailhead. Passable with any vehicle, but the West Fork Road will be tough on a low-clearance vehicle. As you approach the West Fork Trailhead, the road narrows, too narrow in places for two vehicles to meet. Snowbank Campground, a Forest Service vehicle campground, is on the main Mill Creek Road 1.3 miles past the West Fork Road intersection. (You can cut about 2 miles off the route by taking the East River Road south from Livingston and turning left on the well-signed Mill Creek Road.) Ample parking. No toilet. **GPS:** 45.13489 N, 110.33251 W

THE HIKE

For me Thompson Lake was a pleasant surprise, a gorgeous little gem nestled in the southern Absaroka Range, which has a shortage of lakes. It's also an easy hike on a well-maintained and well-traveled trail. The heavy stock traffic has helped keep this trail very distinct. There were no mileage signs, but based on my normal hiking pace, it's close to 5 miles to the lake.

The route starts out in a forest burned by the 1988 forest fires, but after about a mile it heads into a mature, unburned forest for the rest of the way. The route is undulating but has no hills worth mentioning. Watch for the Monitor Peak Trail junction in a large meadow on the top of a ridge, the only meadow on this route. About a mile before the lake, you cross Thompson Creek, and you might be able to cross on unofficial log bridges built by earlier hikers without getting wet feet.

OPTIONS

If you're ambitious and wilderness-wise, you can make Thompson Lake part of a long, adventurous loop by continuing past the lake to the junction with Trail 64, possibly taking the spur trail up to Charlie White Lake for the second night out. Turn right (west) onto Trail 64 and right again onto Trail 67, spending the third night at Fish Lake before heading back to the trailhead on Trail 67. I haven't done this route, but the Forest Service tells me it's open but not well maintained. Check with the Forest Service before attempting it.

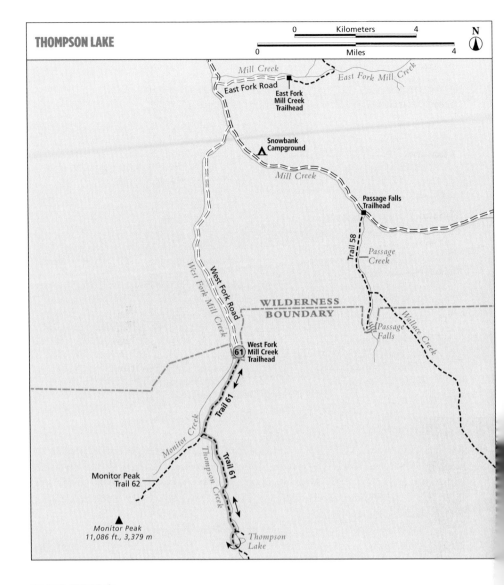

SIDE TRIPS

If you stay two nights at Thompson Lake, you can use the extra day to check out Charlie White Lake.

CAMPING

The south end of the lake has several good campsites, but some of them have been trashed by stock parties tying horses to trees too close to the lakeshore and campsites. This ruins it for everybody. The Forest Service has a prominent notice on the trailhead information board prohibiting this, but some stock parties have obviously ignored the regulation. This lake receives surprisingly heavy use, so be sure to set up a zero-impact camp and help undo some of the damage done by others.

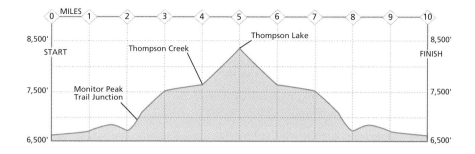

FISHING

Thompson Lake has a nice cutthroat population, but the fish have seen lots of flies, so they can be fussy and can send you home skunked.

MILES AND DIRECTIONS

0.0   Start at West Fork Mill Creek Trailhead.

2.2   Junction with Monitor Peak Trail 62; turn left.

4.0   Thompson Creek.

5.0   Thompson Lake.

10.0   Arrive back at West Fork Mill Creek Trailhead.

Moose can be found throughout the Absaroka Range, which, in general, has higher wildlife populations than the Beartooths.

62 PASSAGE FALLS

An easy day hike to a gorgeous waterfall.

Start: Passage Falls Trailhead
Distance: 4 miles out and back
Difficulty: Easy

Maps: USGS The Pyramid; RMS
Gardiner–Mount Wallace; and at least
1 wilderness-wide map

FINDING THE TRAILHEAD

Drive south from Livingston on US 89 for 16 miles and turn left (east) at a well-marked turn onto Mill Creek Road. You cross the Yellowstone River after 0.5 mile. Continue driving southeast on Mill Creek Road (FR 486), which turns to gravel after 5.6 miles. (You can cut about 2 miles off the route by taking the East River Road south from Livingston and turning left onto the well-signed Mill Creek Road.) For the Passage Falls Trailhead, continue 4 miles past the West Fork Road turnoff or 2.7 miles past Snowbank Campground. Large trailhead with a one-way road through it with ample parking. No toilet. **GPS:** 45.274584 N, 110.501674 W

Never too young to enjoy backpacking.

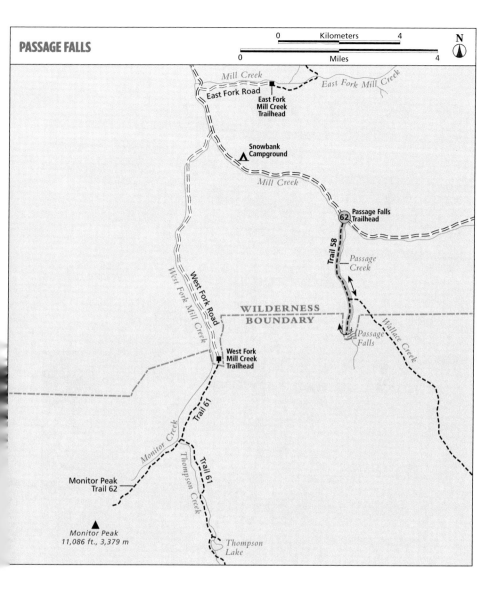

THE HIKE

This is a delightful, short hike to the magnificent Passage Falls on Passage Creek, a fairly large stream. The falls is most spectacular in the spring but worth the trip any time.

The trail is double-wide except for the last 0.2 mile where you turn left onto a single-track for a small drop down to the waterfall. This last section has a few steep spots, so hang onto the kids. The route follows the stream until the junction with the Wallace Creek Trail. It's quite heavily traveled, so don't plan on being alone. The trail goes right down to the falls for an up-close and personal view.

The waterfall is on national forest, but right on the edge of an inholding that's being developed for wilderness cabin sites. Be sure to respect the landowners' rights and stay on the trail.

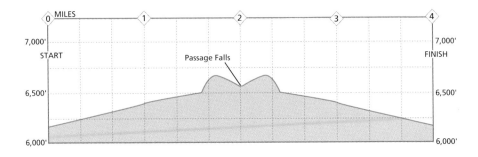

Unfortunately, this trail is open to motorized vehicles, so you might see a dirt bike or ATV along the way.

MILES AND DIRECTIONS

0.0   Start at Passage Falls Trailhead.

1.2   Junction with Wallace Creek Trail; turn right.

1.8   Boundary of private property.

2.0   Passage Falls.

4.0   Arrive back at Passage Falls Trailhead.

63 PINE CREEK LAKE

A moderate day hike or overnighter to a beautiful mountain lake with attractive side trips.

Start: Pine Creek Trailhead
Distance: 10 miles out and back
Difficulty: Moderate

Maps: USGS Emigrant and Mount Cowen; RMS Gardiner–Mount Wallace; and at least 1 wilderness-wide map

FINDING THE TRAILHEAD

Drive south from Livingston on US 89 for 3 miles. Turn left (east) onto East River Road (Highway 540) and head south for 7.5 miles; at 0.7 mile past the cabin community of Pine Creek, turn left (east) onto paved FR 202. Go to the end of this road (2.6 miles, paved all the way, but narrow and curvy). Trail 47 starts at the far end of the campground. For an alternate route from US 89, take Pine Creek Road, between mile markers 43 and 44. Large parking area (often full) and drinking water, but no toilet at trailhead. The Forest Service vehicle campground at trailhead with toilet. **GPS:** 45.49752 N, 110.51965 W

THE HIKE

From the trailhead the first mile of Trail 47 is mostly flat, and it seems like a long mile. At the end of the flat stretch, you stand at the foot of beautiful Pine Creek Falls. This is a very popular hike, so plan on sharing the falls with lots of people. This is far enough

Hiking into Pine Creek Lake.

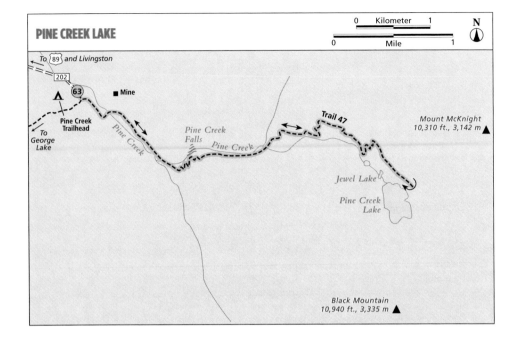

0   Kilometer   1

0   Mile   1

N

To 89 and Livingston

202

63   ■ Mine

Pine Creek
Trailhead

To
George
Lake

Pine Creek

Pine Creek

Pine Creek
Falls

Pine Creek

Trail 47

Mount McKnight
10,310 ft., 3,142 m ▲

Jewel Lake

Pine Creek
Lake

Black Mountain
10,940 ft., 3,335 m ▲

for many hikers, who may have heard about the next 4 miles of trail, which climbs more than 3,000 feet to Pine Creek Lake. For others, however, the allure of a mountain lake held in a glacial cirque is too much to resist. The trail is usually dry, so filter some water at the falls.

Because the trail climbs about 1,000 feet per mile, most people take between 3 and 4 hours to reach the lake. On the bright side, coming out takes only 2 hours.

The lake lies beneath 10,940-foot Black Mountain in an obvious glacial cirque. On the north side of the lake, the bedrock shows pronounced striations where the glacier shoved its rocky load across the granite. At the outlet, a broad slab of granite impounds the lake. Overly friendly ground squirrels, marmots, pikas, and a few mountain goats are common around the lake.

Wait until mid-July to see Pine Creek Lake. To attempt it any earlier will mean wading through snowdrifts on the last part of the trail; in October those drifts may reappear quickly. If you prize solitude, wait until after Labor Day. Before school starts, youth camps use the trail heavily.

If you have extra time, hike around to the east end of the lake and climb the divide to look into Lake McKnight and the Davis Creek drainage. There is no trail into Lake McKnight, and the country is so rough and remote that few hikers ever walk its shores.

One of the pleasures of camping at Pine Creek Lake is the possibility of seeing alpenglow on the peaks. As the sun moves lower in the west and begins to set behind the Gallatin Range, the atmosphere deflects a portion of the color in the spectrum, leaving a pronounced reddish hue in the last few moments of sunlight. When the conditions are right and this red light bounces off the polished rock surfaces just north of the lake's outlet, the effect is startling. With only a little poetic license, one could say it looks like the peaks are on fire.

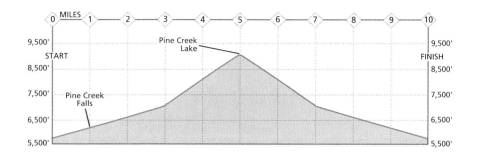

SIDE TRIPS

Experienced hikers will like the off-trail trip over to Lake McKnight.

CAMPING

Good campsites are scarce, but you can find one at the lower end of Pine Creek Lake or near the small tarn below the lake.

FISHING

Pine Creek Lake has a nice population of cutthroats, but these fish see lots of flies and lures, so they can be difficult to catch.

MILES AND DIRECTIONS

0.0 Start at Pine Creek Trailhead.

0.2 Junction with George Lake Trail; turn left.

1.0 Pine Creek Falls.

5.0 Pine Creek Lake.

10.0 Arrive back at Pine Creek Trailhead.

HIKING GUIDEBOOKS: A BAD IDEA?

It has been whispered here and there—usually by "locals"—that books like this one are a bad idea. The theory goes something like this: Guidebooks bring more people into the wilderness; more people cause more environmental damage, and the wildness we all seek gradually evaporates.

I used to think like that, too. And here's why I changed my mind.

When I wrote and published my first guidebook in 1979 (*Hiking Montana*), some of my hiking buddies disapproved, saying I was contributing to the demise of the wilderness I adored and worked so hard to save. Since then, I've written a dozen more hiking guidebooks and published more than a hundred by other authors, and I'm very proud of it. I also hope these books have greatly increased wilderness use.

Experienced hikers sometimes have a lofty attitude toward the inexperienced masses. They think anybody who wants to backpack can buy a topo map and find their own way through the wilderness. But the fact is most beginning hikers want a guide. Sometimes new hikers prefer a real, live guide to show them the way and help them build confidence, but most of the time they can get by with a trail guide like this one.

All FalconGuides (and most guidebooks published by other publishers) encourage wilderness users to respect and support the protection of wild country. Sometimes, this is direct editorializing. Sometimes, this invitation takes the more subtle form of simply helping people experience wilderness. And it's a rare person who leaves the wilderness without a firmly planted passion for wild country—and a desire to vote for more of it.

In classes on backpacking taught for the Yellowstone Institute, I have taken hundreds of people into the wilderness. Many of them had on a backpack for the first time. Many of them were not convinced that we need more wilderness when they left the trailhead, but they were all convinced when they arrived back at the trailhead. Many, many times, I've seen it happen without saying a single word about protecting wilderness.

It doesn't take preaching. Instead, we just need to get people out into the wilderness where the essence of wildness sneaks up on them and takes root—and before they even realize it, the ranks of those who support wilderness has grown.

But what about overcrowding? Yes, it's a problem in many places and probably will be in many more. The answer to overcrowded, overused wilderness is not limiting use of wilderness and restrictive regulations. The answer is more wilderness. A trampled campsite can be rested and reclaimed, but once roads are built and cabins go up, the land no longer qualifies as wilderness.

How can we convince people to support more wilderness when they have never experienced wilderness? In my opinion, we can't. Without the support of people who have

Author and his son, Greg, on their last morning of this wilderness trip, always a remorseful time.

experienced wilderness, I doubt we will have much success in permanently protecting any more wild land.

That's why we need hiking guidebooks. And that's why I changed my mind. I believe guidebooks have done as much to build support for wilderness as pro-wilderness organizations have ever done through political advocacy and public relations campaigns.

And if that's not enough, here's another reason. All FalconGuides (and again, most guidebooks from other publishers) contain sections on zero-impact ethics and wilderness safety. Guidebooks provide an ideal medium for communicating such vital information.

In fifty-plus years of hiking, I have seen dramatic changes in how hikers care for wilderness. I've seen it go from appalling to exceptional. Today, almost everybody walks softly in the wilderness. And I believe the information contained in guidebooks has been partly responsible for this dramatic change.

So, in sum, I hope many thousands of people use this book to enjoy as many fun-filled hikes as possible—and then, of course, vote for wilderness preservation the rest of their lives.

ABSAROKA-BEARTOOTH WILDERNESS FOUNDATION

The Absaroka-Beartooth Wilderness Foundation supports stewardship of the Absaroka-Beartooth Wilderness and appreciation of all wildlands through volunteer projects, education and outreach, and community collaboration. ABWF partners with the US Forest Service and other wilderness stakeholders coordinating boots-on-the-ground projects like trail maintenance, weed pulls, and restoration work, while its outreach efforts include volunteer-driven trail ambassador, educational hikes, and winter webinar programs.

From weeklong backcountry projects swinging Pulaskis and pulling crosscut saws, to blister-less frontcountry projects at trailheads, back in town, or online, ABWF has volunteer opportunities for everyone. One of its most impactful programs is its Wilderness Steward internship: sixteen-week positions working alongside a Custer-Gallatin National Forest trail crew from the Beartooth, Gardiner, or Yellowstone ranger districts. In 2022, the ABWF intern in the Gardiner District alone helped maintain nearly 150 miles of trail while clearing more than 1,000 downed trees. Between 2012 and 2022, ABWF hosted a total of 217 volunteers on 110 projects for 33,000 hours of volunteer service valued at $1.5 million in-kind value, while charging $0 in participant fees.

ABWF envisions a future for the Absaroka-Beartooth Wilderness where its wilderness integrity is maintained because diverse communities value, protect, and connect to this special place through volunteerism, education, experience, and stewardship. To learn about upcoming opportunities and how to support ABWF's mission, visit https://abwilderness.org.

absaroka | beartooth
WILDERNESS FOUNDATION

HIKE INDEX

ABOUT THE AUTHOR

Bill Schneider has spent more than fifty years on the hiking trails of Montana. It started during college in 1965 when he worked on a trail crew in Glacier National Park. He spent the 1970s publishing the Montana Outdoors magazine for the Montana Department of Fish, Wildlife & Parks—and covering as many miles of trails as possible on weekends and holidays.

In 1979 Bill and his partner Mike Sample founded Falcon Publishing, where he worked as publisher for twenty years. Since then, Bill has written twenty-four books and hundreds of magazine and newspaper articles on wildlife, outdoor recreation, and environmental issues.

For twelve years, Bill also taught classes on bicycling, backpacking, zero-impact camping, and hiking in bear country for the Yellowstone Institute, a nonprofit educational organization in Yellowstone National Park.

The author with one of his favorite hiking buddies.

In 2000 Bill retired from his position as publisher of Falcon Publishing, which has grown into the premier publisher of outdoor recreation guidebooks with more than 800 titles in print. He spent the next ten years working as an online columnist, travel writer, and publishing consultant until finally discovering the true concept of retirement.

He now lives in Helena, Montana, with his wife Marnie; works as little as possible; and stays focused on trying to hike, bicycle, and fish himself to death.

BOOKS BY BILL SCHNEIDER

Where the Grizzly Walks, 1977
Hiking Montana, 1979, last revised 2014
The Dakota Image, 1980
The Yellowstone River, 1985
Best Hikes on the Continental Divide, 1988
The Flight of the Nez Perce, 1988
The Tree Giants, 1988
Hiking the Beartooths, 1995
Bear Aware: A Quick Reference Bear Country Survival Guide, 1996, last revised 2012
Hiking Carlsbad Caverns & Guadalupe Mountains National Parks, 1996, last revised 2005
Hiking Canyonlands and Arches National Parks, 1997, last revised 2014
Best Easy Day Hikes Canyonlands and Arches, 1997, last revised 2014
Best Easy Day Hikes Yellowstone, 1997, last revised 2012
Hiking Yellowstone National Park, 1997, last revised 2012
Backpacking Tips (coauthor), 1998
Best Easy Day Hikes Absaroka-Beartooth Wilderness, 1998, last revised 2015
Best Easy Day Hikes Grand Teton, 1999, last revised 2010
Hiking Grand Teton National Park, 1999, last revised 2010
Best Backpacking Vacations Northern Rockies, 2002
Hiking the Absaroka-Beartooth Wilderness, 1998, last revised 2015
Where the Grizzly Walks, 2003 (complete re-write)
Bear Country Behavior (a Backpacker magazine book), 2012
Hiking Montana Bozeman, 2015
Glacier National Park: Reflections, 2020

THE TEN ESSENTIALS OF HIKING

American Hiking Society

American Hiking Society recommends you pack the "Ten Essentials" every time you head out for a hike. Whether you plan to be gone for a couple of hours or several months, make sure to pack these items. Become familiar with these items and know how to use them. Learn more at **AmericanHiking.org/hiking-resources**

 1. Appropriate Footwear

 6. Safety Items (light, fire, and a whistle)

 2. Navigation

 7. First Aid Kit

 3. Water (and a way to purify it)

 8. Knife or Multi-Tool

 4. Food

 9. Sun Protection

 5. Rain Gear & Dry-Fast Layers

 10. Shelter

PROTECT THE PLACES YOU LOVE TO HIKE

Become a member today and take $5 off
an annual membership using the code **Falcon5**.

AmericanHiking.org/join

American Hiking Society is the only national nonprofit
organization dedicated to empowering all to enjoy,
share, and preserve the hiking experience.